P9-DCX-347

Classic Readings in Cultural Anthropology

Classic Readings in Cultural Anthropology

FOURTH EDITION

GARY FERRARO
The University of North Carolina at Charlotte

CENGAGE
Learning·

Australia • Brazil • Mexico • Singapore • United Kingdom • United States

CENGAGE
Learning®

Classic Readings in Cultural Anthropology, Fourth Edition
Gary Ferraro

Product Director: Jon-David Hague

Product Manager: Elizabeth Beiting-Lipps

Content Developer: Erik Fortier

Product Assistant: Stephen Lagos

Marketing Manager: Margaux Cameron

Content Project Manager: Rita Jaramillo

Art Director: Michael Cook

Manufacturing Planner: Judy Inouye

Intellectual Property Project Manager: Farah J. Fard

Production Service: MPS Limited, Charu Khanna

Text Researcher: Pinky Subi

Cover Designer: Irene Morris

Cover Image: © Peter Menzel/ www.menzelphoto.com

Compositor: MPS Limited

© 2016, 2012 Cengage Learning

WCN: 01-100-101

ALL RIGHTS RESERVED. No part of this work covered by the copyright herein may be reproduced, transmitted, stored, or used in any form or by any means graphic, electronic, or mechanical, including but not limited to photocopying, recording, scanning, digitizing, taping, Web distribution, information networks, or information storage and retrieval systems, except as permitted under Section 107 or 108 of the 1976 United States Copyright Act, without the prior written permission of the publisher.

> For product information and technology assistance, contact us at **Cengage Learning Customer & Sales Support, 1-800-354-9706.**
>
> For permission to use material from this text or product, submit all requests online at **www.cengage.com/permissions**.
>
> Further permissions questions can be e-mailed to **permissionrequest@cengage.com**.

Library of Congress Control Number: 2015936371

Student Edition:
ISBN: 978-1-285-73850-5

Cengage Learning
20 Channel Center Street
Boston, MA 02210
USA

Cengage Learning is a leading provider of customized learning solutions with employees residing in nearly 40 different countries and sales in more than 125 countries around the world. Find your local representative at **www.cengage.com**.

Cengage Learning products are represented in Canada by Nelson Education, Ltd.

To learn more about Cengage Learning Solutions, visit **www.cengage.com**.

Purchase any of our products at your local college store or at our preferred online store **www.cengagebrain.com**.

Printed in the United States of America
Print Number: 01   Print Year: 2015

Contents

Preface

Cultural anthropologists have estimated that there are more than five thousand different cultures in the world today that speak mutually unintelligible languages. With such enormous linguistic and cultural variability in the world, it is virtually impossible to become conversant with *all* of the details of *all* of these different cultures. Thus, by necessity, the study of cultural anthropology at the introductory level needs to take a more conceptual approach. Beginning students, in other words, are exposed typically to certain core ideas that provide a conceptual framework for studying comparative cultures. Introductory textbooks, for example, are organized around such chapters as marriage and family, which, in turn, cover such key concepts as polygyny, levirate, arranged marriages, sororate, cross-cousin marriage, and bridewealth. These central concepts are defined and illustrated with ethnographic data from around the world.

Admittedly, introductory textbooks in cultural anthropology take a broad-brush approach to a vast subject matter. The emphasis, by necessity, is to expose beginning students to the enormity of cultural variability, while also allowing them to see universal similarities among the cultures of the world. This general approach to studying other cultures, however, can be enhanced by supplemental readings, which permit the student to explore some areas of the subject matter in greater depth. It is with this idea of "post holing" in mind that *Classic Readings in Cultural Anthropology* was conceived.

This reader was carefully designed to include those articles and segments from books that best represent the discipline over the course of the past century. These readings were not selected because they represent the most recent research and cutting-edge thinking of twenty-first-century scholars. Rather, they represent writings that have been assigned to introductory students for over forty years. While being eminently relevant for cultural anthropology today, these selections have endured the decades to become classics in the field. As one anthropologist has put it, these readings are the "gold standard" for modern cultural anthropology.

The readings found in *Classic Readings in Cultural Anthropology* were selected after consulting with a number of cultural anthropologists, including some leading authors of introductory textbooks. Included in this fourth edition are pieces dating back to as early as 1971 (those of Edward and Mildred Hall and George Gmelch) and as recently as 2013 (Ferraro's and Briody's). It should be pointed out that selections were not excluded for containing terminology that is considered politically incorrect today. In some of the earlier writings, for example, we will see such terms as *man* used to refer generically to humans or the use of the term *Eskimo* instead of the more current term *Inuit*. Nevertheless, the use of these outdated terms (which were not politically incorrect at the time they were written) does not invalidate the relevance of these writings for contemporary cultural anthropology.

Classic Readings in Cultural Anthropology is organized according to the major categories found in most introductory courses of cultural anthropology. These include perspectives on culture, language and communication, economics and ecology, marriage and family, gender, politics and social control, supernatural beliefs, and issues of culture change. Because these eight subheadings are also found in many traditional textbooks in cultural anthropology, adopting professors of this fourth edition of *Classic Readings* should find it relatively easy in coordinating reading assignments.

There are six new selections in this fourth edition of *Classic Readings*. First, investigative journalist Mark Jacobson's piece entitled *Dharavi: Mumbai's Shadow City*, originally published in the *National Geographic Magazine*, serves as a reminder to both anthropology students and their professors that one need not be a cultural anthropologist by training to adequately describe the parameters of a radically different culture; tell the story of culturally different people through their eyes rather than your own; and be able to clearly state the policy implications for government or NGO programs of planned change. Second, drawing upon the perspective of behavioral ecology, Richard Sosis presents a strong argument that religion is much more than an irrational set of values, ideas, and rituals, but rather functions as a highly adaptive institution for peoples from all cultures. Third, included in the section on politics and social control, applied anthropologist Anne Sutherland, serving in the role of expert witness to a court in St. Paul, Minnesota, helps defend a Gypsy man accused of purchasing an automobile by using someone else's Social Security number. This is a classic example of how minority cultural values and practices can conflict with the civil statutes of the larger society. In the section on gender, Lila Abu-Lughod, an expert on gender roles among Muslim women in Egypt, wrote the new selection shortly after 9/11, when the United States was building the case for war against the Taliban regime in Afghanistan. This piece questions the logic of the argument of going to war against the Taliban for the purpose of liberating Afghan women from the tyranny of the "Taliban terrorists" because the argument relies on some spurious ethnographic information and diverts attention away from examining the history of repressive regimes in Muslim countries and the role the United States played in this history. Nancy Scheper-Hughes's classic piece, entitled "Death Without Weeping," which has appeared in the first three editions of *Classic Readings in*

Cultural Anthropology, is being replaced in this edition by a more recent (2013) updated version of the original theme of mother–child bonds in a Brazilian shantytown. Beginning with her original observations from the mid-1960s, Dr. Scheper-Hughes confirms her original thesis of the relationship between extreme poverty and the weakening of the mother–child bond by including data collected between 2001 and 2009.

And finally, two business anthropologists, Gary Ferraro and Elizabeth Briody, offer an analysis of *culture shock* (the psychological disorientation experienced when living in a radically different culture) by looking at its symptoms and stages, and making suggestions for how to minimize its (oftentimes) debilitating effects. Interestingly, this topic of culture shock, although stunningly relevant to ethnographic fieldwork and learning about different cultures experientially, has not received much systematic coverage in the anthropological literature.

The reader contains a number of pedagogical features designed to help the beginning student learn the content of cultural anthropology more efficiently. First, each reading is preceded by a brief introduction, which helps the reader better understand both the article's relevance and context. Second, a series of Discussion Questions at the end of each piece serves not only as a check on understanding but also as a means to stimulate lively class discussions and encourage readers to make connections to their everyday lives.

The purpose of this book is to provide beginning students of cultural anthropology with a set of readings that have stood the test of time. To ensure that this selection of readings meets your needs as both students and instructors, I encourage you to send me your thoughts on how we can improve upon this volume. Please send your comments to me at garyferraro425@gmail.com.

Gary Ferraro
University of North Carolina at Charlotte

Introduction

In a recent article in *Anthropology Newsletter*, anthropologists Elizabeth Bird and Carolena Von Trapp report on a nonscientific survey they conducted among one hundred undergraduates who had never taken a course in anthropology. Many of the common stereotypes about anthropology were confirmed. The majority of respondents associated the discipline with stones and bones exclusively; very few could cite the name of a real anthropologist other than the fictional Indiana Jones; and the image of the anthropologist that emerged was a person who was drab, eccentric, elderly, bookish, unbusinesslike, disheveled, wore shabby clothes, and had very little to do with anything outside of academia. All of these impressions are misleading stereotypes that do nothing but obscure the nature of the discipline and its relevance beyond academia.

Of all of the social sciences, anthropology is the most broadly defined. Some anthropologists do, in fact, deal primarily with stones and bones. One branch of anthropology *(archaeology)* searches for artifacts and other cultural remains of people who lived in the distant past. The subfield of *physical anthropology* unearths fossil remains for the purpose of reconstructing the human evolutionary record. Yet, there are other anthropologists *(cultural anthropologists* and *linguists)* whose focus is on live, warm bodies (i.e., living cultures). Even though these different branches of anthropology have different research agendas, they are all directed at a single purpose: the scientific study of humans, both biologically and culturally, wherever and whenever they may be found. This volume deals only with cultural anthropology, defined most simply as the comparative study of contemporary peoples throughout the world.

Even cultural anthropology, when contrasted with other social sciences, tends to be a wide-ranging discipline. Political scientists focus on power relationships among a group of people. Economists confine their studies to how people produce, distribute, and consume goods and services. Sociologists concentrate on social interaction as their major theoretical construct. Cultural anthropologists, on the other hand, do not limit themselves to a single domain of activity.

Rather, by focusing on the concept of culture, cultural anthropologists look at *all* aspects of behavior, attitudes, beliefs, and material possessions. This comprehensive perspective on the study of human behavior makes cultural anthropology particularly effective at helping us better understand people different from ourselves.

What do we mean by the term *culture*? Although we all think we know what culture is, anthropologists have a considerably different definition from the one popularly held. In everyday usage, the term *culture* refers to the finer things in life, such as symphonies, great works of art, and fine wines. In other words, the so-called cultured person prefers Bach to Britney Spears, spends time at art openings rather than at the NASCAR track, and drinks expensive French champagne rather than Bud Light. Cultural anthropologists, however, define the term *culture* much more broadly to include the total lifeways of a group of people. This anthropological definition of culture involves much more than playing cello in a string quartet or eating pheasant under glass. For the anthropologist, a culture encompasses all aspects of a group's behavior, attitudes, beliefs, and material possessions—both the artistic and the mundane. Shaking hands, brushing one's teeth, visiting Aunt Maude, or eating a hot dog are all part of the widely defined anthropological definition of the term *culture*.

But what is it that enables the discipline of cultural anthropology to so effectively reveal human nature? To be certain, cultural anthropologists over the past century have adhered to certain guiding principles that have distinguished them from other social scientists. First, anthropologists take a highly comparative approach by examining cultural similarities and differences throughout the world. Such an approach serves as a valuable corrective against the pitfall of explaining all human behavior in terms of one's own culture. A case in point is the revision of a prominent psychological theory in the early twentieth century in light of comparative, cross-cultural data from Melanesia. Bronislaw Malinowski, one of the founders of modern anthropology, spent four years of uninterrupted fieldwork among the Trobriand Islanders of the Pacific between 1914 and 1918. At the time, a widely held theory of psychotherapy was the Oedipus complex, in which Sigmund Freud explained the sociopsychological tension between fathers and sons as the result of sexual jealousy over the mother. Freud reasoned that because all males have an innate desire to have sexual relations with their mother, they are jealous of their fathers, who, in fact, do have such sexual relations.

However, Malinowski's research among the matrilineal Trobrianders revealed no social or psychological tension between a man and his biological father, as was common in Western Europe where Freud made his observations. The Trobriand Islanders made the distinction between a man's *biological* father (who actually impregnated the mother) and his *social* father (who is actually the man's maternal uncle). Malinowski found that in Trobriand society there was considerable tension with the social father (the man actually responsible for his upbringing) and little or no tension with the biological father, who was more like an older brother. Clearly, everyone understood that it was the biological father who slept with the mother to produce the child. Malinowski concluded that the tension between fathers and sons observed by Freud in Europe was, in fact, the result of authority rather than sexual jealousy, and as a result, the so-called Oedipus complex was a culture-bound explanation of human behavior. Here, then, is an example of how the broad, comparative approach of cultural anthropology served as a check against an oversimplified explanation of human behavior based solely on evidence from one's own culture.

A second principle that has guided cultural anthropology over the past hundred years has been firsthand observation and inquiry. Many social scientists rely primarily on secondary data such as census data or survey information collected from respondents with whom the scientists never have any face-to-face contact. Cultural anthropologists, by way of contrast, rely on participant observation to a greater extent than any other single data-gathering technique. As its name implies, participant observation involves living in the culture under study while also making systematic observations about it. By engaging in participant observation, cultural anthropologists share in the everyday activities of the local people while making detailed observations of people working, playing, eating, talking, trading, educating, or performing any other cultural activity. The methodological advantages of hands-on research should be obvious. Because most people appreciate any attempt from outsiders to at least try to live according to their culture, participant observation will, in most cases, improve both rapport and the quality of the data received. Moreover, firsthand research allows the anthropologist to distinguish between what people actually do and what they say they do. Participant-observers, in other words, have the advantage of observing actual behavior rather than relying on hearsay.

Perhaps the single most important feature that cultural anthropologists bring to the study of other cultures is the insistence upon viewing a foreign cultural object within its proper *cultural context*. Whenever people encounter a foreign cultural item (such as an idea, a material object, or a behavior pattern), the usual tendency is to make sense of it in terms of their own cultural assumptions. They generally ask themselves the question: How does this foreign idea or thing fit into my culture? Of course, because it is not part of their culture, there is absolutely no reason why it should fit in. There is, in other words, nothing in their own culture that would tend to support that particular cultural item. If you really want to understand why this particular idea or thing is part of that foreign culture, it must be examined in terms of that culture rather than your own.

Perhaps an example would help. Most middle-class North Americans, men and women alike, see no sense in the practice of polygyny (a man having more than one wife at a time). They see it as nonsensical or, worse yet, downright immoral and illegal. And viewed from the perspective of their own cultural assumptions, they would be right. There is very little in our culture that would support or reinforce the practice of polygyny. In fact, there are many parts of our culture that would be in direct conflict with polygyny, such as our legal system and the norms of Christian churches. Even our economic system is at odds with polygyny, because in a cash economy such as our own, it makes no economic sense whatsoever to have large numbers of wives and large numbers of children.

However, if we view polygyny from its original cultural context—let us say from the cultural perspective of an East African mixed farming community—it makes a good deal of sense. In fact, given all of the other parts of *that* culture, polygyny is the most logical form of marriage imaginable. First, there is nothing illegal about having more than one wife at a time in East Africa. Second, their traditional agricultural system encourages men to take more than one wife to maximize the size of the family. Unlike in the United States where large families are economically irrational, in East Africa the more family members there are to cultivate crops, the better off the entire group will be. Third, the system of social prestige in East Africa is based on the number of wives and overall family size, not material wealth as is the case in our own society. Even women in traditional African societies, wanting to be part of a high-status household, supported their husbands' efforts to take additional wives. And finally, the practice of polygyny is supported in many East African societies by the traditional religious practice of ancestor worship. Because men are often elevated to the status of ancestor-god upon death, it is only logical that men would want to have large families so they will have large numbers of people worshiping them after they die. A man with one wife and one child would have only a "congregation" of two people!

Thus, cultural anthropology teaches us that if we view a foreign cultural item through our own cultural lens, it is not likely to make much sense. When polygyny is wrenched from its original cultural context in East Africa, there is no way that it can seem rational. The best way to truly understand an item from another culture is to view it from within its proper cultural content. No one is asking you to practice a foreign cultural norm (such as polygyny). In fact, you are not even required to like it. But if you want to understand the inherent logic of why people in another culture think and behave the way they do (which is the primary objective of the discipline of cultural anthropology), then it is imperative that you follow the lead of cultural anthropology, which from its beginnings has insisted on analyzing the parts of different cultures within their original contexts.

1

Coping with Culture Shock

GARY P. FERRARO

Professor Emeritus of Anthropology, University of North Carolina–Charlotte

ELIZABETH K. BRIODY

Cultural Keys, LLC

From its earliest beginnings in the nineteenth century, the subdiscipline of cultural anthropology has relied primarily on direct, experiential fieldwork (lasting a year or two at a time) for conducting research. For much of this history, the profession acknowledged that all fieldworkers would experience a certain amount of psychological discomfort when living and working in a culture radically different from their own. It was simply considered part of the job description. If the problems of adjusting to a new culture became too difficult, the anthropologist would no doubt be advised to stay at home and become a certified public accountant. It wasn't until 1960 that the term culture shock even made its way into the anthropological literature. Up until the present time, anthropologists were not spending a whole lot of time studying the very real phenomenon of culture shock. However, increasingly, applied anthropologists (such as medical, business, or educational anthropologists) who work with non-anthropologists in culturally diverse settings have been much more attentive to analyzing the nature of culture shock and suggesting ways of minimizing its more deleterious effects.

This selected reading, written by two business anthropologists, is a short chapter from a book titled The Cultural Dimension of Global Business (7th edition). Although written for international businesspeople, the concepts and strategies found in this chapter are no less relevant for educators, medical practitioners, engineers, international aid workers, architects, diplomats, agronomists, or members of any professional groups working in unfamiliar cultural environments. This selected reading is not a step-by-step "cookbook" on avoiding culture shock in any and every culture of the world, but rather is a conceptual piece that looks at the nature of culture shock, its usual stages, and its complex set of symptoms, and then provides a number of generalized suggestions for reducing the harmful effects of culture shock in order to adjust effectively to a new cultural environment. It also describes a frequently unanticipated phenomenon called reentry shock, a type of reverse culture shock, whereby the person who has made a successful adjustment to a new work environment has difficulty adjusting to his or her original culture when returning home. The bottom line of this selection

SOURCE: FERRARO, GARY; BRIODY, ELIZABETH, CULTURAL DIMENSION OF GLOBAL BUSINESS, THE, 7th Edition, © 2013. Reprinted by permission of Pearson Education, Inc., Upper Saddle River, NJ.

is that cultural shock is real, can be devastating to one's career if ignored, will affect everyone working in a different culture to some degree, and can be managed (and indeed overcome) with the proper level of motivation and information.

Tom Walters, a 46-year-old fast-track executive from a high-tech company based in Denver, was selected to oversee the construction of a large manufacturing plant in rural China. After discussing the three-year relocation with his wife Laura and two teenage daughters, Tom decided to take the job because it would be a good career move. After several months of attending to the many details involved in any international move, the Walters family arrived at their new home; it was located about 120 miles from Shanghai, China.

Although the company provided the family with a luxurious home, Tom started his job within three days after arrival, leaving most of the details of "settling in" to Laura. With Tom spending long hours at the job site each day, Laura needed to enroll the girls in school, get a driver's license, deal with some immigration issues, find the best places to buy groceries, and generally learn how to navigate in a radically new and different culture. At first Laura was excited about being in such a dynamic, and culturally different, part of the world. It was very much like being on vacation in an interesting and exotic country. But it didn't take long before the "magic" of being in a foreign country began to wear thin. Working with various civil servants proved to be agonizingly slow. Navigating grocery stores, which seemed like a maze to Laura, became increasingly frustrating. Local people seemed unfriendly and unwilling to answer her questions, largely due to the fact that Laura spoke no Chinese other than such basics as "hello" and "thank you." She began to dread having to leave her house because she was having so much difficulty dealing with "those people." In an attempt to preserve her sanity, she joined an organization for expatriate unemployed spouses, where she spent an increasing amount of her time with similarly unhappy foreign dependents. Moreover, their two teenage daughters were not adjusting well to their new school and were suffering from "separation anxiety" from their friends back home in Denver.

Within several months the unhappiness of his wife and daughters began to affect Tom's job performance. He began to feel guilty that his desire for his own career advancement was a major cause of his family's inability to adjust to the new and different cultural environment. Owing to Tom's distractions from his job, the building project he was overseeing fell so far behind schedule that the Chinese partnering company eventually backed out of the project. The upshot was that the building project was cancelled, Tom and his family were sent back to the States, and Tom's company lost tens of millions of dollars in the aborted joint venture.

This unfortunate scenario of Tom Walters and his family is neither hypothetical nor particularly rare. For decades, global businesspeople worldwide have had to overcome numerous challenges of cultural adjustment when living and working abroad on long-term assignments. In Tom's case, the consequences for his company and his own career were indeed serious, and the financial losses were disastrous. Most often, however, foreign assignees do not become "premature returnees," but their job performance is negatively impacted nevertheless. What all of these cases have in common, however, is that the employees and/or their families contract a malady known as "culture shock"—psychological stress resulting from trying to adjust to major differences in lifestyles, living conditions, and business practices in another cultural setting.

THE NATURE OF CULTURE SHOCK

Definition

Culture shock, a term first popularized by anthropologist Kalvero Oberg, refers to the psychological disorientation experienced by people who suddenly find themselves living and working in radically different cultural environments. Oberg describes culture shock as the anxiety that results when all familiar cultural props have been knocked out from under a person who is entering a new culture:

> Culture shock is precipitated by the anxiety that results from losing all our familiar signs and symbols of social intercourse. These signs or cues include the thousand and one ways in which we orient ourselves to the situations of daily life: when to shake hands and what to say when we meet people, when and how to give tips, how to give orders to servants, how to make purchases, when to accept and when to refuse invitations, when to take statements seriously and when not. Now these cues which may be words, gestures, facial expressions, customs, or norms are acquired by all of us in the course of growing up and are as much a part of our culture as the language we speak or the beliefs we accept. All of us depend for our peace of mind and our efficiency on hundreds of these cues, most of which we do not carry on the level of conscious awareness (1960: 177).

Culture shock ranges from mild irritation to a deep-seated psychological panic or crisis. Culture shock occurs when people such as U.S. businesspersons and their family members, all of a sudden, try to play a game abroad in which they have little or no understanding of the basic rules. Here are some examples of statements (from interview data collected by Elizabeth Briody and Judith Beeber Chrisman) made by American expatriates about the early period of their overseas assignment:

- **Expatriate Spouse:** "I was pregnant. We were not looking forward to moving and had no idea we would be going (on an overseas assignment). It was a surprise ... I was sick for two months from the pregnancy. We are at such a high altitude here (in Mexico). We have to boil our water. We eat at home always."

(She began to cry and it took her several minutes to regain composure.)

- **Expatriate Spouse:** "We were afraid for him (my husband). He would cry at dinner. We didn't want to tell him about our problems. He was feeling guilty that he got us into this."

- **Expatriate Child:** "Hearing the kids talking to the teachers in Spanish was hard. I thought that they were supposed to be talking in English since it was the American School."

Expatriates must struggle to uncover what is meaningful in this new cultural environment, while acknowledging that many of their own familiar cultural cues may be irrelevant. They are forced to try out new and unfamiliar modes of behavior, all the while never really knowing when they might be unwittingly committing a gross social indiscretion. Culture shock usually carries with it feelings of helplessness and irritability, while producing fears of being cheated, injured, contaminated, or discounted. Even though everyone, to some extent, suffers the anxiety of culture shock when first arriving in an unfamiliar cultural setting, the very success or failure of an overseas living assignment depends largely on how well one can make the psychological adjustment and get beyond the frequently debilitating effects.

Both social scientists and laypeople use the term *culture shock* to define in very broad terms the unpleasant consequences of experiencing a foreign culture. Since the 1960s a number of writers in the field have attempted to elaborate on Oberg's (1960) original formulation by using such terms as *role shock* (Byrnes 1966), *culture fatigue* (Guthrie 1975), and *pervasive ambiguity* (Ball-Rokeach 1973). Yet despite these variations on Oberg's original theme, there is general agreement that culture shock involves the following dimensions:

- A sense of confusion over expected role behavior

- A sense of surprise, even disgust, after encountering some of the features of the new culture

- A sense of loss of the old familiar surroundings (friends, possessions, and routines)

- A sense of loss of self-esteem because the inability to function in the new culture results in an imperfect meeting of professional objectives

- A feeling of impotence at having little or no control over the environment

- A strong sense of doubt when old values (which had always been held as absolute) are brought into question.

Despite the use of the word *shock*, which implies a sudden jolt, culture shock does not occur quickly, nor is it the result of a single event. Rather, it results from a series of cumulative experiences. When you first arrive in a new culture, usually flying into a major city, the cultural contrasts do not seem too obvious. There are usually traffic lights, taxis, tall buildings with elevators, banks, and modern hotels with English-speaking desk clerks. But before long, the very real cultural differences become painfully apparent. People push in front of you in line rather than lining up in an orderly fashion; when people say yes, they don't always mean yes; you try to be thoughtful by asking about the health of your business partner's wife, and he acts offended; you invite local acquaintances to your home for dinner, but they don't reciprocate; you cannot buy things that you are accustomed to having every day at home; people promise to have something done by tomorrow, but it doesn't get done; you tell a humorous story to your colleague at the office and he responds with a blank look on his face; you try to be friendly, but people don't respond. As those first days and weeks pass, the differences become more apparent, and the anxiety and sense of frustration build slowly. Trying to cope with all the newness is beginning to sap you of your energy. Eventually, the cultural differences become the focus of attention. You no longer perceive the foreign ways of thinking and acting as quaint and fascinating alternative ways of living but rather as pathological and clearly inferior to your own. When this occurs, culture shock has set in.

Impact While Abroad

Robert Kohls (1984: 65) and Elisabeth Marx (1999: 32) provide a fairly comprehensive list of the major symptoms that have been observed in relatively severe cases of culture shock:

- Homesickness

- Boredom

- Withdrawal (e.g., spending excessive amounts of time reading; seeing only other Americans; avoiding contact with host nationals) Need for excessive amounts of sleep

- Compulsive eating

- Compulsive drinking

- Irritability

- Exaggerated cleanliness

- Marital stress

- Family tension and conflict

- Chauvinistic excesses

- Stereotyping of host nationals

- Hostility toward host nationals

- Loss of ability to work effectively

- Unexplainable fits of weeping

- Physical ailments (psychosomatic illnesses)

- Feelings of isolation

- Weight loss

- Feelings of helplessness

- Tenseness, moodiness, and irritability

- Loss of confidence

- Fear of the worst happening.

Because culture shock is characterized by a large and diverse set of symptoms, the malady is frequently difficult to predict and control. It is important to point out, however, that not everyone will experience all the symptoms, but almost all people will experience some. Moreover, some symptoms, or combination of symptoms, will vary in severity from one case to another. Yet, whenever any of the symptoms manifest themselves while one is living and working abroad, one can be sure that culture shock has set in.

Individual international businesspeople vary greatly in the extent to which they suffer from culture shock. A few people are so ill suited to working in culturally different environments that they repatriate shortly after arriving in the host country. Others manage to get by with a minimum of psychological discomfort. But for most Westerners, operating abroad involves a fairly severe bout with culture shock. According to Oberg (1960), culture shock usually occurs in the following four stages:

1. *The honeymoon stage:* Most people begin their foreign assignment with a positive attitude, so this initial stage is usually characterized by euphoria. At this point, all that is new is exotic and exciting. Attitudes about the host country, and one's capacity to operate in it successfully, are unrealistically positive. During this initial stage, which may last from several days to several weeks, the recent arrival is probably staying temporarily at a Western-style hotel or staff guesthouse where food, conditions of cleanliness, and language are not appreciably different from those at home. The sojourner's time is devoted to getting established—finding a house, a car, and perhaps schools for the children. It is possible that the family's standard of living in this foreign land will be more opulent than they were accustomed to while living in the United States. By and large, it is the similarities between this new country and the United States that stand out—which leads one to the erroneous conclusion that people are really all alike under the skin.

2. *Irritation and hostility:* But as with marriages, honeymoons do not last forever. Within several weeks or perhaps months, problems arise at work, at home, and at the marketplace. Things taken for granted at home simply don't occur. A number of small problems become insurmountable obstacles. Now, all of a sudden, it is the cultural differences, not the similarities, that loom so large. For the first time it becomes

clear that, unlike a two-week vacation, one will be in this situation for the next 12–18 months. The second stage of culture shock has set in; this second stage represents the crisis stage of the "disease." Small problems are blown out of proportion. It is during this stage that one or more of the symptoms mentioned are manifested to some degree. A commonly used mode for dealing with this crisis stage is to band together with other expatriates to disparage the local people: "How can they be so lazy?" "So dirty?" "So stupid?" "So slow?" Now is when ethnic jokes proliferate. The speed with which one passes through this crisis stage of culture shock will vary directly with the ultimate success of the international assignment. Unfortunately, some never get past stage 2, and they become premature return statistics or somehow manage to stick it out but at a high cost to themselves, their families, and their companies. Inadequate job performance leads to a "loss of business, low morale among host country national employees, and poor corporate image generally" (Briody and Chrisman 1991: 277).

3. *Gradual adjustment:* Stage 3 marks the passing of the crisis and a gradual recovery. This stage may begin so gradually that the "patient" is unaware that it is even happening. An understanding slowly emerges of how to operate within the new culture. Some cultural cues now begin to make sense; patterns of behavior begin to emerge, which enable a certain level of predictability; some of the language is becoming comprehensible; and some of the problems of everyday living—which seemed so overwhelming in stage 2—are beginning to be resolved. In short, the culture seems more natural and more manageable. A capacity to laugh at one's situation is a sure sign that adjustment—and ultimate recovery—are well under way.

4. *Biculturalism:* The fourth and final stage, representing full or near full recovery, involves the ability to function effectively in two different

cultures. The local customs that were so unsettling months earlier are now both understood and appreciated. Without having to "go native," the international businessperson now accepts many of the new cultural ways for what they are. This is not to imply that all strains in intercultural relationships have disappeared, but the high-level anxiety caused by living and working in a different cultural environment is reduced. Moreover, in a number of situations, those making a full recovery from culture shock find that there are many local customs to which they have become accustomed and which will be missed upon returning home. Again, many people never reach stage 4. It is possible to "get by" with a modicum of success by never going beyond stage 3. But for those who do become bicultural, the international assignment can be a truly positive, growth-producing experience.

A lot has happened in the realm of global business since Oberg's seminal work. More companies are doing business overseas; international assignments continue to rise, as Aahad Osman-Gani and Thomas Rockstuhl point out in their recent review of the expatriate literature (2008). Many firms send employees and their families abroad, particularly as new partnerships are being established (e.g., joint ventures) or as infrastructure is being built (e.g., new plants). Many are on assignment for about three years; they may take subsequent assignments. Others may take short-term assignments of a year or less in duration. Those who are successful will have developed an ability to negotiate and operate not only biculturally, as suggested by Oberg, but also triculturally—within the local host country national culture, within the expatriate community culture, and within their home culture once they have repatriated.

The description of culture shock presented here so far paints a rather bleak picture of the helpless victim suffering from the debilitating psychological effects of a serious illness. Although not glossing over the very serious consequences of culture shock, we can view it more positively as a potentially profound experience leading to cultural learning, self-awareness, and personal growth. For example, Peter Adler (1975) suggested that the conflicts, problems, and frustrations associated with culture shock can result in "transitional experiences" for the international businessperson and accompanying family members, which "can be the source of higher levels of personality and professional development." Cultural learning is most likely to occur under situations of high anxiety, such as is common in moderate to severe cases of culture shock. At lower levels of anxiety, the motivation to learn about the host culture is absent. But when anxiety, frustration, and pain are high, the motivation will be powerful to acquire new knowledge and skills, which can be used to reduce the anxiety. Moreover, culture shock encourages the sufferers to confront their own cultural heritage and to develop a new awareness of the degree to which they are products of it.

Although we are indebted to Adler for reminding us of the more positive consequences of culture shock, the suggestion that it can be growth-producing does have its limitations. As Richard Brislin has suggested, if the anxiety of culture shock is too high, "people may be so upset that they are unable to focus on new learning possibilities" (1981: 158). While a certain amount of anxiety can be positive, there is a point at which it can become dysfunctional. The anxiety of culture shock can interrupt work patterns, increase the number of bad solutions to problems, and impair decision making, planning, and personal relationships on one's overseas assignments.

Ironically, some of the personality characteristics traditionally considered positive for businesspeople at home are the very traits that can most readily contribute to culture shock. To illustrate, many business leaders are type-A personalities, characterized by a high motivation to achieve, competitiveness, and a high level of time consciousness. However desirable these traits are at home, they can become liabilities when attempting to work globally. Wanting to achieve the greatest results in the shortest period of time, type-A personalities tend to be impatient, overly aggressive, domineering, and self-centered. They often do not take the time to listen to others or study and adapt to the local cultural environment.

Impact upon Repatriation

As has been too often the case, many Western businesspeople fail to meet their overseas objectives because they are ill prepared to cope with culture shock. Yet, even for those who are successful at managing culture shock during their foreign assignment (i.e., by reaching stage 3 or 4), the phenomenon has an additional surprise in store—reverse culture shock, or what has come to be known as *reentry shock*. Nan Sussman found that expatriates who were the least prepared for repatriation, experienced greater distress than those who had a better understanding of it (2001). Most Westerners are not prepared for the enormous letdown they feel when returning home after an overseas assignment. In some cases, reentry shock—the disorientation faced when trying to reorient oneself to life and work in your own culture—can be more anxiety producing than the original culture shock. Here are some examples (from research done by Elizabeth Briody and Judith Beeber Chrisma) of reentry shock statements made by expatriates upon their return home:

- **Former Expatriate:** "I experienced a good deal of reverse culture shock in coming back (from Japan) … There is disinterest on the part of the Americans with regard to how the Japanese do things. The attitude is, 'Those (expletive) Japs!' There is resentment about having to hear about the Japanese and how they are taking us to the cleaners. This occurs both in my social life where people essentially do not want to hear about the last four years of your life, and in my work life … When you return to the U.S., you encounter a closed social system. Even with your former friends, it is hard to fit in with them. The disparity of your experience and their lack of experience with a foreign culture make it difficult to fit in."

- **Former Expatriate Spouse:** "I was not happy when I first came back to the U.S. Jack was gone a lot. If we had still been overseas, friends would have known that Jack was away and would have called me to do things. This did not happen when we moved back. In addition, we were living quite close to my parents and they were always dropping in—a lot. I would have to drop whatever I was doing in order to entertain them. This turned out to be pretty stressful. Also, I was thrown right back in with suburban life— talking about idiotic things in a small town. In general, overseas people were more into foreign affairs, paying more attention to it. No one cared about foreign affairs in Ridgewood since they lived in their own little world there. A lot of the suburbia wives would find out that we had lived overseas and would poo poo it and then say how difficult it must have been for the kids to adjust.…"

- **Former Expatriate Child:** "I noticed that American kids were more aggressive. I knew that I couldn't fit in. I didn't like football and baseball because I couldn't understand them. I only knew soccer. It took me a long while to make friends (about 4 years)."

Although most international businesspeople will anticipate a certain number of problems and discomforts when entering a new cultural environment, they are frequently unprepared for the myriad of problems they will face when returning home. First, upon return, home life feels relatively boring and confining. Many foreign assignments of a year or more can be exciting in that they involve travel and learning all sorts of new things. Since coming home to "life as usual" can seem uninteresting by comparison, many returnees experience a generalized malaise or lack of interest in their lives.

Second, many U.S. businesspeople, after returning from a long assignment abroad, soon realize that one problem is finding a new niche in the corporate structure at home. Those who originally decided to send them abroad may no longer be on the scene; consequently, the corporation's plan for how it would use them now may no longer exist.

Third) while trying to overcome the original dose of culture shock, many U.S. businesspeople tend to embellish (in some cases, grossly exaggerate) their fond memories of life in the United States. They remember that things are better made, cheaper, and cleaner and people are more efficient, polite, and competent. But upon reentry to the United States, many of these myths are shattered. One of the by-products of a successful adjustment to the host culture is that our old notions of our culture will never again be the same. After one lives for a while in Switzerland, the United States no longer seems to be the epitome of cleanliness; when compared with the Japanese, the typical American seems loud and boisterous; after returning from an extended stay in Germany you become painfully aware of how unprepared most Americans are to engage in an informed political discussion; after a stint in a developing nation, people in the United States seem rushed and impersonal. Somehow home isn't what one had remembered.

Fourth, one's standard of living may actually decrease when returning to the United States. Such luxuries as servants, large company houses, chauffeurs, live-in babysitters, and other perks used to entice people into an international assignment are likely to disappear. One is now faced with cutting one's own lawn and spending several hours each day commuting to and from work.

Fifth, in those cases in which U.S. businesspeople have made a successful adaptation to a third-world cultural environment, there can be additional problems of adjustment. The returnee and his or her family have seen, on a daily basis, the economic standards of people living in the host country. Per capita income may be no more than several hundred dollars a year; infant mortality may be 15 times as high as it is in the United States; disease and lack of medical facilities keep the average life expectancy to less than 40 years of age; government attention to human rights might be nonexistent; and the prospects of changing these conditions in any meaningful way are highly unlikely. And then, upon return, they encounter friends, colleagues, neighbors, and relatives complaining bitterly that they are unable to find at the grocery store the correct color of toilet tissue for the downstairs bathroom. Such complaints stir up (1) considerable anger at how unaware and unappreciative most Americans are of their own material well-being and (2) guilt for having mouthed many of these same inane complaints at an earlier time.

Sixth, perhaps the most unsettling aspect of reentry shock is the almost total dearth of psychological support for the returnee and his or her household. When encountering the initial stage 2 culture shock during the foreign assignment, there were (it is hoped) some preparations, an understanding (however inadequately developed) that there would be rough times, and other expatriates (who were experiencing many of the same frustrations) who could provide reassurance and support. But when returning home, U.S. businesspeople and their families feel alone and unable to express their feelings with someone who has not been through the same type of experience. Friends and relatives whom they have not seen for months or even years will say, "Oh, I can't wait to hear about your stint in Singapore." But after listening half-heartedly for about two minutes, they will change the subject to a new TV show they have just seen. In short, returnees have a great need to share their overseas experiences (some of which may have been life-altering) with others, but frequently no one seems to be interested. Since the returnees have had the unusual experience of living and working abroad, many of their friends and acquaintances, whose lives may have gone on uninterrupted or changed in other ways, have no way of relating to these experiences. The result is a feeling of alienation from the returnees' own culture because they feel that they are not being understood.

MINIMIZING CULTURE SHOCK

Just about everyone living and working abroad for extended periods of time can expect to experience culture shock to some degree. Tourists and occasional (short-term) business travelers are by and large shielded from some of the more debilitating effects of culture shock because their experiences are limited to hotels and restaurants geared to Westerners. Yet, those who must live and work in a foreign culture for extended periods of time are faced with new ways of behaving, thinking, and communicating. Even U.S. businesspeople who have lived and worked in a number of different countries claim that they have experienced culture shock in each country. For some, each subsequent assignment becomes a little easier, but for many, culture shock must be confronted for each new situation. Although there is no "quick fix" for culture shock, you can take a number of purposeful steps to minimize its negative impact.

Weigh the Alternatives

One very effective way of totally avoiding culture shock is to choose (or have your employer choose) to stay "stateside" or at home in the U.S. rather than enter the global business arena. Some people simply do not have the desire, inclination, or temperament for international assignments. There may be others who are suited for some foreign cultures but not others. Family matters (e.g., medical concerns, education issues, care of elderly parents) need to be considered carefully during the decision-making process because they may be "show stoppers". The old Greek adage "Know thyself" could not be more appropriate than in the process of self-selection for an international assignment. Before deciding to live abroad, it is imperative to have a realistic grasp of your motives and feelings. If individuals possess a high degree of cross-cultural motivation, their adjustment and job performance abroad will be better (Black and Gregersen 1991; Mohr and Klein 2004; Chen et al. 2010). If people decide to move into the global arena solely on the basis of the lure of more money, a possible promotion, or worst of all, to put a little excitement into their less-than-adequate marriage, they will probably do themselves (and their organizations) a favor by staying home. International businesspeople (and any accompanying family members) who are most likely to do well abroad (1) have a realistic understanding of the problems and promises

of international business, (2) possess a number of important cross-cultural coping skills, and (3) see the world marketplace as providing vast opportunities for professional and personal growth. Those who cannot meet these criteria may be so ill-suited to living and working abroad that they would be virtually unable to overcome the debilitating effects of culture shock.

Prepare Carefully

For those who do select the international business arena, the best single piece of advice for minimizing culture shock is to be prepared. The more thorough the preparation for an overseas assignment, the fewer surprises there will be, and, consequently, the smaller will be the accumulated negative effect. A major factor in adjusting to a foreign cultural environment is the degree of familiarity with the host culture. It is important to recognize that culture shock will never be totally avoided, but it can be minimized through careful preparation. To prepare for an international business encounter, refer to the major substantive chapters of this book, which really suggest a fourfold approach.

First, as suggested in Chapter 1, a general understanding of the concept of culture can provide a fuller appreciation of other cultures, regardless of where one might be conducting business. For example, that cultures are learned (as opposed to being acquired genetically) should remind the international businessperson and expatriate family members that although culturally different people have learned different things, they are no less capable of learning efficiently. The concept of an integrated culture—where many or most of the parts of the culture are interconnected—should serve to convince us that all cultures, no matter how incomprehensible they may appear at first, do in fact have a consistently logical structure and should not be given such disparaging epithets as "primitive," "savage," "crazy," "stupid," and so on. And we should realize that our culture is so thoroughly internalized that it can have very real effects on our physiological functioning. These and other general concepts—which hold equally true for

Indonesians, the French, Bolivians, or Japanese—can be helpful in gaining a greater understanding of the foreign cultural environment.

A second way of preparing for culture shock is to become familiar with local patterns of communication—both nonverbal and verbal (see Chapters 3 and 4). Because any type of business depends on communication to such a significant degree, learning to communicate in a foreign business context is absolutely essential. For the international business person, it enhances rapport with host country national and expatriate colleagues; it enables the international businessperson to understand the full context of the negotiations and transactions; it frequently gives access to otherwise exclusive realms of local business; and it opens a window onto the rest of the culture. For the expatriate family members, learning to communicate in the new cultural environment is also beneficial. It enables adjustment to the local culture—its institutions, economic, political, and social systems, and daily living. Communication facilitates interaction with individuals and groups in the new locale. It also positions the expatriate family to learn, in an in-depth way, about the history and culture of the area.

But proficiency in communications can also play a major role in adjusting to culture shock. Because living in a foreign culture involves doing hundreds of things a day—from taking taxis, to making appointments, to having a watch repaired—knowing how to communicate efficiently can both minimize the frustrations, misunderstandings, and aggravations that always face the linguistic outsider and provide a sense of safety, mastery, and self-assurance. In addition to the mastery of the local language, a vital part of communicating in an international business and living situation involves being able to send and receive nonverbal messages accurately. As mentioned in Chapter 3, any communication event is incomplete without a consideration of the additional layers of meaning conveyed by nonverbal behavior.

The third segment of the fourfold approach, as spelled out in Chapter 2, involves a healthy dose of cultural self-awareness. Before it is possible to understand the internal structure and logic of another culture, it is essential to first understand our own culture and how it influences who we are and what we do. We are as much products of our culture as the Chinese, Indians, and Cubans are products of theirs. All people face a number of universal societal problems, from how to make decisions to how to help young people make the transition to responsible adulthood, from how to gain a livelihood to how to explain the unexplainable.

How any particular culture solves these problems varies widely. Middle-class Americans have worked out one set of cultural patterns, whereas the Indonesians may have developed a radically different set of solutions. In most cases, one solution is probably not more inherently rational than another. They simply represent different responses to similar societal problems. Only after we understand why we do the things we do can we appreciate the internal logic of why other, culturally different people do what they do.

Fourth, before entering the international business scene, it is important to become familiar with as much specific cultural information as possible about the country or countries with which one is conducting business (see Appendix B). There is no shortcut to the acquisition of culture-specific data. It will take time, effort, and no small amount of creativity, but the effort will be worth it. It is important not to be limiting when learning about a new culture. The number of sources of culture-specific information is nearly endless. There are, for example, many scholarly sources (e.g., books, journal articles) from such disciplines as anthropology, religious studies, intercultural communication, cross-cultural psychology, and comparative sociology. Besides the scholarly literature (which is not always easily accessible or comprehensible), there are many other sources of excellent information, including commercially published sources for the business traveler, State Department publications, newspapers, and information published and distributed by the various foreign embassies. And, in recent years a wide variety of information (in terms of both quality and breadth of content) now appears on the Internet. Cross-cultural training classes may be useful for new expatriates, though recent research by John Okpara and Jean Kabongo suggests that cross-cultural training is most effective when focused on the specific host country culture (2011). In addition, people who have spent time in that location, or at least overseas, are also valid sources of information. Work colleagues, expatriate family members, foreign exchange students and faculty, and volunteers and staff of nongovernmental organizations are among the kinds of people who can be particularly helpful. In short, it is advisable to draw on as wide a range of culture-specific sources as possible. The more cultural information at hand, the fewer surprises there are likely to be; consequently, serious culture shock can more likely be avoided.

Additional Suggestions

This approach to understanding the cultural environment constitutes the cornerstone of the *cognitive* approach. By conscientiously pursuing these content areas—general cultural concepts, local communication patterns, cultural self-awareness, and culture-specific information—the global businessperson and expatriate family members will avoid total alienation and some of the more debilitating consequences of culture shock, as well as reentry shock. But one's preparation for coping with, and eventually adjusting to, radically different cultural environments involves more than the mere acquisition of information or new colleagues, friends, and acquaintances. Also required is the development of life-long skills and competencies that are useful irrespective of the country in which you might be conducting business. These essential competencies, which will be discussed in some detail in the following chapter, include developing a broad perspective, balancing contradictions, appreciating other perspectives, emphasizing global teamwork, and becoming perceptually acute, among others. When developed together, these global skills and competencies establish a global mindset, which is essential for the global business person in the 21st century. What follows are some additional suggestions for reducing culture shock and enhancing the international business experience.

1. *Understand that learning about the host culture is a process that continues throughout your stay in the host culture and beyond.* Far more learning will occur after your arrival in the country than prior to leaving home. Make certain that you use a wide variety of information sources to learn about the host culture. Include local people, newspapers, tourist information, libraries, and your own observations. Find a friend or colleague (either a local resident or an experienced expatriate) to serve as a guide and mentor in helping you learn as quickly as possible.

2. *As soon after arrival as possible, become familiar with your immediate physical surroundings.* Armed with a good map of the vicinity, leave your hotel and walk in a number of different directions, exploring the city or town on foot. Identify local buildings, what they are used for, where they are in relation to one another, the pattern, if any, of how streets are configured, and where people seem to congregate. A familiarity with the "lay of the land," while very tangible and concrete, will provide an excellent base for learning about other aspects of the culture.

3. *Within the first several days of arrival, work on familiarizing yourself with some of the basic, everyday survival skills that your hosts take for granted.* These include such capacities as using the local currency, using the public transportation system, buying stamps, interacting with shopkeepers, and ordering from a menu. By mastering these seemingly simple tasks, you will minimize frustrations and embarrassment quickly, as well as gain the self-confidence to master some of the more subtle aspects of the host culture.

4. *As difficult as it may be, try to understand your hosts in terms of their culture rather than your own.* When you encounter a behavior or an attitude that appears strange or even offensive, try to make sense of it in terms of their cultural assumptions rather than your own. This is not to suggest that you should adopt their attitudes or behaviors, or even like them, but you will better understand aspects of the local culture when

viewed from within their proper cultural context.

5. *Particularly in the beginning, learn to live with the ambiguity of not having all the answers.* Trying to operate in a new culture is, by definition, a highly ambiguous situation. The person who insists on having immediate and clear-cut answers for everything is likely to be frustrated. Just like the person who is expected to play a game without knowing all the rules, it is important for the cultural neophyte to know that there will be many unanswered questions. By being patient and learning to live with ambiguity, the new arrival is both preserving his or her mental health and "buying time" to learn more answers, reduce the ambiguity, and thus eventually adjust to the new culture.

6. *As a way of enhancing your relationships with your hosts, make a conscious effort to be empathetic; that is, put yourself in the other person's shoes.* People are often attracted to those individuals who can see things from their point of view. Empathy can be practiced by becoming an active listener. First try to understand— then try to be understood.

7. *Understand that flexibility and resourcefulness are key elements to adapting to a new culture.* When living and working in a different culture, the best-laid plans often are not realized. When plans do not work out as expected (as they have a tendency to do more than at home), you need to make and execute new plans quickly and efficiently without becoming overstressed. Resourceful people are familiar with what is available in the host culture, are comfortable calling on others for help, and know how to take advantage of available opportunities.

8. *Learn to postpone making a judgment or decision until you have sufficient information.* Effective administrators in the United States are defined by their ability to decide quickly and effectively and to bring successful closure to problem-solving tasks. When operating in another culture, however, the capacity of "wrapping things up" or "getting the show on the road"

can be a liability rather than an asset. Because people have an imperfect grasp of the rules, norms, and procedures in the host culture, they need to postpone decisions and conclusions until enough facts are at hand.

9. *At least at the beginning of your stay, don't evaluate yourself according to your usual standards of accomplishment.* Any recent arrival to a new culture is bound to be less efficient, productive, or socially competent. The learning curve takes time, so don't be unrealistically hard on yourself.

10. *Work hard at building new social relationships with host country nationals.* Because existing social networks from home have been suspended (at least in a "face-to-face" sense), the sojourner must understand that it is vital to build, nurture, and maintain new social networks in the host country. While it is relatively easy to broaden one's social networks with other expatriates, the cultural adjustment process will be greatly facilitated by focusing on building social relationships with local host country nationals.

11. *Don't lose your sense of humor.* People in any situation, either at home or abroad, tend to get themselves in trouble if they take themselves too seriously. When struggling to learn a new culture, everyone makes mistakes that may be discouraging, embarrassing, or downright laughable. In most situations, your hosts will be disarmingly forgiving of your social faux pas. The ability to laugh at your own mistakes (or at least not lose sight of the humorous side) may be the ultimate defense against despair.

12. *Avoid U.S. ghettos abroad.* Perhaps the best way to ensure an unsuccessful international experience is to limit your social life to an isolated and insulated U.S. enclave where you can get a hamburger and ice in your soft drink but little else. Ghettos are formed when some U.S. travelers attempt to recreate their former lifestyle, while complaining about the lack of amenities, pace of life, and inconveniences of the host culture. Ghetto dwellers might as well have stayed home, for they are neither learning much about the host culture nor about the

expatriate culture. By remaining isolated in an American ghetto, expatriates send the local population the message that they feel superior. At the same time, they reinforce their own negative stereotypes.

13. *Avoid going native.* At the opposite extreme of isolating oneself in a U.S. ghetto—and equally as inadvisable—is to "go native." This involves throwing oneself into and idolizing the host culture to such an extent that one loses one's own sense of cultural identity. Expatriates who attempt to imitate the local people are most often met with suspicion, are not taken seriously, and often reject their own cultures so thoroughly that they fail to meet their original personal and professional objectives.

14. *Be adventurous.* All too often, Americans abroad view their overseas assignments as a hardship post that must be endured and will eventually pass, particularly if they become immersed in the job. But living and working abroad should be much more than an experience to be endured. Instead, it can and should be a positively life-altering experience. As long as there is a willingness to experiment and learn about new things, an overseas experience can provide an exciting new world. There are places to explore, people to meet, customs to learn, food to eat, and music and art to experience. These are all available if the traveler is willing to experiment and take risks.

15. *Learn how best to manage stress.* Culture shock results from the anxiety brought about by (1) the loss of familiar cultural cues and (2) trying to operate in an unfamiliar cultural setting. How one responds to such anxiety varies considerably, as do the techniques for coping with stress. Some manage stress through regular physical exercise, such as jogging, playing tennis, or taking an aerobics class. Others use such techniques as biofeedback, yoga, or meditation. Still others rely on more spiritual techniques for reducing stress, such as prayer and worship. Whatever technique you choose, it is important to have an effective mechanism for reducing stress, which will in turn enhance the adjustment process.

16. *Take appropriate health precautions.* There is nothing that can ruin an international assignment quicker than serious illness or death. While we cannot eliminate the possibility of illnesses, a number of preventive measures will reduce their occurrence. For example, prior to leaving home, be certain that all required and recommended immunizations are current. If traveling to a malaria-infested area, be certain to take the required malarial suppressant(s) prior to, during, and after your stay abroad. While away from home, follow the same good health habits recommended generally—eat well-balanced meals, allow yourself sufficient rest, exercise regularly, and avoid excesses of alcohol, tobacco, and drugs. Moreover, obtain accurate information about which local foods can be eaten safely and which should be avoided. During home stays, attend to physician and dental visits.

17. *Let go of home (for now).* Before leaving home, it is important to properly say goodbye to friends, relatives, and your familiar way of life that you are temporarily leaving behind. Saying goodbye provides the traveler with a symbolic way of moving from home, a necessary step before you can step into a new culture. This is not to say that you need to cut yourself off from home. In fact, it is advisable to work out ways ahead of time to maintain contact with people at home through letters, telephone calls, or e-mails. Also, before leaving, travelers need to understand that they (and those remaining at home) will have changed in significant ways upon return to the United States.

18. *Keep in mind that when studying other cultures there are no absolutes.* In a sense, every culture is unique, as is every situation and person within a culture. Moreover, each sojourner brings her or his unique perceptions based on past experiences. In other words, there is no way of predicting with absolute certainty how people will behave in any given situation, irrespective of

how well prepared one may be. The generalizations that we read in books written by social scientists should not be viewed as ironclad rules but rather as general statements that are valid for most people, most of the time. The advice we get in training sessions and in our reading should not be viewed as a step-by-step set of prescriptions to be used like a cookbook.

19. *Keep the faith.* After preparing yourself for an international assignment as thoroughly as possible, you need to have confidence in yourself as well as in your hosts. All new arrivals are bound to experience frustrations and make mistakes. Yet, eventually your goodwill and basic humanity will come across to the local people—provided, of course, you make an honest effort to participate in the local culture. At the same time, having faith in the inherent goodwill of the local population is important. By and large, people the world over are tolerant of our indiscretions when they result from an honest attempt to learn about the local culture. If you genuinely communicate that you are the student (interested in learning about their culture) and they are the teachers, very few people in the world would refuse to share their expertise. They are the experts, whereas the visitors are the uneducated, at least in terms of local cultural knowledge. If the sojourner is able to acknowledge openly his or her own subordinate (or at least nondominant) position when dealing with local people, many doors of learning and friendship will be open.

20. *Be conscious about maintaining a healthy balance between work and other aspects of your life such as family, recreation, and social networks.* When working abroad, the demands of working in an unfamiliar setting are likely to make even more demands on your time than would be case at home. The chances of excessive work having a negative effect on one's friends and family are considerably greater than the other way around. Maintaining a healthy work–life balance is particularly important for female expatriates (Fischlmayr and Kollinger 2010).

To be certain, no bottled remedies for culture shock are to be found at the pharmacy. But, by simply knowing that culture shock exists, that it happens to everyone to some extent, and that it is not permanent is likely to reduce the severity of the symptoms and speed the recovery. Don't think you are pathological or inadequate if you experience some culture shock. The anxiety resulting from trying to operate in a different environment is normal. Give yourself permission to feel frustration, homesickness, or irritability. Eventually, you will work through these symptoms and emerge with a much richer appreciation of the host culture. But it is also important to remain realistic. There will be some people, for whatever reason, who will not become close friends. There may be others who, for purely personal reasons, you will not like, and vice versa. And there are some things that may never be understood. But once you understand that these problems, while real and frustrating, are perfectly normal reactions for any sojourner, you can begin to search for solutions.

DISCUSSION QUESTIONS

1. Have you ever experienced any of the symptoms of culture shock mentioned in this selected reading when spending time in a culture radically different from your own? If so, please describe.

2. Why have practitioners of the discipline of cultural anthropology—which involves living

and working in radically different cultures—spent so little time actually studying culture shock? Is it because cultural anthropologists are immunized against culture shock?

3. Do you think that culture shock is less or more of a problem in the twenty-first century than it was in the twentieth century? Why?

2

Not a Real Fish: The Ethnographer as Inside Outsider

ROGER M. KEESING

Australian National University/McGill University

Before the 1960s, cultural anthropologists conducted fieldwork, that is, they studied and lived with specific cultural groups wherever they may have been throughout the world. After months, or even years, of analyzing the field notes, a book or journal article would appear, describing that culture in considerable detail. Yet, these earlier written accounts don't have any information on how the field research was conducted, for what period of time, or what problems were encountered while living in the field. Fortunately, since the 1960s cultural anthropologists have been much more willing to discuss these fieldwork issues because these matters have a bearing on the validity and reliability of the studies themselves. Moreover, cultural anthropologists are writing more personal essays dealing with (1) the conflicting values and perceptions among the cultures of the people they are studying and their own, and (2) what they, as anthropologists, have learned from the experience of conducting intense field research based on participant observation.

One such personalized essay, published in 1992 in an anthology titled The Naked Anthropologist, edited by Philip De Vita, is by Australian-born anthropologist Roger Keesing. This piece, like many of the other essays in De Vita's edited volume, demonstrates the difficulties involved in the ethnographic enterprise. Cultural anthropologists spend long periods of time living with culturally different peoples throughout the world in hopes of making sense of and describing these cultures. Most credible anthropologists, however, soon learn that what is abhorrent in one's own culture makes perfect sense according to the worldview and cultural assumption of those people being studied, and vice versa. Trying to find the rationality behind the behavior of the "other" brings us face to face with the rationality (or lack thereof) of our own cultural assumptions. Once confronted, many experienced cultural anthropologists come to the same conclusion as did Keesing (1992:77) several decades ago: the best that any ethnographer can ever hope to become is "an outsider who knows something of what it is to be an insider."

It was to be my first night in a Solomon Island village ... At Bina, on the west Malaita coast, where I had been dropped by a government ship, I unpacked my two backpacks before the gaze of all the village children and many of the adults. Out came the mosquito netting, then the Abercrombie

SOURCE: From "Not a Real Fish: The Ethnographer as Inside Outsider," by Keesing, Roger M. In Philip R. De Vita (ed.), *The Naked Anthropologist: Tales from Around the World* (pp. 73–78). Belmont, CA: Wadsworth, 1992. Reprinted with permission of the author.

and Fitch air mattress and its foot pump. I spread the mattress on the ground, screwed the pump into the valve, and pumped, but nothing happened, in front of the expectant crowd as the sweating white stranger pumped away. Finally, after endless fiddling with the valve and sotto voce cursing, Western technology at last unfolded its mysteries.

Awakening on the thatched verandah to find a steady rain, I watched where the locals were going off, along the beach and around the point, bent under pandanus leaf umbrellas, for morning pees. I followed the same path. I discovered only by later observation that it was the women's latrine; the men's latrine, separated (as I was to learn) even in such Christian villages by strict rules of gender segregation, was a structure built over the water. My hosts were too polite to comment on— or claim compensation for—what I later realized had been a massive breach of propriety.

There had been no way to learn any Pidgin in advance, and after less than a week in the Solomons I could scarcely communicate at all with the villagers (although a couple spoke a bit of English). By midmorning, the carriers arranged by the district officer to guide me across the middle of the island had not arrived. Eventually, in late morning I succeeded in persuading two young men to carry my bags and lead the way; but after an hour and a half of walking into the foothills they announced that they would take me no further. Not until I had spent another reluctant night in a Christian village could I persuade anyone to take me further.

The still pagan Kwaio of the mountains above Sinalagu on the east coast, who had perpetrated the 1927 massacre of a district officer and his entourage,[1] were feared by the colonial government as wild and dangerous. Their hostility to outsiders, especially missionaries and government, was legendary in the Solomons. Yet the lure of the mist-shrouded Kwaio mountains had been reinforced a few days earlier as I had traveled down the coast on a small ship with a Malaitan government clerk.

"You wouldn't want to go up *there*!" he advised me. "The people live in houses on the bare ground, like pigs, and they don't wear any clothes!"

After conferring with the district officer, who claimed to know the Kwaio and their mountain fastnesses well, it seemed that their potential hostility might best be defused if I approached their heartland from a different direction than Europeans usually did: by land rather than by sea. But with no maps, little information, and no way of communicating effectively, I was relatively helpless in seeking to enlist cooperation and explain my intentions. All I knew was that I was supposed to get to a place called 'Aenaafou, which the district officer had told me was the key midpoint on the path to "Sinerango."[2]

My guides the next morning set off, but not toward 'Aenaafou. "You can't get there from here," an English-speaking Christian man had explained, translating for me. "The river is up." I had been in no position to argue, and at least I was moving inland—and upward. For the next nine hours, I struggled and sweated up and down precipitous paths: an hour and a half of climbing straight upward to a long-deserted mountaintop settlement site, then a plunge down the other side, on slippery red clay, into the gorge below. Looking back at the maps (which in 1962 did not exist), the maze of elevation lines shows this to be the steepest, most broken terrain in the Solomons, almost vertical in many places. Rather than following the contours, the path zigzagged from peak tops to watering places a thousand or more feet below.

We did not pass a settlement all day. But exotic it was, not least of all because my tour guides were two cheerful and pretty teenage girls, smoking pipes and stark naked. They bounded up and down the path like mountain goats; my fifty-pound packs were a trifle. At the end of the afternoon, exhausted, I was led into a mountaintop clearing with several thatch buildings. It was clear from the response of the men gathered there, surly-looking and carrying long machetes, bows and arrows, and clubs, that I

1. See Keesing and Corris 1980.

2. The government had been getting all the place names wrong for fifty years.

was neither expected nor particularly welcome. Trying to explain my presence through linguistic filters, I learned that this was a marriage feast. I was told I would have to stay inside one of the houses, from which I could only peek through narrow gaps in the thatch. Having been warned by the government that I might well be killed by Kwaio warriors, who had dispatched a dozen Europeans through the years (and were to dispatch another, a New Zealand missionary, three years later), I was less than relaxed.

What followed through most of the night was uninterpretable and often terrifying. Perhaps two hundred people, the women and many of the men naked except for shell ornaments and woven pouches, streamed into the clearing as dusk fell. Several times, a warrior clutching a machete or club ran screaming around the house from which I was peering, shouting with what seemed hostility; one chopped down a banana tree beside the house with fierce whacks. Shouts and speeches, then falsetto screams echoing out on all sides, naked bodies back and fro in the flickering firelight. Eventually, persuaded by the sheer lapse of time that I was not to be the main course and numbed by physical exhaustion, I strung my mosquito net in a corner of the house and collapsed into sleep, only to be awakened in terror when someone stumbled into my net and he and it collapsed on top of me.

In late 1964, after almost two years of fieldwork, I could look back and smile at my early anxieties and innocence. I had been to a dozen wedding feasts, had helped to finance some with my own strung shell valuables, and knew now about the conventionalized mock threats and food distributions that had terrified me that first time. I spoke Kwaio fluently and had been received by these fiercely conservative mountaineers with a warmth and enthusiasm that had been amazing. (Only later did I more clearly understand the extent to which I had, through accidents of history, been incorporated into their historic project of anticolonial struggle;

when I arrived they were trying to write down their customs in emulation of colonial legal statutes, and I was to be their scribe.)[3] Taking part in feasting prestations, incorporated into kinship and neighborhood networks, allowed into shrines to take part in rituals,[4] I felt like a comfortable "insider."

But of course, I wasn't. I could never leave my own cultural world despite my partial successes in entering theirs. In fact, the lonely isolation, after ten months with scarcely a word of English (and mail service only once a month), was taking me near the edge of psychological balance. I choose two small episodes late in my fieldwork to illustrate both my precarious state and the unbridged and unbridgeable gulf between their world and mine. Both began while I was sitting in my thatch house typing field notes (I was very good about that in those days and have been degenerating ever since).

As I sat typing one day, a wizened little man I hadn't seen before—he turned out to be from the mountains ten miles down the coast—slipped rather furtively beside me and whispered, "Come outside, I want to tell you something important." I put him off several times while I finished my journal entry, but eventually I followed as he led us secretively into a dark corner of an empty adjoining house. He leaned over to me and asked me portentously, in a hoarse voice scarcely loud enough to be heard, "Do you know where we all come from?" "What do you mean?" I asked. "Do you know where we Malaita people came from?" "Not exactly," I said, "but we're finding out something about that." "We all come from the same place, you Americans and we Malaita people. Do you know that?" Aha, I thought. A visionary glimpse of the human past ... I shifted into lecturing mode, and for five minutes or so I gave him a condensed explanation of the evolution of humankind and the prehistory of the Pacific. He heard me out politely. "I didn't think you knew," he said. "I'll tell you. You know that mountain at Iofana, beyond 'Ubuni—that's where we all came from. We Malaita people and you

3. See Keesing 1978, 1988; and Fifi'i 1989.

4. In the category of small-boy-who-doesn't-know-any-better, a status into which I was inducted after my wife's return to the United States at the end of 1963.

Americans." And then he gave *his* five-minute lecture, about the snake ancestress 'Oi'oifi'ona from whose eight human children the Malaitans—and Americans, by way of a migration to and beyond Tulagi—are descended. He was right. I didn't know.[5]

A few weeks later, I was again at my typewriter. I heard a commotion in the harbor a thousand feet below and went out to look. Loud voices, splashing of human—and other—bodies in the water. "They're driving *kirio* [dolphins] onto the beach and killing them," explained a local lad. A couple of minutes later, some young men from a settlement just up the hill came bounding down. "We're going down to kill a dolphin!" they announced. I was horrified: I had just been reading Lilly's early accounts of dolphin intelligence and had spent hours with my former teacher Gregory Bateson before I left California, discussing his plans for dolphin research. "Don't kill a dolphin! They're intelligent! They're like people!" I called out. But they paid no heed and went bounding down the precipitous path to the harbor.

Two hours later, they were back, carrying a huge leaf package. "We got one!" they called cheerfully. I was still horrified. Although Malaitans eat dolphins, that is a fringe benefit; they kill them for the teeth, which are used as exchange valuables and ornamentation. The young men unwrapped their package, to display a big butchered dolphin. I confess to a moment of ambivalence at the sight of red mammalian steaks—I had had no meat but an occasional strip of pork fat for months. But my outrage on behalf of a fellow sentient being far outweighed my urge for steak, and I abandoned my typewriter in favor of rhetoric.

"Don't eat that thing! You shouldn't eat *kirio*. They're not fish [*i'a*, in Kwaio]! They're like people, not fish! Look at its blood—it's red, and warm, like ours!" My friends went on cutting logs and building up a fire to heat the stones for a leaf oven, oblivious

to my rhetoric (but giving me odd glances). My rhetoric was impeded somewhat by language problems. Dolphins may not be fish, but they are *i'a*. "But they're not *i'a to'ofunga'a*, 'real' *i'a*," I insisted (but they are: The category includes dolphins and whales as well as fish). The locals were unimpressed, so I reiterated the argument about warm, red blood. "And look," I said, "they can talk. *Kirio* can talk, the way we do."

This was too much, and they stopped building the fire. "What do you mean, they can talk?" I remembered that in the *Life* magazines in my house, there was an issue with a Lockheed ad showing a scuba diver tape-recording dolphin squeaks; and I bounded into the house to look for it. A few minutes later, I returned in triumph to the firebuilders, who had returned to the task and were heating stones. The ad was perfect. Fortuitously, the microphone the scuba diver was holding looked exactly like my tape-recorder microphone. "Look at this," I said. "The *kirio* is talking onto [*sic*] the tape recorder. They talk just the way humans do. That's why you shouldn't eat them."

At last, I had their interest. "We didn't know they could talk! How do you talk to them? What language do they speak? How can they talk under water?" I explained as best I could about dolphin bleeps and the efforts to decode them. But they went on with their stone-heating and then put the tasty-looking meat into a leaf oven. "You shouldn't eat them," I pressed again. "They're not like fish, they're like us. They're intelligent. They talk." But after the possibility of humans talking with dolphins had faded, so had their interest. But not their appetites. Eventually I went back to my typewriter, wondering why my logic and rhetorical force hadn't persuaded them to bury the poor kindred spirit rather than eating it.

Only after typing fretfully at my notes for another fifteen minutes did it dawn on me that until 1927, when the government imposed the *Pax Britannica* after the massacre, the Kwaio ate *people*....

5. This episode was brought back to mind in 1989 during a session taping stories of ancient ancestors and human origins with the brilliant young pagan priest Maenaa'adi and my longtime Kwaio collaborator, the late Jonathan Fifi'i. During a pause, Fifi'i turned to me and said, "When I was in California with you [in 1966–67], I met some people who said they were descended from apes and monkeys. I thought that was really interesting. I'm descended from a snake."

Last year, a quarter of a century later, on my eighth fieldwork trip into Kwaio country, chewing betel and squatting around a fire reflecting with Maenaa'adi about the outcome of the divination he had just performed and the ritual about to be staged, I was still all I will ever be: an outsider who knows something of what it is to be an insider.

REFERENCES

Fifi'i, J. 1989. *From Pig-Theft to Parliament: My Life Between Two Worlds*. R. M. Keesing, trans. and ed. Honiara: University of the South Pacific and Solomon Islands College of Higher Education.

Keesing, R. M. 1978. *'Elota's Story: The Life and Times of a Solomon Island Big Man*. St. Lucia: University of Queensland Press (2d ed. 1983, New York: Holt, Rinehart & Winston).

Keesing, R. M. 1988. *The Anthropologist as Messiah*. Etnofoor 1:78–81.

Keesing, R. M., and P. Corris. 1980. *Lightning Meets the West Wind: The Malaita Massacre*. Melbourne: Oxford University Press.

DISCUSSION QUESTIONS

1. How did author Roger Keesing get caught with his ethnocentrism showing?

2. Keesing tried to argue that dolphins should not be eaten because they are mammals. Do you believe that Western anthropologists come from cultures that prohibit eating the flesh of mammals?

3. In a single sentence, state the significance of this short article for the beginning student of cultural anthropology.

3

Rapport-Talk and Report-Talk

DEBORAH TANNEN

Professor of Linguistics, Georgetown University

In the selection, Deborah Tannen, a professor of sociolinguistics at Georgetown University, explores the real differences in linguistic style between men and women in the United States. Women feel that men never express their feelings, are critical, and tend to operate in "lecture mode." Men, on the other hand, feel that their wives nag them and never get to the point. Often women and men walk away from a conversation with totally different impressions of what has just transpired. In many respects, Tannen suggests that discourse between men and women takes on some of the difficulties of cross-cultural communication.

Tannen distinguishes between the female mode of "rapport-talk" and the male mode of "report-talk." Women, according to Tannen, use talk for the purpose of building rapport with others. This rapport-talk involves a good deal of emotional self-disclosure and emphasizes matching experiences and showing empathy and understanding. Report-talk, on the other hand, the prominent linguistic style of men, uses talk to establish and maintain status and power. Personal disclosures are avoided because they can make the highly combative male appear vulnerable. For men discourse is competitive, information oriented, and geared to solving problems and accomplishing goals. Men feel more comfortable engaging in public speaking, whereas women operate more effectively in the private domain.

It is no coincidence that the book from which this selection is taken stayed on the New York Times best-seller list for nearly four years. Tannen combines a keen eye for observation with the power of original analysis to provide an excellent description of gender discourse in the United States. But Tannen's work is also relevant to applied anthropology because of its usefulness for helping us better understand and improve our discourse with members of the opposite sex.

I was sitting in a suburban living room, speaking to a women's group that had invited men to join them for the occasion of my talk about communication between women and men. During the discussion, one man was particularly talkative, full of lengthy comments and explanations. When I made the observation that women often complain that their husbands don't talk to them enough, this man volunteered that he heartily agreed. He gestured toward his wife, who had sat silently beside him on the couch throughout the evening, and said, "She's the talker in our family."

Everyone in the room burst into laughter. The man looked puzzled and hurt. "It's true," he

SOURCE: Excerpt from pp. 74–81 from YOU JUST DON'T UNDERSTAND by DEBORAH TANNEN. COPYRIGHT © 1990 BY DEBORAH TANNEN. Reprinted by permission of HarperCollins Publishers.

explained. "When I come home from work, I usually have nothing to say, but she never runs out. If it weren't for her, we'd spend the whole evening in silence." Another woman expressed a similar paradox about her husband: "When we go out, he's the life of the party. If I happen to be in another room, I can always hear his voice above the others. But when we're home, he doesn't have that much to say. I do most of the talking."

Who talks more, women or men? According to the stereotype, women talk too much. Linguist Jennifer Coates notes some proverbs:

A woman's tongue wags like a lamb's tail.
Foxes are all tail and women are all
tongue. The North Sea will sooner be
found wanting in water than a woman be
at a loss for a word.

Throughout history, women have been punished for talking too much or in the wrong way. Linguist Connie Eble lists a variety of physical punishments used in Colonial America: Women were strapped to dunking stools and held underwater until they nearly drowned, put into the stocks with signs pinned to them, gagged, and silenced by a cleft stick applied to their tongues.

Though such institutionalized corporal punishments have given way to informal, often psychological ones, modern stereotypes are not much different from those expressed in the old proverbs. Women are believed to talk too much. Yet study after study finds that it is men who talk more—at meetings, in mixed-group discussions, and in classrooms where girls or young women sit next to boys or young men. For example, communications researchers Barbara and Gene Eakins tape-recorded and studied seven university faculty meetings. They found that, with one exception, men spoke more often and, without exception, spoke for a longer time. The men's turns ranged from 10.66 to 17.07 seconds, while the women's turns ranged from 3 to 10 seconds. In other words, the women's longest turns were still shorter than the men's shortest turns.

When a public lecture is followed by questions from the floor, or a talk show host opens the phones, the first voice to be heard asking a question is almost always a man's. And when they ask questions or offer comments from the audience, men tend to talk longer. Linguist Marjorie Swacker recorded question-and-answer sessions at academic conferences. Women were highly visible as speakers at the conferences studied; they presented 40.7 percent of the papers at the conferences studied and made up 42 percent of the audiences. But when it came to volunteering and being called on to ask questions, women contributed only 27.4 percent. Furthermore, the women's questions, on the average, took less than half as much time as the men's. (The mean was 23.1 seconds for women, 52.7 for men.) This happened, Swacker shows, because men (but not women) tended to preface their questions with statements, ask more than one question, and follow up the speaker's answer with another question or comment.

I have observed this pattern at my own lectures, which concern issues of direct relevance to women. Regardless of the proportion of women and men in the audience, men almost invariably ask the first question, more questions, and longer questions. In these situations, women often feel that men are talking too much. I recall one discussion period following a lecture I gave to a group assembled in a bookstore. The group was composed mostly of women, but most of the discussion was being conducted by men in the audience. At one point, a man sitting in the middle was talking at such great length that several women in the front rows began shifting in their seats and rolling their eyes at me. Ironically, what he was going on about was how frustrated he feels when he has to listen to women going on and on about topics he finds boring and unimportant.

RAPPORT-TALK AND REPORT-TALK

Who talks more, then, women or men? The seemingly contradictory evidence is reconciled by the difference between what I call *public* and *private speaking*. More men feel comfortable doing "public speaking," while more women feel comfortable doing "private" speaking. Another way of capturing these differences is by using the terms *report-talk* and *rapport-talk*.

For most women, the language of conversation is primarily a language of rapport: a way of establishing connections and negotiating relationships. Emphasis is placed on displaying similarities and matching experiences. From childhood, girls criticize peers who try to stand out or appear better than others. People feel their closest connections at home, or in settings where they *feel* at home—with one or a few people they feel close to and comfortable with—in other words, during private speaking. But even the most public situations can be approached like private speaking.

For most men, talk is primarily a means to preserve independence and negotiate and maintain status in a hierarchical social order. This is done by exhibiting knowledge and skill, and by holding center stage through verbal performance such as storytelling, joking, or imparting information. From childhood, men learn to use talking as a way to get and keep attention. So they are more comfortable speaking in larger groups made up of people they know less well—in the broadest sense, "public speaking." But even the most private situations can be approached like public speaking, more like giving a report than establishing rapport.

PRIVATE SPEAKING:
THE WORDY WOMAN AND
THE MUTE MAN

What is the source of the stereotype that women talk a lot? Dale Spender suggests that most people feel instinctively (if not consciously) that women, like children, should be seen and not heard, so any amount of talk from them seems like too much. Studies have shown that if women and men talk equally in a group, people think the women talked more. So there is truth to Spender's view. But another explanation is that men think women talk a lot because they hear women talking in situations where men would not: on the

telephone; or in social situations with friends, when they are not discussing topics that men find inherently interesting; or, like the couple at the women's group, at home alone—in other words, in private speaking.

Home is the setting for an American icon that features the silent man and the talkative woman. And this icon, which grows out of the different goals and habits I have been describing, explains why the complaint most often voiced by women about the men with whom they are intimate is "He doesn't talk to me"—and the second most frequent is "He doesn't listen to me."

A woman who wrote to Ann Landers is typical:

> My husband never speaks to me when he comes home from work. When I ask, "How did everything go today?" he says, "Rough..." or "It's a jungle out there." (We live in Jersey and he works in New York City.)
>
> It's a different story when we have guests or go visiting. Paul is the gabbiest guy in the crowd—a real spellbinder. He comes up with the most interesting stories. People hang on every word. I think to myself, "Why doesn't he ever tell *me* these things?"
>
> This has been going on for 38 years. Paul started to go quiet on me after 10 years of marriage. I could never figure out why. Can you solve the mystery?

—THE INVISIBLE WOMAN

Ann Landers suggests that the husband may not want to talk because he is tired when he comes home from work. Yet women who work come home tired too, and they are nonetheless eager to tell their partners or friends everything that happened to them during the day and what these fleeting, daily dramas made them think and feel.

Sources as lofty as studies conducted by psychologists, as down to earth as letters written to advice columnists, and as sophisticated as movies and plays come up with the same insight: Men's silence at home is a disappointment to women. Again and again, women complain, "He seems to have everything to say to everyone else, and nothing to say to me."

The film *Divorce American Style* opens with a conversation in which Debbie Reynolds is claiming that she and Dick Van Dyke don't communicate, and he is protesting that he tells her everything that's on his mind. The doorbell interrupts their quarrel, and husband and wife compose themselves before opening the door to greet their guests with cheerful smiles.

Behind closed doors, many couples are having conversations like this. Like the character played by Debbie Reynolds, women feel men don't communicate. Like the husband played by Dick Van Dyke, men feel wrongly accused. How can she be convinced that he doesn't tell her anything, while he is equally convinced he tells her everything that's on his mind? How can women and men have such different ideas about the same conversations?

When something goes wrong, people look around for a source to blame: either the person they are trying to communicate with ("You're demanding, stubborn, self-centered") or the group that the other person belongs to ("All women are demanding"; "All men are self-centered"). Some generous-minded people blame the relationship ("We just can't communicate"). But underneath, or overlaid on these types of blame cast outward, most people believe that something is wrong with them.

If individual people or particular relationships were to blame, there wouldn't be so many different people having the same problems. The real problem is conversational style. Women and men have different ways of talking. Even with the best intentions, trying to settle the problem through talk can only make things worse if it is ways of talking that are causing trouble in the first place.

BEST FRIENDS

Once again, the seeds of women's and men's styles are sown in the ways they learn to use language while growing up. In our culture, most people, but especially women, look to their closest

relationships as havens in a hostile world. The center of a little girl's social life is her best friend. Girls' friendships are made and maintained by telling secrets. For grown women too, the essence of friendship is talk, telling each other what they're thinking and feeling, and what happened that day: who was at the bus stop, who called, what they said, how that made them feel. When asked who their best friends are, most women name other women they talk to regularly. When asked the same question, most men will say it's their wives. After that, many men name other men with whom they do things such as play tennis or baseball (but never just sit and talk) or a chum from high school whom they haven't spoken to in a year.

When Debbie Reynolds complained that Dick Van Dyke didn't tell her anything, and he protested that he did, both were right. She felt he didn't tell her anything because he didn't tell her the fleeting thoughts and feelings he experienced throughout the day—the kind of talk she would have with her best friend. He didn't tell her these things because to him they didn't seem like anything to tell. He told her anything that seemed important—anything he would tell his friends.

Men and women often have very different ideas of what's important—and at what point "important" topics should be raised. A woman told me, with lingering incredulity, of a conversation with her boyfriend. Knowing he had seen his friend Oliver, she asked, "What's new with Oliver?" He replied, "Nothing." But later in the conversation it came out that Oliver and his girlfriend had decided to get married. "That's nothing?" the woman gasped in frustration and disbelief.

For men, "Nothing" may be a ritual response at the start of a conversation. A college woman missed her brother but rarely called him because she found it difficult to get talk going. A typical conversation began with her asking, "What's up with you?" and his replying, "Nothing." Hearing his "Nothing" as meaning "There is nothing personal I want to talk about," she supplied talk by filling him in on her news and eventually hung up in frustration. But when she thought back, she remembered that later in the conversation he had mumbled, "Christie and I got into another fight." This came so late and so low that she didn't pick up on it. And he was probably equally frustrated that she didn't.

Many men honestly do not know what women want, and women honestly do not know why men find what they want so hard to comprehend and deliver.

DISCUSSION QUESTIONS

1. How would you summarize Tannen's characterization of gender differences in linguistic styles found in the United States?

2. Have you seen any of these gender differences in linguistic style operating in your own conversations with members of the opposite gender? Be specific.

3. Based on Tannen's description of female and male communication styles, what practical suggestions would you make to men and women in the United States to help them improve their cross-gender communication?

4

The Sounds of Silence

EDWARD T. HALL AND MILDRED REED HALL

Northwestern University

When we think of human communication, it is usually language that first comes to mind. As important as language is to the communications process, humans also send and receive an enormous number of messages without ever uttering words. Humans communicate nonverbally in a number of different ways. We communicate through "body language," such as gestures, facial expressions, posture, gait, body movement, and eye contact. We communicate by touching others or by withholding physical contact. Certain physical qualities of our bodies (such as body type, height, weight, skin color, and body odor, among others) also convey different meanings in different parts of the world. We communicate by the artifacts we put on our bodies, such as clothing, makeup, perfumes, jewelry, and eyeglasses. We communicate by using time when we keep people waiting or arrive early to a party. And as the Halls point out in this selection, spatial distancing, such as conversational distances and seating arrangements, also sends various messages in different cultures.

In this article, written more than forty years ago, the Halls remind us that people from all cultures communicate without words; there are many different modes of nonverbal communication (such as facial expressions, hand gestures, eye contact, posture, and touching, among others); and the actual details of nonverbal communication vary enormously from culture to culture. Mastering the realm of nonverbal communication becomes even more challenging when we realize that there are some cultures that tend to emphasize nonverbal communication over language. US culture, for example, places greater importance on the spoken word, whereas many Eastern cultures, the Japanese in particular, look to nonverbal messages as the primary conveyer of meaning. North Americans, therefore, are likely to underestimate the importance of nonverbal cues in a cross-cultural setting. As important as language is in all human communication, it is imperative that, if we are to become globally savvy in the twenty-first century, we need to learn to "hear" the silent messages and "read" the invisible words of nonverbal communication wherever we may encounter them.

Bob leaves his apartment at 8:15 a.m. and stops at the corner drug-store for breakfast. Before he can speak, the counterman says, "The usual?" Bob nods yes. While he savors his Danish, a fat man pushes onto the adjoining stool and overflows into his space. Bob scowls and the man pulls himself in as much as he can. Bob has sent two messages without speaking a syllable.

SOURCE: From "The Sounds of Silence," by Edward T. Hall and Mildred R. Hall. Copyright © 1971 by Edward T. Hall and Mildred R. Hall. Reprinted with permission of the author.

Henry has an appointment to meet Arthur at 11 o'clock; he arrives at 11:30. Their conversation is friendly, but Arthur retains a lingering hostility. Henry has unconsciously communicated that he doesn't think the appointment is very important or that Arthur is a person who needs to be treated with respect.

George is talking to Charley's wife at a party. Their conversation is entirely trivial, yet Charley glares at them suspiciously. Their physical proximity and the movements of their eyes reveal that they are powerfully attracted to each other.

José Ybarra and Sir Edmund Jones are at the same party and it is important for them to establish a cordial relationship for business reasons. Each is trying to be warm and friendly, yet they will part with mutual distrust and their business transaction will probably fall through. José, in Latin fashion, moved closer and closer to Sir Edmund as they spoke, and this movement was miscommunicated as pushiness to Sir Edmund, who kept backing away from this intimacy, and this was miscommunicated to José as coldness. The silent languages of Latin and English cultures are more difficult to learn than their spoken languages.

In each of these cases, we see the subtle power of nonverbal communication. The only language used throughout most of the history of humanity (in evolutionary terms, vocal communication is relatively recent), it is the first form of communication you learn. You use this preverbal language, consciously and unconsciously, every day to tell other people how you feel about yourself and them. This language includes your posture, gestures, facial expressions, costume, the way you walk, even your treatment of time and space and material things. All people communicate on several different levels at the same time but are usually aware of only the verbal dialog and don't realize that they respond to nonverbal messages. But when a person says one thing and really believes something else, the discrepancy between the two can usually be sensed. Nonverbal-communication systems are much less subject to the conscious deception that often occurs in verbal systems. When we find ourselves thinking, "I don't know what it is about him, but he doesn't seem sincere," it's usually this lack of congruity between a person's words and his behavior that makes us anxious and uncomfortable.

Few of us realize how much we all depend on body movement in our conversation or are aware of the hidden rules that govern listening behavior. But we know instantly whether or not the person we're talking to is "tuned in" and we're very sensitive to any breach in listening etiquette. In white middle-class American culture, when someone wants to show he is listening to someone else, he looks either at the other person's face or, specifically, at his eyes, shifting his gaze from one eye to the other.

If you observe a person conversing, you'll notice that he indicates he's listening by nodding his head. He also makes little "Hmm" noises. If he agrees with what's being said, he may give a vigorous nod. To show pleasure or affirmation, he smiles; if he has some reservations, he looks skeptical by raising an eyebrow or pulling down the corners of his mouth. If a participant wants to terminate the conversation, he may start shifting his body position, stretching his legs, crossing or uncrossing them, bobbing his foot, or diverting his gaze from the speaker. The more he fidgets, the more the speaker becomes aware that he has lost his audience. As a last measure, the listener may look at his watch to indicate the imminent end of the conversation.

Talking and listening are so intricately intertwined that a person cannot do one without the other. Even when one is alone and talking to oneself, there is part of the brain that speaks while another part listens. In all conversations, the listener is positively or negatively reinforcing the speaker all the time. He may even guide the conversation without knowing it, by laughing or frowning or dismissing the argument with a wave of his hand.

The language of the eyes—another age-old way of exchanging feelings—is both subtle and complex. Not only do men and women use their eyes differently but there are class, generation, regional, ethnic, and national cultural differences. Americans often complain about the way foreigners stare at people or hold a glance too long. Most Americans look away from someone who is using his eyes in an unfamiliar way because it makes them self-conscious. If a man looks at another man's wife in a certain way, he's asking for trouble, as indicated earlier. But he might not be ill-mannered or seeking to challenge the husband. He might be a European in this country who hasn't learned our visual mores. Many American women visiting France or Italy are acutely embarrassed because, for the first time in their lives, men really look at them—their eyes, hair, nose, lips, breasts, hips, legs, thighs, knees, ankles, feet, clothes, hairdo, even their walk. These same women, once they have become used to being looked at, often return to the United States and are overcome with the feeling that "No one ever really looks at me anymore."

Analyzing the mass of data on the eyes, it is possible to sort out at least three ways in which the eyes are used to communicate: dominance versus submission, involvement versus detachment and positive versus negative attitude. In addition there are three levels of consciousness and control, which can be categorized as follows: (1) conscious use of the eye to communicate, such as the flirting blink and the intimate nose-wrinkling squint; (2) the very extensive category of unconscious but learned behavior governing where the eyes are directed and when (this unwritten set of rules dictates how and under what circumstances the sexes, as well as people of all status categories, look at each other); and (3) the response of the eye itself, which is completely outside both awareness and control— changes in that cast (the sparkle) of the eye and the pupillary reflex.

The eye is unlike any other organ of the body, for it is an extension of the brain. The unconscious pupillary reflex and the cast of the eye have been known by people of Middle Eastern origin for years—although most are unaware of their knowledge. Depending on the context Arabs and others look either directly at the eye or deeply *into* the eyes of their interlocutor. We became aware of this in the Middle East several years ago while looking at jewelry. The merchant suddenly started to push a particular bracelet at a customer and said, "You buy this one." What interested us was that the bracelet was not the one that had been consciously selected by the purchaser. But the merchant, watching the pupils of the eyes, knew what the purchaser really wanted to buy. Whether he specifically knew *how* he knew is debatable.

A psychologist at the University of Chicago, Eckhard Hess, was the first to conduct systematic studies of the pupillary reflex. His wife remarked one evening, while watching him reading in bed, that he must be very interested in the text because his pupils were dilated. Following up on this, Hess slipped some pictures of nudes into a stack of photographs that he gave to his male assistant. Not looking at the photographs but watching his assistant's pupils, Hess was able to tell precisely when the assistant came to the nudes. In further experiments, Hess retouched the eyes in a photograph of a woman. In one print, he made the pupils small, in another, large; nothing else was changed. Subjects who were given the photographs found the woman with the dilated pupils much more attractive. Any man who has had the experience of seeing a woman look at him as her pupils widen with reflex speed knows that she's flashing him a message.

The eye-sparkle phenomenon frequently turns up in our interviews of couples in love. It's apparently one of the first reliable clues in the other person that love is genuine. To date, there is no scientific data to explain eye sparkle; no investigation of the pupil, the cornea or even the white sclera of the eye shows how the sparkle originates. Yet we all know it when we see it.

One common situation for most people involves the use of the eyes in the street and in public. Although eye behavior follows a definite set of rules, the rules vary according to the place, the needs and feelings of the people, and their ethnic background. For urban whites, once they're within definite recognition distance (16–32 feet for people with average eyesight), there is mutual avoidance of eye contact—unless they want something specific; a pickup, a handout or information of some kind. In the West and in small towns generally, however, people are much more likely to look at and greet one another, even if they're strangers.

It's permissible to look at people if they're beyond recognition distance; but once inside this sacred zone, you can only steal a glance at strangers. You *must* greet friends, however; to fail to do so is insulting. Yet, to stare too fixedly at them is considered rude and hostile. Of course, all of these rules are variable.

A great many blacks, for example, greet each other in public even if they don't know each other. To blacks, most eye behavior of whites has the effect of giving the impression that they aren't there, but this is due to white avoidance of eye contact with *anyone* in the street.

Another very basic difference between people of different ethnic backgrounds is their sense of territoriality and how they handle space. This is the silent communication, or miscommunication, that caused friction between Mr. Ybarra and Sir Edmund Jones in our earlier example. We know from research that everyone has around himself an invisible bubble of space that contracts and expands depending on several factors: his emotional state, the activity he's performing at the time and his cultural background. This bubble is a kind of mobile territory that he will defend against intrusion. If he is accustomed to close personal distance between himself and others, his bubble will be smaller than that of someone who's accustomed to greater personal distance. People of North European heritage— English, Scandinavian, Swiss, and German—tend to avoid contact. Those whose heritage is Italian, French, Spanish, Russian, Latin American, or Middle Eastern like close personal contact.

People are very sensitive to any intrusion into their spatial bubble. If someone stands too close to you, your first instinct is to back up. If that's not possible, you lean away and pull yourself in, tensing your muscles. If the intruder doesn't respond to these body signals, you may then try to protect yourself, using a briefcase, umbrella or raincoat. Women—especially when traveling alone—often plant their pocketbook in such a way that no one gets very close to them. As a last resort, you may move to another spot and position yourself behind a desk or a chair that provides screening. Everyone tries to adjust the space around himself in a way that's comfortable for him; most often, he does this unconsciously.

Emotions also have a direct effect on the size of a person's territory. When you're angry or under stress, your bubble expands and you require more space. New York psychiatrist Augustus Kinzel found a difference in what he calls Body-Buffer Zones between violent and nonviolent prison inmates. Dr. Kinzel conducted experiments in which a prisoner was placed in the center of a small room and then Dr. Kinzel slowly walked toward him. Nonviolent prisoners allowed him to come quite close, while prisoners with a history of violent behavior couldn't tolerate his proximity and reacted with some vehemence.

Apparently, people under stress experience other people as looming larger and closer than they actually are. Studies of schizophrenic patients have indicated that they sometimes have a distorted perception of space, and several psychiatrists have reported patients who experience their boundaries as filling up an entire room. For these patients, anyone who comes into the room is actually inside their body, and such an intrusion may trigger a violent outburst.

Unfortunately, there is little detailed information about normal people who live in highly congested urban areas. We do know, of course, that the noise, pollution, dirt, crowding, and confusion of our cities induce feelings of stress in more of us, and stress leads to a need for greater space. The man who's packed into a subway, jostled in the street, crowded into an elevator and forced to work all day in a bull pen or in a small office without auditory or visual privacy is going to be very stressed at the end of his day. He needs places that provide relief from constant overstimulation of his nervous system. Stress from overcrowding is cumulative and people can tolerate more crowding early in the day than later; note the increased bad temper during the evening rush hour as compared with the morning melee. Certainly one factor in people's desire to commute by car is the need for privacy and relief from crowding (except, often, from other cars); it may be the only time of the day when nobody can intrude.

In crowded public places, we tense our muscles and hold ourselves stiff, and thereby communicate to others our desire, not to intrude on their space and, above all, not to touch them. We also avoid eye contact, and the total effect is that of someone who has "tuned out." Walking along the street, our bubble expands slightly as we move in a stream of strangers, taking care not to bump into them. In the office, at meetings, in restaurants, our bubble keeps changing as it adjusts to the activity at hand.

Most white middle-class Americans use four main distances in their business and social relations: intimate, personal, social, and public. Each of these distances has a near and a far phase and is accompanied by changes in the volume of the voice. Intimate distance varies from direct physical contact with another person to a distance of six to eighteen inches and is used for our most private activities—caressing another person or making love. At this distance, you are overwhelmed by sensory inputs from the other person—heat from the body, tactile stimulation from the skin, the fragrance of perfume, even the sound of breathing—all of which literally envelop you. Even at the far phase, you're still within easy touching distance. In general, the use of intimate distance in public between adults is frowned on. It's also much too close for strangers, except under conditions of extreme crowding.

In the second zone—personal distance—the close phase is one and a half to two and a half feet; it's at this distance that wives usually stand from their husbands in public. If another woman moves into this zone, the wife will most likely be disturbed. The far phase—two and a half to four feet—is the distance used to "keep someone at arm's length" and is the most common spacing used by people in conversation.

The third zone—social distance—is employed during business transactions or exchanges with a clerk or repairman. People who work together tend to use close social distance—four to seven feet. This is also the distance for conversation at social gatherings. To stand up at this distance from someone who is seated has a dominating effect (e.g., teacher to pupil, boss to secretary). The far phase of the third zone—seven to twelve feet—is

where people stand when someone says, "Stand back so I can look at you." This distance lends a formal tone to business or social discourse. In an executive office, the desk serves to keep people at this distance.

The fourth zone—public distance—is used by teachers in classrooms or speakers at public gatherings. At its farthest phase—25 feet and beyond—it is used for important public figures. Violations of this distance can lead to serious complications. During his 1970 U.S. visit, the president of France, Georges Pompidou, was harassed by pickets in Chicago, who were permitted to get within touching distance. Since pickets in France are kept behind barricades a block or more away, the president was outraged by this insult to his person, and President Nixon was obliged to communicate his concern as well as offer his personal apologies.

It is interesting to note how American pitchmen and panhandlers exploit the unwritten, unspoken conventions of eye and distance. Both take advantage of the fact that once explicit eye contact is established, it is rude to look away, because to do so means to brusquely dismiss the other person and his needs. Once having caught the eye of his mark, the panhandler then locks on, not letting go until he moves through the public zone, the social zone, the personal zone and, finally, into the intimate sphere, where people are most vulnerable.

Touch also is an important part of the constant stream of communication that takes place between people. A light touch, a firm touch, a blow, a caress are all communications. In an effort to break down barriers among people, there's been a recent upsurge in group-encounter activities, in which strangers are encouraged to touch one another. In special situations such as these, the rules for not touching are broken with group approval and people gradually lose some of their inhibitions.

Although most people don't realize it, space is perceived and distances are set not by vision alone but with all the senses. Auditory space is perceived with the ears, thermal space with the skin, kinesthetic space with the muscles of the body and olfactory space with the nose. And, once again, it's one's culture that determines how his senses are pro-grammed—which sensory information ranks highest and lowest. The important thing to remember is that culture is very persistent. In this country, we've noted the existence of culture patterns that determine distance between people in the third and fourth generations of some families, despite their prolonged contact with people of very different cultural heritages.

Whenever there is great cultural distance between two people, there are bound to be problems arising from difference in behavior and expectations. An example is the American couple who consulted a psychiatrist about their marital problems. The husband was from New England and had been brought up by reserved parents who taught him to control his emotions and to respect the need for privacy. His wife was from an Italian family and had been brought up in close contact with all the members of her large family, who were extremely warm, volatile and demonstrative.

When the husband came home after a hard day at the office, dragging his feet and longing for peace and quiet, his wife would rush to him and smother him. Clasping his hands, rubbing his brow, crooning over his weary head, she never left him alone. But when the wife was upset or anxious about her day, the husband's response was to withdraw completely and leave her alone. No comforting, no affectionate embrace, no attention—just solitude. The woman became convinced her husband didn't love her, and, in desperation, she consulted a psychiatrist. Their problem wasn't basically psychological but cultural.

Why has man developed all these different ways of communicating messages without words? One reason is that people don't like to spell out certain kinds of messages. We prefer to find other ways of showing our feelings. This is especially true in relationships as sensitive as courtship. Men don't like to be rejected and most women don't want to turn a man down bluntly. Instead, we work out subtle ways of encouraging or discouraging each other that save face and avoid confrontations.

How a person handles space in dating others is an obvious and very sensitive indicator of how he

or she feels about the other person. On a first date, if a woman sits or stands so close to a man that he is acutely conscious of her physical presence—inside the intimate-distance zone—the man usually construes it to mean that she is encouraging him. However, before the man starts moving in on the woman, he should be sure what message she's really sending; otherwise, he risks bruising his ego. What is close to someone of North European background may be neutral or distant to someone of Italian heritage. Also, women sometimes use space as a way of misleading a man and there are few things that put men off more than women who communicate contradictory messages—such as women who cuddle up and then act insulted when a man takes the next step.

How does a woman communicate interest in a man? In addition to such familiar gambits as smiling at him, she may glance shyly at him, blush, and then look away. Or she may give him a real come-on look and move in very close when he approaches. She may touch his arm and ask for a light. As she leans forward to light her cigarette, she may brush him lightly, enveloping him in her perfume. She'll probably continue to smile at him and she may use what ethologists call preening gestures—touching the back of her hair, thrusting her breasts forward, tilting her hips as she stands or crossing her legs if she's seated, perhaps even exposing one thigh or putting a hand on her thigh and stroking it. She may also stroke her wrists as she converses or show the palm of her hand as a way of gaining his attention. Her skin may be unusually flushed or quite pale, her eyes brighter, the pupils larger.

If a man sees a woman whom he wants to attract, he tries to present himself by his posture and stance as someone who is self-assured. He moves briskly and confidently. When he catches the eye of the woman, he may hold her glance a little longer than normal. If he gets an encouraging smile, he'll move in close and engage her in small talk. As they converse, his glance shifts over her face and body. He, too, may make preening gestures—straightening his tie, smoothing his hair or shooting his cuffs.

How do people learn body language? The same way they learn spoken language—by observing and imitating people around them as they're growing up. Little girls imitate their mothers or an older female. Little boys imitate their fathers or a respected uncle or a character in television. In this way, they learn the gender signals appropriate for their sex. Regional, class, and ethnic patterns of body behavior are also learned in childhood and persist throughout life.

Such patterns of masculine and feminine body behavior vary widely from one culture to another. In America, for example, women stand with their thighs together. Many walk with their pelvis tipped slightly forward and their upper arms close to their body. When they sit, they cross their ankles. American men hold their arms away from their body, often swinging them as they walk. They stand with their legs apart (an extreme example is the cowboy, with legs apart and thumbs tucked into his belt). When they sit, they put their feet on the floor with legs apart and, in some parts of the country, they cross their legs by putting one ankle on the other knee.

Leg behavior indicates sex, status, and personality. It also indicates whether or not one is at ease or is showing respect or disrespect for the other person. Young Latin-American males avoid crossing their legs. In their world of *machismo*, the preferred position for young males when with one another (if there is no older dominant male present to whom they must show respect) is to sit on the base of their spine with their leg muscles relaxed and their feet wide apart. Their respect position is like our military equivalent; spine straight, heels and ankles together—almost identical to that displayed by properly brought up young women in New England in the early part of this century.

American women who sit with their legs spread apart in the presence of males are *not* normally signaling a come-on—they are simply (and often unconsciously) sitting like men. Middle-class women in the presence of other women to whom they are very close may on occasion throw themselves down on a soft chair or sofa and let themselves go. This is a signal that nothing serious will be taken up. Males, on the other hand, lean back and prop their legs up on the nearest object.

The way we walk, similarly, indicates status, respect, mood, and ethnic or cultural affiliation. The many variants of the female walk are too well known to go into here, except to say that a man would have to be blind not to be turned on by the way some women walk—a fact that made Mae West rich before scientists ever studied these matters. To white Americans, some French middle-class males walk in a way that is both humorous and suspect. There is a bounce and looseness to the French walk, as though the parts of the body were somehow unrelated. Jacques Tati, the French movie actor, walks this way; so does the great mime, Marcel Marceau.

Blacks and whites in America—with the exception of middle- and upper-middle-class professionals of both groups—move and walk very differently from each other. To the blacks, whites often seem incredibly stiff, almost mechanical in their movements. Black males, on the other hand, have a looseness and coordination that frequently makes whites a little uneasy; it's too different, too integrated, too alive, too male. Norman Mailer has said that squares walk from the shoulders, like bears, but blacks and hippies walk from the hips, like cats.

All over the world, people walk not only in their own characteristic way but have walks that communicate the nature of their involvement with whatever it is they're doing. The purposeful walk of North Europeans is an important component of proper behavior on the job. Any male who has been in the military knows how essential it is to walk properly (which makes for a continuing source of tension between blacks and whites in the Service). The quick shuffle of servants in the Far East in the old days was a show of respect. On the island of Truk, when we last visited, the inhabitants even had a name for the respectful walk that one used when in the presence of a chief or when walking past a chief's house. The term was *sufan*, which meant to be humble and respectful.

The notion that people communicate volumes by their gestures, facial expressions, posture and walk is not new; actors, dancers, writers and psychiatrists have long been aware of it. Only in recent years, however, have scientists begun to make systematic observations of body motions. Ray L. Birdwhistell of the University of Pennsylvania is one of the pioneers in body-motion research and coined the term kinesics to describe this field. He developed an elaborate notation system to record both facial and body movements, using an approach similar to that of the linguist, who studies the basic elements of speech. Birdwhistell and other kinesicists such as Albert Sheflen, Adam Kendon and William Condon take movies of people interacting. They run the film over and over again, often at reduced speed for frame-by-frame analysis, so that they can observe even the slightest body movements not perceptible at normal interaction speeds. These movements are then recorded in notebooks for later analysis.

To appreciate the importance of nonverbal-communication systems, consider the unskilled inner-city black looking for a job. His handling of time and space alone is sufficiently different from the white middle-class pattern to create great misunderstandings on both sides. The black is told to appear for a job interview at a certain time. He arrives late. The white interviewer concludes from his tardy arrival that the black is irresponsible and not really interested in the job. What the interviewer doesn't know is that the black time system (often referred to by blacks as C.P.T.—colored people's time) isn't the same as that of whites. In the words of a black student who had been told to make an appointment to see his professor: "Man, you *must* be putting me on. I never had an appointment in my life."

The black job applicant, having arrived late for his interview, may further antagonize the white interviewer by his posture and his eye behavior. Perhaps he slouches and avoids looking at the interviewer; to him this is playing it cool. To the interviewer, however, he may well look shifty and sound uninterested.

The interviewer has failed to notice the actual signs of interest and eagerness in the black's behavior, such as the subtle shift in the quality of the voice—a gentle and tentative excitement—an almost imperceptible change in the cast of the eyes and a relaxing of the jaw muscles.

Moreover, correct reading of black–white behavior is continually complicated by the fact that both groups are comprised of individuals—some of whom [sic] try to accommodate and some of whom make it a point of pride *not* to accommodate. At present, this means that many Americans, when thrown into contact with one another, are in the precarious position of not knowing which pattern applies. Once identified and analyzed, nonverbal-communication systems can be taught, like a foreign language. Without this training, we respond to nonverbal communications in terms of our own culture; we read everyone's behavior as if it were our own, and thus we often misunderstand it.

Several years ago in New York City, there was a program for sending children from predominantly black and Puerto Rican low-income neighborhoods to summer school in a white upper-class neighborhood on the East Side. One morning, a group of young black and Puerto Rican boys raced down the street, shouting and screaming and overturning garbage cans on their way to school. A doorman from an apartment building nearby chased them and cornered one of them inside a building. The boy drew a knife and attacked the doorman. This tragedy would not have occurred if the doorman had been familiar with the behavior of boys from low-income neighborhoods, where such antics are routine and socially acceptable and where pursuit would be expected to invite a violent response.

The language of behavior is extremely complex. Most of us are lucky to have under control one subcultural system—the one that reflects our sex, class, generation, and geographic region within the United States. Because of its complexity, efforts to isolate bits of nonverbal communication and generalize from them are in vain; you don't become an instant expert on people's behavior by watching them at cocktail parties. Body language isn't something that's independent of the person, something that can be donned and doffed like a suit of clothes.

Our research and that of our colleagues has shown that, far from being a superficial form of communication that can be consciously manipulated, nonverbal-communication systems are interwoven into the fabric of the personality and, as sociologist Erving Goffman had demonstrated, into society itself. They are the warp and wool of daily interactions with others and they influence how one expresses oneself, how one experiences oneself as a man or a woman.

Nonverbal communications signal to members of your own group what kind of person you are, how you feel about others, how you'll fit into and work in a group, whether you're assured or anxious, the degree to which you feel comfortable with the standards of your own culture, as well as deeply significant feelings about the self including the state of your own psyche. For most of us it's difficult to accept the reality of another's behavioral system. And, of course, none of us will ever become fully knowledgeable of the importance of every nonverbal signal. But as long as each of us realizes the power of these signals, this society's diversity can be a source of great strength rather than a further—and subtly powerful—source of division.

DISCUSSION QUESTIONS

1. How many modes of human nonverbal communication can you identify?

2. How does nonverbal communication function in regulating human interaction?

3. In US culture, how can you tell (from nonverbal forms of communication) whether someone is listening to you?

5

The Worst Mistake in the History of the Human Race

JARED DIAMOND
UCLA School of Medicine

Approximately 10,000 years ago, humans made the revolutionary transition from food collecting to food production (the domestication of plants and animals). For hundreds of thousands of years before this time, humans had subsisted exclusively on what they obtained naturally from the environment through hunting and gathering. Although no definitive explanation has emerged for why the Neolithic (food-producing) Revolution occurred, most archaeologists agree that it was a response to certain environmental or demographic conditions, such as variations in rainfall or population increases. Whatever the cause or causes may have been, there is little doubt of the monumental consequences of the Neolithic Revolution, which produced the world's first population explosion. Not only did populations become larger as a result of the Neolithic Revolution, but they also became more sedentary, more occupationally diversified, and more highly stratified. It is generally believed that without these enormous sociocultural changes brought about by the Neolithic Revolution, civilization (or urban society), the Industrial Revolution, and the global Information Age of the twenty-first century would never have been possible.

The enormity of the changes brought about by the Agricultural Revolution cannot be overstated. Most people take for granted the enormous prosperity humans have enjoyed during the last 10,000 years because of the Neolithic Revolution. And yet some anthropologists (including Jared Diamond) who have identified many of the negative consequences of the Neolithic Revolution conclude that it may have been a colossal mistake for the subsequent evolution of humanity. What do you think?

To science we owe dramatic changes in our smug self-image. Astronomy taught us that our earth isn't the center of the universe but merely one of billions of heavenly bodies. From biology we learned that we weren't specially created by God but evolved along with millions of other species. Now archaeology is demolishing another sacred belief: that human history over the past million years has been a long tale of progress. In particular, recent discoveries suggest that the adoption of agriculture, supposedly our most decisive step toward a better life, was in many ways a catastrophe from which we have never recovered. With agriculture came the gross social and sexual

SOURCE: Diamond, Jared, "The Worst Mistake in the History of the Human Race." *First appeared in Discover*, 8(5), 1987, pp. 64–66. Reprinted with permission of the author.

inequality, the disease and despotism, that curse our existence.

At first, the evidence against this revisionist interpretation will strike twentieth century Americans as irrefutable. We're better off in almost every respect than people of the Middle Ages, who in turn had it easier than cavemen, who in turn were better off than apes. Just count our advantages. We enjoy the most abundant and varied foods, the best tools and material goods, some of the longest and healthiest lives, in history. Most of us are safe from starvation and predators. We get our energy from oil and machines, not from our sweat. What neo-Luddite among us would trade his life for that of a medieval peasant, a caveman, or an ape?

For most of our history we supported ourselves by hunting and gathering: we hunted wild animals and foraged for wild plants. It's a life that philosophers have traditionally regarded as nasty, brutish, and short. Since no food is grown and little is stored, there is (in this view) no respite from the struggle that starts anew each day to find wild foods and avoid starving. Our escape from this misery was facilitated only 10,000 years ago, when in different parts of the world people began to domesticate plants and animals. The agricultural revolution spread until today it's nearly universal and few tribes of hunter-gatherers survive.

From the progressivist perspective on which I was brought up, to ask "Why did almost all our hunter-gatherer ancestors adopt agriculture?" is silly. Of course they adopted it because agriculture is an efficient way to get more food for less work. Planted crops yield far more tons per acre than roots and berries. Just imagine a band of savages, exhausted from searching for nuts or chasing wild animals, suddenly grazing for the first time at a fruit-laden orchard or a pasture full of sheep. How many milliseconds do you think it would take them to appreciate the advantages of agriculture?

The progressivist party line sometimes even goes so far to credit agriculture with the remarkable flowering of art that has taken place over the past few thousand years. Since crops can be stored, and since it takes less time to pick food from a garden than to find it in the wild, agriculture gave

us free time that hunter-gatherers never had. Thus it was agriculture that enabled us to build the Parthenon and compose the B-minor Mass.

While the case for the progressivist view seems overwhelming, it's hard to prove. How do you show that the lives of people 10,000 years ago got better when they abandoned hunting and gathering for farming? Until recently, archaeologists had to resort to indirect tests, whose results (surprisingly) failed to support the progressivist view. Here's one example of an indirect test: Are twentieth century hunter-gatherers really worse off than farmers? Scattered throughout the world, several dozen groups of so-called primitive people, like the Kalahari bushmen, continue to support themselves that way. It turns out that these people have plenty of leisure time, sleep a good deal, and work less hard than their farming neighbors. For instance, the average time devoted each week to obtaining food is only 12 to 19 hours for one group of Bushmen, 14 hours or less for the Hadza nomads of Tanzania. One Bushman, when asked why he hadn't emulated neighboring tribes by adopting agriculture, replied, "Why should we, when there are so many mongongo nuts in the world?"

While farmers concentrate on high-carbohydrate crops like rice and potatoes, the mix of wild plants and animals in the diets of surviving hunter-gatherers provides more protein and a better balance of other nutrients. In one study, the Bushmen's average daily food intake (during a month when food was plentiful) was 2,140 calories and 93 grams of protein, considerably greater than the recommended daily allowance for people of their size. It's almost inconceivable that Bushmen, who eat 75 or so wild plants, could die of starvation the way hundreds of thousands of Irish farmers and their families did during the potato famine of the 1840s.

So the lives of at least the surviving hunter-gatherers aren't nasty and brutish, even though farmers have pushed them into some of the world's worst real estate. But modern hunter-gatherer societies that have rubbed shoulders with farming societies for thousands of years don't tell us about conditions before the agricultural revolution. The progressivist view is really making a claim about the distant past: that the lives of primitive people improved when they switched from gathering to farming. Archaeologists can date that switch by distinguishing remains of wild plants and animals from those of domesticated ones in prehistoric garbage dumps.

How can one deduce the health of the prehistoric garbage makers, and thereby directly test the progressivist view? That question has become answerable only in recent years, in part through the newly emerging techniques of paleopathology, the study of signs of disease in the remains of ancient peoples.

In some lucky situations, the paleopathologist has almost as much material to study as a pathologist today. For example, archaeologists in the Chilean deserts found well preserved mummies whose medical conditions at time of death could be determined by autopsy (*Discover*, October). And feces of long-dead Indians who lived in dry caves in Nevada remain sufficiently well preserved to be examined for hookworm and other parasites.

Usually the only human remains available for study are skeletons, but they permit a surprising number of deductions. To begin with, a skeleton reveals its owner's sex, weight, and approximate age. In the few cases where there are many skeletons, one can construct mortality tables like the ones life insurance companies use to calculate expected life span and risk of death at any given age. Paleopathologists can also calculate growth rates by measuring bones of people of different ages, examine teeth for enamel defects (signs of childhood malnutrition), and recognize scars left on bones by anemia, tuberculosis, leprosy, and other diseases.

One straightforward example of what paleopathologists have learned from skeletons concerns historical changes in height. Skeletons from Greece and Turkey show that the average height of hunter-gatherers toward the end of the ice ages was a generous 5' 9" for men, 5' 5" for women. With the adoption of agriculture, height crashed, and by 3000 B.C. had reached a low of only 5' 3" for men, 5' for women. By classical times heights were very slowly on the rise again, but modern

Greeks and Turks have still not regained the average height of their distant ancestors.

Another example of paleopathology at work is the study of Indian skeletons from burial mounds in the Illinois and Ohio river valleys. At Dickson Mounds, located near the confluence of the Spoon and Illinois rivers, archaeologists have excavated some 800 skeletons that paint a picture of the health changes that occurred when a hunter-gatherer culture gave way to intensive maize farming around A.D. 1150. Studies by George Armelagos and his colleagues then at the University of Massachusetts show these early farmers paid a price for their new-found livelihood. Compared to the hunter-gatherers who preceded them, the farmers had a nearly 50 percent increase in enamel defects indicative of malnutrition, a fourfold increase in iron-deficiency anemia (evidenced by a bone condition called porotic hyperostosis), a threefold rise in bone lesions reflecting infectious disease in general, and an increase in degenerative conditions of the spine, probably reflecting a lot of hard physical labor. "Life expectancy at birth in the pre-agricultural community was about twenty-six years," says Armelagos, "but in the post-agricultural community it was nineteen years. So these episodes of nutritional stress and infectious disease were seriously affecting their ability to survive."

The evidence suggests that the Indians at Dickson Mounds, like many other primitive peoples, took up farming not by choice but from necessity in order to feed their constantly growing numbers. "I don't think most hunter-gatherers farmed until they had to, and when they switched to farming they traded quality for quantity," says Mark Cohen of the State University of New York at Plattsburgh, co-editor with Armelagos, of one of the seminal books in the field, *Paleopathology at the Origins of Agriculture*. "When I first started making that argument ten years ago, not many people agreed with me. Now it's become a respectable, albeit controversial, side of the debate."

There are at least three sets of reasons to explain the findings that agriculture was bad for health. First, hunter-gatherers enjoyed a varied diet, while early farmers obtained most of their food from one or a few starchy crops. The farmers gained cheap calories at the cost of poor nutrition. (Today just three high-carbohydrate plants—wheat, rice, and corn—provide the bulk of the calories consumed by the human species, yet each one is deficient in certain vitamins or amino acids essential to life.) Second, because of dependence on a limited number of crops, farmers ran the risk of starvation if one crop failed. Finally, the mere fact that agriculture encouraged people to clump together in crowded societies, many of which then carried on trade with other crowded societies, led to the spread of parasites and infectious disease. (Some archaeologists think it was the crowding, rather than agriculture, that promoted disease, but this is a chicken-and-egg argument, because crowding encourages agriculture and vice versa.) Epidemics couldn't take hold when populations were scattered in small bands that constantly shifted camp. Tuberculosis and diarrheal disease had to await the rise of farming[;] measles and bubonic plague[,] the appearance of large cities.

Besides malnutrition, starvation, and epidemic diseases, farming helped bring another curse upon humanity: deep class divisions. Hunter-gatherers have little or no stored food, and no concentrated food sources, like an orchard or a herd of cows: they live off the wild plants and animals they obtain each day. Therefore, there can be no kings, no class of social parasites who grow fat on food seized from others. Only in a farming population could a healthy, non-producing élite set itself above the disease-ridden masses. Skeletons from Greek tombs at Mycenae ca. 1500 B.C. suggest that royals enjoyed a better diet than commoners, since the royal skeletons were two or three inches taller and had better teeth (on the average, one instead of six cavities or missing teeth). Among Chilean mummies from ca. A.D. 1000, the élite were distinguished not only by ornaments and gold hair clips but also by a fourfold lower rate of bone lesions caused by disease.

Similar contrasts in nutrition and health persist on a global scale today. To people in rich countries like the U.S., it sounds ridiculous to extol the virtues of hunting and gathering. But Americans are an élite, dependent on oil and minerals that must often be imported from countries with poorer health and nutrition. If one could choose between being a peasant farmer in Ethiopia or a bushman gatherer in the Kalahari, which do you think would be the better choice?

Farming may have encouraged inequality between the sexes, as well. Freed from the need to transport their babies during a nomadic existence, and under pressure to produce more hands to till the fields, farming women tended to have more frequent pregnancies than their hunter-gatherer counterparts—with consequent drains on their health. Among the Chilean mummies for example, more women than men had bone lesions from infectious disease.

Women in agricultural societies were sometimes made beasts of burden. In New Guinea farming communities today I often see women staggering under loads of vegetables and firewood while the men walk empty-handed. Once while on a field trip there studying birds, I offered to pay some villagers to carry supplies from an airstrip to my mountain camp. The heaviest item was a 110-pound bag of rice, which I lashed to a pole and assigned to a team of four men to shoulder together. When I eventually caught up with the villagers, the men were carrying light loads, while one small woman weighing less than the bag of rice was bent under it, supporting its weight by a cord across her temples.

As for the claim that agriculture encouraged the flowering of art by providing us with leisure time, modern hunter-gatherers have at least as much free time as do farmers. The whole emphasis on leisure time as a critical factor seems to me misguided. Gorillas have had ample free time to build their own Parthenon, had they wanted to. While post-agricultural technological advances did make new art forms possible and preservation of art easier, great paintings and sculptures were already being produced by hunter-gatherers 15,000 years ago, and were still being produced as recently as the last century by such hunter-gatherers as some Eskimos and the Indians of the Pacific Northwest.

Thus with the advent of agriculture the élite became better off, but most people became worse off. Instead of swallowing the progressivist party line that we chose agriculture because it was good for us, we must ask how we got trapped by it despite its pitfalls.

One answer boils down to the adage "Might makes right." Farming could support many more people than hunting, albeit with a poorer quality of life. (Population densities of hunter-gatherers are rarely over one person per ten square miles, while farmers average 100 times that.) Partly, this is because a field planted entirely in edible crops lets one feed far more mouths than a forest with scattered edible plants. Partly, too, it's because nomadic hunter-gatherers have to keep their children spaced at four-year intervals by infanticide and other means, since a mother must carry her toddler until it's old enough to keep up with the adults. Because farm women don't have that burden, they can and often do bear a child every two years.

As population densities of hunter-gatherers slowly rose at the end of the ice ages, bands had to choose between feeding more mouths by taking the first steps toward agriculture, or else finding ways to limit growth. Some bands chose the former solution, unable to anticipate the evils of farming, and seduced by the transient abundance they enjoyed until population growth caught up with increased food production. Such bands outbred and then drove off or killed the bands that chose to remain hunter-gatherers, because a hundred malnourished farmers can still outfight one healthy hunter. It's not that hunter-gatherers abandoned their life style, but that those sensible enough not to abandon it were forced out of all areas except the ones farmers didn't want.

At this point it's instructive to recall the common complaint that archaeology is a luxury, concerned with the remote past, and offering no lessons for the present. Archaeologists studying the rise of farming have reconstructed a crucial stage at which we made the worst mistake in human history. Forced to choose between limiting population or [sic] trying to increase food production, we chose the latter and ended up with starvation, warfare, and tyranny.

Hunter-gatherers practiced the most successful and longest-lasting lifestyle in human history. In contrast, we're still struggling with the mess into which agriculture has tumbled us, and it's unclear whether we can solve it. Suppose that an archaeologist who had visited from outer space were trying to explain human history to his fellow spacelings. He might illustrate the results of his digs by a 24-hour clock on which one hour represents 100,000 years of real past time. If the history of the human race began at midnight, then we would now be almost at the end of our first day. We lived as hunter-gatherers for nearly the whole of that day, from midnight through dawn, noon, and sunset. Finally, at 11:54 p.m. we adopted agriculture. As our second midnight approaches, will the plight of famine-stricken peasants gradually spread to engulf us all? Or will we somehow achieve those seductive blessings that we imagine behind agriculture's glittering façade, and that have so far eluded us?

DISCUSSION QUESTIONS

1. How did the introduction of food production (agriculture and animal husbandry) affect the health of the world's population?

2. Do you agree with the idea that food production was a prerequisite for civilization (large, differentiated, stratified societies with bureaucratic forms of government)? Why or why not?

3. Even if food production was not "the worst mistake in the history of the human race," why is this brief article by Jared Diamond important to read?

6

The Domestication of Wood in Haiti: A Case Study in Applied Evolution

GERALD F. MURRAY

Professor Emeritus, University of Gainesville

During the 1980s, Haiti, like many other developing countries, faced a major problem of deforestation. Owing to market demands for lumber and charcoal, some 50 million trees per year were being harvested, posing the dual problem of denuding the country of trees and lowering farm productivity through soil erosion. Previous attempts to stem the tide of deforestation took a conservationist approach, rewarding people for planting and penalizing them for cutting trees down. Anthropologist Gerald Murray, hired by USAID to direct the reforestation efforts in Haiti, took a different, and quite unorthodox, approach to the problem. Wanting to capitalize on the strong tradition of cash cropping among Haiti's small farmers, he suggested that local farmers be given seedlings to plant as a cash crop. Wood trees, in Murray's view, should be planted, harvested, and sold in the same way as corn or beans.

This project in applied anthropology drew heavily not only on past ethnographic studies of Haitian farmers but also on evolutionary theory. Cultural evolutionists remind us that humans were foragers for approximately 99.8 percent of their time on earth and, as such, ran the risk of wiping out their food supply if they became too efficient. Thus, foragers had built-in limits to the amount of food they could procure and, consequently, the size of their populations. It wasn't until humans began to domesticate plants and animals around 10,000 years ago that the world's food supply expanded exponentially. In other words, the age-old problem of food shortages was not solved by a conservationist approach, but rather by encouraging human populations to increase food supplies through their own efforts. This approach to reforestation, informed by both anthropological data and theory, was enormously successful. By the end of the four-year project, more than 20 million trees had been planted.

PROBLEM AND CLIENT

Expatriate tree lovers, whether tourists or developmental planners, often leave Haiti with an upset stomach. Though during precolonial times the island Arawaks had reached a compromise with the forest, their market-oriented colonial successors saw trees as something to be removed. The Spaniards specialized in exporting wood from the eastern side of the island, whereas the French on the western third found it more profitable to clear the wood and produce sugar cane, coffee, and indigo for

SOURCE: *Anthropological praxis: translating knowledge into action* by Wulff, Robert M. and Fiske, Shirley J. Reproduced with permission of WESTVIEW PRESS in the format Republish in a book via Copyright Clearance Center.

European markets. During the nineteenth century, long after Haiti had become an independent republic, foreign lumber companies cut and exported most of the nation's precious hardwoods, leaving little for today's peasants.

The geometric increase in population since colonial times—from an earlier population of fewer than half a million former slaves to a contemporary population of more than six million—and the resulting shrinkage of average family holding size have led to the evolution of a land use system devoid of systematic fallow periods. A vicious cycle has set in—one that seems to have targeted the tree for ultimate destruction. Not only has land pressure eliminated a regenerative fallow phase in the local agricultural cycle; in addition, the catastrophic declines in per hectare food yields have forced peasants into alternative income-generating strategies. Increasing numbers crowd into the capital city, Port-au-Prince, creating a market for construction wood and charcoal. Poorer sectors of the peasantry in the rural areas respond to this market by racing each other with axes and machetes to cut down the few natural tree stands remaining in remoter regions of the republic. The proverbial snowball in Hades is at less risk than a tree in Haiti.

Unable to halt the flows either of wood into the cities or of soil into the oceans, international development organizations finance studies to measure the volume of these flows (50 million trees cut per year is one of the round figures being bandied about) and to predict when the last tree will be cut from Haiti. Reforestation projects have generally been entrusted by their well-meaning but short-sighted funders to Duvalier's Ministry of Agriculture, a kiss-of-death resource channeling strategy by which the Port-au-Prince jobs created frequently outnumber the seedlings produced. And even the few seedlings produced often died in the nurseries because peasants were understandably reluctant to cover their scarce holdings with state-owned trees. Project managers had been forced to resort to "food for work" strategies to move seedlings out of nurseries onto hillsides. And peasants have endeavored where possible to plant the trees on somebody else's hillsides and to enlist their

livestock as allies in the subsequent removal of this potentially dangerous vegetation.

This generalized hostility to tree projects placed the U.S. Agency for International Development (AID)/Haiti mission in a bind. After several years of absence from Haiti in the wake of expulsion by Francois Duvalier, AID had reestablished its presence under the government of his son Jean Claude. But an ambitious Integrated Agricultural Development Project funded through the Ministry of Agriculture had already given clear signs of being a multimillion-dollar farce. And an influential congressman chairing the U.S. House Ways and Means Committee—and consequently exercising strong control over AID funds worldwide—had taken a passionate interest in Haiti. In his worldwide travels this individual had become adept at detecting and exposing developmental charades. And he had been blunt in communicating his conviction that much of what he had seen in AID/Haiti's program was precisely that. He had been touched by the plight of Haiti and communicated to the highest AID authorities his conviction about the salvific power of contraceptives and trees and his determination to have AID grace Haiti with an abundant flow of both. And he would personally visit Haiti (a convenient plane ride from Washington, D.C.) to inspect for himself, threatening a worldwide funding freeze if no results were forthcoming. A chain reaction of nervous "yes sirs" speedily worked its way down from AID headquarters in Washington to a beleaguered Port-au-Prince mission.

The pills and condoms were less of a problem. Even the most cantankerous congressman was unlikely to insist on observing them in use and would probably settle for household distribution figures. Not so with the trees. He could (and did) pooh-pooh nursery production figures and ask to be taken to see the new AID forests, a most embarrassing request in a country where peasants creatively converted daytime reforestation projects into nocturnal goat forage projects. AID's reaction was twofold—first, to commission an immediate study to explain to the congressman and others why peasants refused to plant trees (for this they called down an

AID economist); and second, to devise some program strategy that would achieve the apparently unachievable: to instill in cash-needy, defiant peasant charcoalmakers a love, honor, and respect for newly planted trees. For this attitudinal transformation, a task usually entrusted to the local armed forces, AID/Haiti invited an anthropologist to propose an alternative approach.

PROCESS AND PLAYERS

During these dynamics, I completed a doctoral dissertation on the manner in which Haitian peasant land tenure had evolved in response to internal population growth. The AID economist referred to above exhaustively reviewed the available literature, also focusing on the issue of Haitian peasant land tenure, and produced for the mission a well-argued monograph (Zuvekas 1978) documenting a lower rate of landlessness in Haiti than in many other Latin American settings but documenting as well the informal, extralegal character of the relationship between many peasant families and their landholdings. This latter observation was interpreted by some in the mission to mean that the principal determinant of the failure of tree planting projects was the absence among peasants of legally secure deeds over their plots. Peasants could not be expected to invest money on land improvements when at mildest the benefits could accrue to another and at worst the very improvements themselves could lead to expropriation from their land. In short, no massive tree planting could be expected, according to this model, until a nationwide cadastral reform granted plot-by-plot deeds to peasant families.

This hypothesis was reputable but programmatically paralyzing because nobody dreamed that the Duvalier regime was about to undertake a major cadastral reform for the benefit of peasants. Several AID officers in Haiti had read my dissertation on land tenure (Murray 1977), and I received an invitation to advise the mission. Was Haitian peasant land tenure compatible with tree planting? Zuvekas' study had captured the internally complex

nature of Haitian peasant land tenure. But the subsequent extrapolations as to paralyzing insecurity simply did not seem to fit with the ethnographic evidence. In two reports (Murray 1978a, 1978b) I indicated that peasants in general feel secure about their ownership rights over their land. Failure to secure plot-by-plot surveyed deeds is generally a cost-saving measure. Interclass evictions did occur, but they were statistically rare; instead most land disputes were intrafamilial. A series of extralegal tenure practices had evolved—preinheritance land grants to young adult dependents, informal inheritance subdivisions witnessed by community members, fictitious sales to favored children, complex community-internal sharecropping arrangements. And though these practices produced an internally heterogeneous system with its complexities, there was strong internal order. Any chaos and insecurity tended to be more in the mind of observers external to the system than in the behavior of the peasants themselves. There was a danger that the complexities of Haitian peasant land tenure would generate an unintended smokescreen obscuring the genuine causes of failure in tree planting projects.

What then were these genuine causes? The mission, intent on devising programming strategies in this domain, invited me to explore further, under a contract aimed at identifying the "determinants of success and failure" in reforestation and soil conservation projects. My major conclusion was that the preexisting land tenure, cropping, and livestock systems in peasant Haiti were perfectly adequate for the undertaking of significant tree planting activities. Most projects had failed not because of land tenure or attitudinal barriers among peasants but because of fatal flaws in one or more key project components. Though my contract called principally for analysis of previous or existing projects, I used the recommendation section of the report to speculate on how a Haiti-wise anthropologist would program and manage reforestation activities if he or she had the authority. In verbal debriefings I jokingly challenged certain young program officers in the mission to give me a jeep and carte blanche access to a $50,000 checking account, and I would prove my anthropological assertions about peasant economic behavior and produce more trees in the ground than their current multimillion-dollar Ministry of Agriculture charade. We had a good laugh and shook hands, and I departed confident that the report would be as dutifully perused and as honorably filed and forgotten as similar reports I had done elsewhere.

To my great disbelief, as I was correcting Anthro 101 exams some two years later, one of the program officers still in Haiti called to say that an Agroforestry Outreach Project (AOP) had been approved chapter and verse as I had recommended it; and that if I was interested in placing my life where my mouth had been and would leave the ivory tower to direct the project, my project bank account would have, not $50,000, but $4 million. After several weeks of hemming and hawing and vigorous negotiating for a leave from my department, I accepted the offer and entered a new (to me) role of project director in a strange upside-down world in which the project anthropologist was not a powerless cranky voice from the bleachers but the chief of party with substantial authority over general project policy and the allocation of project resources. My elation at commanding resources to implement anthropological ideas was dampened by the nervousness of knowing exactly who would be targeted for flak and ridicule if these ideas bombed out, as most tended to do in the Haiti of Duvalier.

The basic structural design of AOP followed a tripartite conceptual framework that I proposed for analyzing projects. Within this framework a project is composed of three essential systemic elements: a technical base, a benefit flow strategy, and an institutional delivery strategy. Planning had to focus equally on all three. I argued that defects in one would sabotage the entire project.

Technical Strategy

The basic technical strategy was to make available to peasants fast-growing wood trees (*Leucaena leucocephala, Cassia siatnea, Azadirachta indica, Casuarina equisedfolia, Eucalyptus camaldulensis*) that were not only drought resistant but also rapid growing,

producing possible four-year harvest rotations in humid lowland areas (and slower rotations and lower survival rates in arid areas) and that were good for charcoal and basic construction needs. Most of the species mentioned also restore nutrients to the soil, and some of them coppice from a carefully harvested stump, producing several rotations before the need for replanting.

Of equally critical technical importance was the use of a nursery system that produced light-weight microseedlings. A project pickup truck could transport over 15,000 of these microseedlings (as opposed to 250 traditional bag seedlings), and the average peasant could easily carry over 500 transportable seedlings at one time, planting them with a fraction of the ground preparation time and labor required for bulkier bagged seedlings. The anthropological implications of this nursery system were critical. It constituted a technical breakthrough that reduced to a fraction the fossil-fuel and human energy expenditure required to transport and plant trees.

But the technical component of the project incorporated yet another element: the physical juxtaposition of trees and crops. In traditional reforestation models, the trees are planted in large unbroken monocropped stands. Such forests or woodlots presuppose local land tenure and economic arrangements not found in Haiti. For the tree to make its way as a cultivate into the economy of Haitian peasants and most other tropical cultivators, reforestation models would have to be replaced by agroforestry models that entail spatial or temporal juxtaposition of crops and trees. Guided by prior ethnographic knowledge of Haitian cropping patterns, AOP worked out with peasants various border planting and intercropping strategies to make tree planting feasible even for small holding cultivators.

Benefit Flow Strategies

With respect to the second systemic component, the programming of benefit flows to participants, earlier projects had often committed the fatal flaw of defining project trees planted as *pyebwa leta* (the state's trees). Authoritarian assertions by project staff concerning sanctions for cutting newly planted trees created fears among peasants that even trees planted on their own land would be government property. And several peasants were frank in reporting fears that the trees might eventually be used as a pretext by the government or the "Company" (the most common local lexeme used to refer to projects) for eventually expropriating the land on which peasants had planted project trees.

Such ambiguities and fears surrounding benefit flows paralyze even the technically soundest project. A major anthropological feature of AOP was a radical frontal attack on the issue of property and usufruct rights over project trees. Whereas other projects had criticized tree cutting, AOP promulgated the heretical message that trees were meant to be cut, processed, and sold. The only problem with the present system, according to project messages, was that peasants were cutting nature's trees. But once a landowner "*mete fos li deyo*" (expends his resources) and plants and cares for his or her own wood trees on his or her own land, the landowner has the same right to harvest and sell wood as corn or beans.

I was inevitably impressed at the impact that this blunt message had when I delivered it to groups of prospective peasant tree planters. Haitian peasants are inveterate and aggressive cash-croppers; many of the crops and livestock that they produce are destined for immediate consignment to local markets. For the first time in their lives, they were hearing a concrete proposal to make the wood tree itself one more marketable crop in their inventory.

But the message would ring true only if three barriers were smashed.

1. The first concerned the feared delay in benefits. Most wood trees with which the peasants were familiar took an impractically long time to mature. There fortunately existed in Haiti four-year-old stands of leucaena, cassia, eucalyptus, and other project trees to which we could take peasant groups to demonstrate the growth speed of these trees.

2. But could they be planted on their scanty holdings without interfering with crops? Border and row planting techniques were demonstrated, as well as intercropping. The average peasant holding was about a hectare and a half. If a cultivator planted a field in the usual crops and then planted 500 seedlings in the same field at 2 meters by 2 meters, the seedlings would occupy only a fifth of a hectare. And they would be far enough apart to permit continued cropping for two or three cycles before shade competition became too fierce. That is, trees would be planted on only a fraction of the peasant's holdings and planted in such a way that they would be compatible with continued food growing even on the plots where they stood. We would then calculate with peasants the potential income to be derived from these 500 trees through sale as charcoal, polewood, or boards. In a best-case scenario, the gross take from the charcoal of these trees (the least lucrative use of the wood) might equal the current annual income of an average rural family. The income potential of these wood trees clearly far offset any potential loss from decreased food production. Though it had taken AID two years to decide on the project, it took about twenty minutes with any group of skeptical but economically rational peasants to generate a list of enthusiastic potential tree planters.

3. But there was yet a third barrier. All this speculation about income generation presupposed that the peasants themselves, and not the government or the project, would be the sole owners of the trees and that the peasants would have unlimited rights to the harvest of the wood whenever they wished. To deal with this issue, I presented the matter as an agreement between the cultivator and the project: We would furnish free seedlings and technical assistance; the cultivators would agree to plant 500 of these seedlings on their own land and permit project personnel to carry out periodic survival counts. We would, of course, pay no wages or "Food for Work" for this planting. But we would guarantee to the planters complete and exclusive ownership of the trees. They did not need to ask for permission from the project to harvest the trees whenever their needs might dictate, nor

would there be any penalties associated with early cutting or low survival. If peasants changed their minds, they could rip out their seedlings six months after planting. They would never get any more free seedlings from us, but they would not be subject to any penalties. There are preexisting local forestry laws, rarely enforced, concerning permissions and minor taxes for tree cutting. Peasants would have to deal with these as they had skillfully done in the past. But from our project's point of view, we relinquish all tree ownership rights to the peasants who accept and plant the trees on their property.

Cash-flow dialogues and ownership assurances such as these were a far cry from the finger-wagging ecological sermons to which many peasant groups had been subjected on the topic of trees. Our project technicians developed their own messages; but central to all was the principle of peasant ownership and usufruct of AOP trees. The goal was to capitalize on the preexisting fuel and lumber markets, to make the wood tree one more crop in the income-generating repertoire of the Haitian peasant.

Institutional Strategy

The major potential fly in the ointment was the third component, the institutional component. To whom would AID entrust its funds to carry out this project? My own research had indicated clearly that Haitian governmental involvement condemned a project to certain paralysis and possible death, and my report phrased that conclusion as diplomatically as possible. The diplomacy was required to head off possible rage, less from Haitian officials than from certain senior officers in the AID mission who were politically and philosophically wedded to an institution-building strategy. Having equated the term "institution" with "government bureaucracy," and having defined their own career success in terms, not of village-level resource flows, but of voluminous and timely bureaucracy-to-bureaucracy cash transfers, such officials were in effect marshaling U.S. resources into the service of extractive ministries with unparalleled track records of squandering and/or pilfering expatriate donor funds.

To the regime's paradoxical credit, however, the blatant openness and arrogance of Duvalierist predation had engendered an angry willingness in much of Haiti's development community to explore other resource flow channels. Though the nongovernmental character of the proposal provoked violent reaction, the reactionaries in the Haiti mission were overridden by their superiors in Washington, and a completely nongovernmental implementing mode was adopted for this project.

The system, based on private voluntary organizations (PVOs), worked as follows.

1. AID made a macrogrant to a Washington-based PVO (the Pan American Development Foundation, PADF) to run a tree-planting project based on the principles that had emerged in my research. At the Haiti mission's urging, PADF invited me to be chief of party for the project and located an experienced accountant in Haiti to be financial administrator. PADF in addition recruited three American agroforesters who, in addition to MA-level professional training, had several years of overseas village field experience under their belts. Early in the project they were supplemented by two other expatriates, a Belgian and a French Canadian. We opened a central office in Port-au-Prince and assigned a major region of Haiti to each of the agroforesters, who lived in their field regions.

2. These agroforesters were responsible for contacting the many village-based PVOs working in their regions to explain the project, to emphasize its microeconomic focus and its difference from traditional reforestation models, to discuss the conditions of entry therein, and to make technical suggestions as to the trees that would be appropriate for the region.

3. If the PVO was interested, we drafted an agreement in which our mutual contributions and spheres of responsibility were specified. The agreements were not drafted in French (Haiti's official language) but in Creole, the only language spoken by most peasants.

4. The local PVO selected *animateurs* (village organizers) who themselves were peasants who

lived and worked in the village where trees would be planted. After receiving training from us, they contacted their neighbors and kin, generated lists of peasants interested in planting a specified number of trees, and informed us when the local rains began to fall. At the proper moment we packed the seedlings in boxes customized to the particular region and shipped them on our trucks to the farmers, who would be waiting at specified drop-off points at a specified time. The trees were to be planted within twenty-four hours of delivery.

5. The animateurs were provided with Creole language data forms by which to gather ecological, land use, and land tenure data on each plot where trees would be planted and certain bits of information on each peasant participant. These forms were used as well to follow up, at periodic intervals, the survival of the trees, the incidence of any problems (such as livestock depredation, burning, disease), and—above all—the manner in which the farmer integrated the trees into cropping and livestock patterns, to detect and head off any unintended substitution of food for wood.

RESULTS AND EVALUATION

The project was funded for four years from October 1981 through November 1985. During the writing of the project paper we were asked by an AID economist to estimate how many trees would be planted. Not knowing if the peasants would in fact plant any trees, we nervously proposed to reach two thousand peasant families with a million trees as a project goal. Fiddling with his programmed calculator, the economist informed us that that output would produce a negative internal rate of return. We would need at least two million trees to make the project worth AID's institutional while. We shrugged and told him cavalierly to up the figure and to promise three million trees on the land of six thousand peasants. (At that time I thought someone else would be directing the project.)

Numbers of Trees and Beneficiaries

Though I doubted that we could reach this higher goal, the response of the Haitian peasants to this new approach to tree planting left everyone, including myself, open mouthed. Within the first year of the project, one million trees had been planted by some 2,500 peasant households all over Haiti. My fears of peasant indifference were now transformed into nervousness that we could not supply seedlings fast enough to meet the demand triggered by our wood-as-a-cash-crop strategy. Apologetic village animateurs informed us that some cultivators who had not signed up on the first lists were actually stealing newly planted seedlings from their neighbors' fields at night. They promised to catch the scoundrels. If they did, I told them, give the scoundrels a hug. Their pilfering was dramatic proof of the bull's-eye nature of the anthropological predictions that underlie the project.

By the end of the second year (when I left the project), we had reached the four-year goal of three million seedlings and the project had geared up and decentralized its nursery capacity to produce several million seedlings per season (each year having two planting seasons). Under the new director, a fellow anthropologist, the geometric increase continued. By the end of the fourth year, the project had planted, not its originally agreed-upon three million trees, but twenty million trees. Stated more accurately, some 75,000 Haitian peasants had enthusiastically planted trees on their own land. In terms of its quantitative outreach, AOP had more than quintupled its original goals.

Wood Harvesting and Wood Banking

By the end of its fourth year the project had already received an unusual amount of professional research attention by anthropologists, economists, and foresters. In addition to AID evaluations, six studies had been released on one or another aspect of the project (Ashley 1986; Balzano 1986; Buffum and King 1985; Conway 1986; Grosenick 1985; McGowan 1986). As predicted, many peasants were harvesting trees by the end of the fourth year. The most lucrative sale of the wood was as polewood in local markets, though much charcoal was also being made from project trees.

Interestingly, however, the harvesting was proceeding much more slowly than I had predicted. Peasants were "clinging" to their trees and not engaging in the clear cutting that I hoped would occur, as a prelude to the emergence of a rotational system in which peasants would alternate crops with tree cover that they themselves had planted. This technique would have been a revival, under a "domesticated" mode, of the ancient swidden sequence that had long since disappeared from Haiti. Though such a revival would have warmed anthropological hearts, the peasants had a different agenda. Though they had long ago removed nature's tree cover, they were extremely cautious about removing the tree cover that they had planted. Their economic logic was unassailable. Crop failure is so frequent throughout most of Haiti, and the market for wood and charcoal so secure, that peasants prefer to leave the tree as a "bank" against future emergencies. This arboreal bank makes particular sense in the context of the recent disappearance from Haiti of the peasant's traditional bank, the pig. A governmentally mandated (and U.S. financed) slaughter of all pigs because of fears of African swine fever created a peasant banking gap that AOP trees have now started to fill.

Strengthening Private Institutions

Before this project, PVOs had wanted to engage in tree planting, and some ineffective ecology-cum-conservation models had been futilely attempted. AOP has now involved large numbers of PVOs in economically dynamic tree planting activities. Though some of the PVOs, many operating with religious affiliation, were originally nervous about the nonaltruistic commercial thrust of the AOP message, the astounding response of their rural clientele has demolished their objections. In fact many have sought their own sources of funding to carry out this new style of tree planting, based on microseedlings made available in large numbers to peasants as one more marketable crop. Although these PVOs are no longer dependent on AOP, it is safe to say that they will never revert to their former way of promoting trees. AOP has effected positive and probably irreversible changes in the behavior of dozens of well-funded, dedicated local institutions. And by nudging these PVOs away from ethereal visions of the functions of trees, AOP has brought them into closer dynamic touch with, and made them more responsive to, the economic interests of their peasant clientele.

Modifying AID's Modus Operandi

AID has not only taken preliminary steps to extend AOP (some talk is heard of a ten-year extension!); it also has adapted and adopted the privatized AOP delivery model for several other important projects. The basic strategy is twofold: to work through private institutions but to do it in a way consistent with AID administrative realities. AID missions prefer to move large chunks of money with one administrative sweep. Missions are reluctant to enter into separate small contract or grant relationships with dozens of local institutions. The AOP model utilizes an "umbrella" PVO to receive and administer a conveniently large macrogrant. This PVO, not AID, then shoulders the burden of administering the minigrants given to local participating PVOs.

Though it would be premature to predict a spread effect from AOP to other AID missions in other countries, such a spread is not unlikely. What is clear, however, is that the modus operandi of the Haiti mission itself has been deeply changed. In the late 1970s we were fighting to give nongovernmental implementing goals a toehold in Haiti. In the mid-1980s, a recent mission director announced that nearly 60 percent of the mission's portfolio was now going out through nongovernmental channels.

The preceding paragraphs discuss positive results of AOP. There have also been problems and the need for midcourse corrections.

Measurement of Survival Rates

A data-gathering system was instituted by which we hoped to get 100 percent information on all trees planted. Each tree-promoting animateur was to fill out data forms on survival of trees on every single project plot. The information provided by village animateurs on survival was inconsistent and in many cases clearly inaccurate. Project staff members themselves had to undertake separate, carefully controlled measures, on a random sample basis, of tree survival and tree growth. Such precise measurement was undertaken in the final two years of the project.

Improvement of Technical Outreach

The original project hope had been for an overall survival rate of 50 percent. The rate appears lower than that. The principal cause of tree mortality has been postplanting drought. Also in the early years the project was catapulted by peasant demand into a feverish tree production and tree distribution mode that underemphasized the need for careful instruction to all participating peasants about how to plant and properly care for the trees planted. In recent years more attention has been given to the production of educational materials.

Reduction of Per Household Planting Requirements

In its earliest mode, the project required that peasants interested in participating agree to plant a minimum of 500 trees. Peasants not possessing the fifth of a hectare were permitted to enter into combinational arrangements that allowed several peasants to apply as a unit. This mechanism, however, was rarely invoked in practice, and in some regions of the country poorer peasants were reported to have been denied access to trees. In more cases, however, peasants simply gave away trees for which there was no room on their holding.

In view of the pressure that the 500-tree requirement was placing on some families and the unexpected demand that the project had triggered, the per family tree allotment was eventually lowered to 250. This reduced the number of trees available to each farmer but doubled the number of families reached.

Elimination of Incentives

I had from the outset a deep anthropological suspicion that Haitian peasants would respond enthusiastically to the theme of wood as a cash crop. But to hedge my bets I recommended that we build into the project an incentive system. Rather than linking recompense to the planting of trees, I recommended a strategy by which participating peasants would be paid a small cash recompense for each tree surviving after nine and eighteen months. Some members of the project team objected, saying that the tree itself would be sufficient recompense. I compromised by accepting an experimental arrangement: We used the incentive in some regions but made no mention of it in others.

After two seasons it became clear that the peasants in the nonincentive regions were as enthusiastic about signing up for trees as those in incentive regions and were as careful in protecting the trees. I was delighted to back down on this incentive issue: The income-generating tree itself, not an artificial incentive, was the prime engine of peasant enthusiasm. This was a spectacular and rewarding confirmation of the underlying anthropological hypothesis on which the entire project had been built.

The Anthropological Difference

Anthropological findings, methods, and theories clearly have heavily influenced this project at all stages. We are dealing, not with an ongoing project affected by anthropological input, but with a project whose very existence was rooted in anthropological research and whose very character was determined by ongoing anthropological direction and anthropologically informed managerial prodding.

My own involvement with the project spanned several phases and tasks:

1. Proposal of a theoretical and conceptual base of AOP, the concept of "wood as a cash crop."

2. Preliminary contacting of local PVOs to assess preproject interest.

3. Identification of specific program measures during project design.

4. Preparation of social soundness analysis for the AID project paper.

5. Participation as an outside expert at the meetings in AID Washington at which the fate of the project was decided.

6. Participation in the selection and in-country linguistic and cultural training of the agro-foresters who worked for the project.

7. Direction and supervision of field operations.

8. Formative evaluation of preliminary results and the identification of needed midcourse corrections.

9. Generation of several hundred thousand dollars of supplemental funding from Canadian and Swiss sources and internationalization of the project team.

10. Preparation of publications about the project. (Murray 1984, 1986)

In addition to my own participation in the AOP, four other anthropologists have been involved in long-term commitments to the project. Fred Conway did a preliminary study of firewood use in Haiti (Conway 1979). He subsequently served for two years as overall project coordinator within AID/Haiti. More recently he has carried out revealing case study research on the harvesting of project trees (Conway 1986). Glenn Smucker likewise did an early feasibility study in the northwest (Smucker 1981) and eventually joined the project as my successor in the directorship. Under his leadership many of the crucial midcourse corrections were introduced. Ira Lowenthal took over the AID coordination of the project at a critical transitional period and has been instrumental in forging plans for its institutional future. And Anthony Balzano has carried out several years of case study fieldwork on the possible impact of the tree-planting activities on the land tenure in participating villages. All these individuals have PhDs, or are PhD candidates, in anthropology. And another anthropologist in the Haiti mission, John Lewis, succeeded in adapting the privatized umbrella agency outreach model for use in a swine repopulation project. With the possible exception of Vicos, it would be

hard to imagine a project that has been as heavily influenced by anthropologists.

But how specifically has anthropology influenced the content of the project? There are at least three major levels at which anthropology has impinged on the content of AOP.

1. *The Application of Substantive Findings.* The very choice of "wood as a marketable crop" as the fundamental theme of the project stemmed from ethnographic knowledge of the cash-oriented foundations of Haitian peasant horticulture and knowledge of current conditions in the internal marketing system. Because of ethnographic knowledge I was able to avoid succumbing to the common-sense inclination to emphasize fruit trees (whose perishability and tendency to glut markets make them commercially vulnerable) and to choose instead the fast-growing wood tree. There is a feverishly escalating market for charcoal and construction wood that cannot be dampened even by the most successful project. And there are no spoilage problems with wood. The peasants can harvest it when they want. Furthermore, ethnographic knowledge of Haitian peasant land tenure—which is highly individualistic—guided me away from the community forest schemes that so many development philosophers seem to delight in but that are completely inappropriate to the social reality of Caribbean peasantries.

2. *Anthropological Methods.* The basic research that led up to the project employed participant observation along with intensive interviewing with small groups of informants to compare current cost/benefit ratios of traditional farming with projected cash yields from plots in which trees are intercropped with food on four-year rotation cycles. A critical part of the project design stage was to establish the likelihood of increased revenues from altered land use behaviors. During project design I also applied ethnographic techniques to the behavior of institutional personnel. The application of anthropological notetaking on 3-by-5 slips, not only with peasants but also with technicians, managers, and officials, exposed the institutional roots of earlier project failures and stimulated

the proposal of alternative institutional routes. Furthermore ethnoscientific elicitation of folk taxonomies led to the realization that whereas fruit trees are classified as a crop by Haitian peasants, wood trees are not so classified. This discovery exposed the need for the creation of explicit messages saying that wood can be a crop, just as coffee, manioc, and corn can. Finally, prior experience in Creole-language instrument design and computer analysis permitted me to design a baseline data-gathering system.

3. *Anthropological Theory.* My own thinking about tree planting was heavily guided by cultural-evolutionary insights into the origins of agriculture. The global tree problem is often erroneously conceptualized in a conservationist or ecological framework. Such a perspective is very short-sighted for anthropologists. We are aware of an ancient food crisis, when humans still hunted and gathered, that was solved, not by the adoption of conservationist practices, but rather by the shift into a domesticated mode of production. From hunting and gathering we turned to cropping and harvesting. I found the analogy with the present tree crisis conceptually overpowering. Trees will reemerge when and only when human beings start planting them aggressively as a harvestable crop, not when human consciousness is raised regarding their ecological importance. This anthropological insight (or bias), nourished by the aggressive creativity of the Haitian peasants among whom I had lived, swayed me toward the adoption of a dynamic "domestication" paradigm in proposing a solution to the tree problem in Haiti. This evolutionary perspective also permitted me to see that the cash-cropping of wood was in reality a small evolutionary step, not a quantum leap. The Haitian peasants already cut and sell natural stands of wood. They already plant and sell traditional food crops. It is but a small evolutionary step to join these two unconnected streams of Haitian peasant behavior, and this linkage is the core purpose of the Agro-forestry Outreach Project.

Broader anthropological theory also motivated and justified a nongovernmental implementing mode for AOP. Not only AID but also most international development agencies tend to operate on a service model of the state. This idealized model views the basic character of the state as that of a provider of services to its population. Adherence to this theoretically naive service model has led to the squandering of untold millions of dollars in the support of extractive public bureaucracies. This waste is justified under the rubric of institution building—assisting public entities to provide the services that they are supposed to be providing.

But my anthropological insights into the origins of the state as a mechanism of extraction and control led me to pose the somewhat heretical position that the predatory behavior of Duvalier's regime was in fact not misbehavior. Duvalier was merely doing openly and blatantly what other state leaders camouflage under rhetoric. AID's search of nongovernmental implementing channels for AOP, then, was not seen as a simple emergency measure to be employed under a misbehaving regime but rather as an avenue of activity that might be valid as an option under many or most regimes. There is little justification in either ethnology or anthropological theory for viewing the state as the proper recipient of developmental funds. This theoretical insight permitted us to argue for a radically nongovernmental mode of tree-planting support in AOP. In short, sensitivity to issues in anthropological theory played a profound role in the shaping of the project.

Would AOP have taken the form it did without these varied types of anthropological input? Almost certainly not. Had there been no anthropological input, a radically different scenario would almost certainly have unfolded with the following elements.

1. AID would probably have undertaken a reforestation project—congressional pressure alone would have ensured that. But the project would have been based, not on the theme of "wood as a peasant cash-crop," but on the more traditional approach to trees as a vehicle of soil conservation. Ponderous educational programs would have been launched to teach the peasants about the value of trees. Emphasis would have been placed on educating the ignorant and on trying to induce peasants to plant commercially marginal (and nutritionally

tangential) fruit trees instead of cash-generating wood trees.

2. The project would have been managed by technicians. The emphasis would probably have been on carrying out lengthy technical research concerning optimal planting strategies and the combination of trees with optimally effective bench terraces and other soil conservation devices. The outreach problem would have been given second priority. Throughout Haiti hundreds of thousands of dollars have been spent on numerous demonstration projects to create terraced, forested hillsides, but only a handful of cooperative local peasants have been induced to undertake the same activities on their own land.

3. The project would almost certainly have been run through the Haitian government. When after several hundred thousand dollars of expenditures few trees were visible, frustrated young AID program officers would have gotten finger-wagging lectures about the sovereign right of local officials to use donor money as they see fit. And the few trees planted would have been defined as *pyebwa leta* (the government's trees), and peasants would have been sternly warned against ever cutting these trees, even the ones planted on their own land. And the peasants would soon turn the problem over to their most effective ally in such matters, the free-ranging omnivorous goat, who would soon remove this alien vegetation from the peasant's land.

Because of anthropology, the Agroforestry Outreach Project has unfolded to a different scenario. It was a moving experience for me to return to the village where I had done my original fieldwork (and which I of course tried to involve in the tree-planting activities) to find several houses built using the wood from leucaena trees planted during the project's earliest phases. Poles were beginning to be sold, although the prices had not yet stabilized for these still unknown wood types. Charcoal made from project trees was being sold in local markets. For the first time in the history of this village, people were "growing" part of their house structures and their cooking fuel. I felt as though I were observing (and had been a participant in) a replay of an ancient anthropological drama, the shift from an extractive to a domesticated mode of resource procurement. Though their sources of food energy had been domesticated millennia ago, my former village neighbors had now begun replicating this transition in the domain of wood and wood-based energy. I felt a satisfaction at having chosen a discipline that could give me the privilege of participating, even marginally, in this very ancient cultural-evolutionary transition.

REFERENCES

Ashley, Marshall D. 1986. A Study of Traditional Agroforestry Systems in Haiti and Implications for the USAID/Haiti Agroforestry Outreach Project. Port-au-Prince: University of Maine Agroforestry Outreach Research Project.

Balzano, Anthony. 1986. Socioeconomic Aspects of Agroforestry in Rural Haiti. Port-au-Prince: University of Maine Agroforestry Outreach Research Project.

Buffum, William, and Wendy King. 1985. Small Farmer Decision Making and Tree Planting: Agroforestry Extension Recommendations. Port-au-Prince: Haiti Agroforestry Outreach Project.

Conway, Frederick. 1979. A Study of the Fuelwood Situation in Haiti. Port-au-Prince: USAID.

Conway, Frederick. 1986. The Decision Making Framework for Tree Planting Within the Agroforestry Outreach Project. Port-au-Prince: University of Maine Agroforestry Outreach Research Project.

Grosenick, Gerald. 1985. Economic Evaluation of the Agroforestry Outreach Project. Port-au-Prince: University of Maine Agroforestry Outreach Research Project.

McGowan, Lisa A. 1986. Potential Marketability of Charcoal, Poles, and Planks Produced by Participants in the Agroforestry Outreach Project. Port-au-Prince: University of Maine Agroforestry Outreach Research Project.

Murray, Gerald F. 1977. The Evolution of Haitian Peasant Land Tenure: A Case Study in Agrarian

Adaptation to Population Growth. Ph.D. dissertation, Columbia University, New York.

Murray, Gerald F. 1978a, Hillside Units, Wage Labor, and Haitian Peasant Land Tenure: A Strategy for the Organization of Erosion Control. Port-au-Prince: USAID.

Murray, Gerald F. 1978b. Informal Subdivisions and Land Insecurity: An Analysis of Haitian Peasant Land Tenure. Port-au-Prince: USAID.

Murray, Gerald F. 1979. Terraces, Trees, and the Haitian Peasant: An Assessment of 25 Years of Erosion Control in Rural Haiti. Port-au-Prince: USAID.

Murray, Gerald F. 1984. The Wood Tree as a Peasant Cash-Crop: An Anthropological Strategy for the Domestication of Energy. In A. Valdman and R. Foster, eds., *Haiti—Today and Tomorrow: An Interdisciplinary Study*. New York: University Press of America.

Murray, Gerald F. 1986. Seeing the Forest While Planting the Trees: An Anthropological Approach to Agroforestry in Rural Haiti. In D. W. Brinkerhoff and J. C. Garcia-Zamor, eds., *Politics, Projects, and Peasants: Institutional Development in Haiti*. New York: Praeger, pp. 193–226.

Smucker, Glenn R. 1981. Trees and Charcoal in Haitian Peasant Economy: A Feasibility Study. Port-au-Prince: USAID.

Zuvekas, Clarence.1978. Agricultural Development in Haiti: An Assessment of Sector Problems, Policies, and Prospects under Conditions of Severe Soil Erosion. Washington, D.C.: USAID.

DISCUSSION QUESTIONS

1. What were the factors that led to Haiti's problem of deforestation?

2. In what ways did an anthropologist (using anthropological insights) contribute to the huge success of the reforestation project in Haiti?

3. What barriers did Murray have to overcome to convince local farmers to participate in the reforestation project?

7

Arranging a Marriage in India

SERENA NANDA

Professor Emeritus, John Jay College of Criminal Justice, CUNY

When viewed from a comparative perspective, middle-class North Americans tend to be fiercely independent. Children growing up in the United States and Canada are encouraged by their parents and teachers to solve their own problems and make their own decisions. Most parents, although they might have their preferences, are not likely to force their children to attend a particular college or enter into a profession against their will. And most North Americans would be repulsed by the thought of their parents determining whom they would marry.

Yet this is exactly what Serena Nanda encountered on her first fieldwork experience in India. At first, Nanda could not understand why Indian women, particularly well-educated ones, would allow this most important (and personal) decision to be made by their parents. But as she became more immersed in Indian culture through the process of fieldwork, she gained a much fuller appreciation of the role of arranged marriages in India. In fact, after a while, Nanda became a willing participant in the system by helping arrange the marriage of the son of one of her Indian friends.

Nanda's article, though hardly as well known as some in this volume, is important because it demonstrates the process of understanding another cultural system. Nanda, born and raised in the United States, tried to understand the system of arranged marriages in India through the lens of her own culture. But like the good ethnographer that she is, she kept an open mind and continued to probe her female informants with more and more questions, until eventually she saw the inherent logic of this particular form of marriage.

> *Sister and doctor brother-in-law invite correspondence from North Indian professionals only, for a beautiful, talented, sophisticated, intelligent sister, 5'; 3", slim, M.A. in textile design, father a senior civil officer. Would prefer immigrant doctors, between 26–29 years. Reply with full details and returnable photo.*
>
> *A well-settled uncle invites matrimonial correspondence from slim, fair, educated South Indian girl, for his nephew, 25 years, smart, M.B.A., green card holder, 5' 6". Full particulars with returnable photo appreciated.*
>
> *Matrimonial Advertisements, India Abroad*

In India, almost all marriages are arranged. Even among the educated middle classes in modern, urban India, marriage is as much a concern of the families as it is of the individuals. So customary is

SOURCE: From Serena Nanda, "Arranging a Marriage in India." In Philip De Vita (ed.), *Stumbling Toward Truth: Anthropologists at Work*, pp. 196–204. Prospect Heights, IL: Waveland, 2000. Reprinted with permission of the author.

the practice of arranged marriage that there is a special name for a marriage which is not arranged: It is called a "love match."

On my first field trip to India, I met many young men and women whose parents were in the process of "getting them married." In many cases, the bride and groom would not meet each other before the marriage. At most they might meet for a brief conversation, and this meeting would take place only after their parents had decided that the match was suitable. Parents do not compel their children to marry a person who either marriage partner finds objectionable. But only after one match is refused will another be sought.

As a young American woman in India for the first time, I found this custom of arranged marriage oppressive. How could any intelligent young person agree to such a marriage without great reluctance? It was contrary to everything I believed about the importance of romantic love as the only basis of a happy marriage. It also clashed with my strongly held notions that the choice of such an intimate and permanent relationship could be made only by the individuals involved. Had anyone tried to arrange my marriage, I would have been defiant and rebellious!

At the first opportunity, I began, with more curiosity than tact, to question the young people I met on how they felt about this practice. Sita, one of my young informants, was a college graduate with a degree in political science. She had been waiting for over a year while her parents were arranging a match for her. I found it difficult to accept the docile manner in which this well-educated young woman awaited the outcome of a process that would result in her spending the rest of her life with a man she hardly knew, a virtual stranger, picked out by her parents.

"How can you go along with this?" I asked her, in frustration and distress. "Don't you care who you marry?"

"Of course I care," she answered. "This is why I must let my parents choose a boy for me. My marriage is too important to be arranged by such an inexperienced person as myself. In such matters, it is better to have my parents' guidance."

I had learned that young men and women in India do not date and have very little social life involving members of the opposite sex. Although I could not disagree with Sita's reasoning, I continued to pursue the subject.

"But how can you marry the first man you have ever met? Not only have you missed the fun of meeting a lot of different people, but you have not given yourself the chance to know who is the right man for you."

"Meeting with a lot of different people doesn't sound like any fun at all," Sita answered. "One hears that in America the girls are spending all their time worrying about whether they will meet a man and get married. Here we have the chance to enjoy our life and let our parents do this work and worrying for us."

She had me there. The high anxiety of the competition to "be popular" with the opposite sex certainly was the most prominent feature of life as an American teenager in the late fifties. The endless worrying about the rules that governed our behavior and about our popularity ratings sapped both our self-esteem and our enjoyment of adolescence. I reflected that absence of this competition in India most certainly may have contributed to the self-confidence and natural charm of so many of the young women I met.

And yet, the idea of marrying a perfect stranger, whom one did not know and did not "love," so offended my American ideas of individualism and romanticism, that I persisted with my objections.

"I still can't imagine it," I said. "How can you agree to marry a man you hardly know?"

"But of course he will be known. My parents would never arrange a marriage for me without knowing all about the boy's family background. Naturally we will not rely only on what the family tells us. We will check the particulars out ourselves. No one will want their daughter to marry into a family that is not good. All these things we will know beforehand."

Impatiently, I responded, "Sita, I don't mean know the family, I mean, know the man. How can you marry someone you don't know personally and don't love? How can you think of spending your life with someone you may not even like?"

"If he is a good man, why should I not like him?" she said. "With you people, you know the boy so well before you marry, where will be the fun to get married? There will be no mystery and no romance. Here we have the whole of our married life to get to know and love our husband. This way is better, is it not?"

Her response made further sense, and I began to have second thoughts on the matter. Indeed, during months of meeting many intelligent young Indian people, both male and female, who had the same ideas as Sita, I saw arranged marriages in a different light. I also saw the importance of the family in Indian life and realized that a couple who took their marriage into their own hands was taking a big risk, particularly if their families were irreconcilably opposed to the match. In a country where every important resource in life—a job, a house, a social circle—is gained through family connections, it seemed foolhardy to cut oneself off from a supportive social network and depend solely on one person for happiness and success.

––––––––––––––

Six years later I returned to India to again do fieldwork, this time among the middle class in Bombay, a modern, sophisticated city. From the experience of my earlier visit, I decided to include a study of arranged marriages in my project. By this time I had met many Indian couples whose marriages had been arranged and who seemed very happy. Particularly in contrast to the fate of many of my married friends in the United States who were already in the process of divorce, the positive aspects of arranged marriages appeared to me to outweigh the negatives. In fact, I thought I might even participate in arranging a marriage myself. I had been fairly successful in the United States in "fixing up" many of my friends, and I was confident that my match-making skills could be easily applied to this new situation, once I learned the basic rules. "After all," I thought, "how complicated can it be? People want pretty much the same things in a marriage whether it is in India or America."

An opportunity presented itself almost immediately. A friend from my previous Indian trip was in the process of arranging for the marriage of her eldest son. In India there is a perceived shortage of "good boys," and since my friend's family was eminently respectable and the boy himself personable, well educated, and nice looking, I was sure that by the end of my year's fieldwork, we would have found a match.

The basic rule seems to be that a family's reputation is most important. It is understood that matches would be arranged only within the same caste and general social class, although some crossing of subcastes is permissible if the class positions of the bride's and groom's families are similar. Although dowry is now prohibited by law in India, extensive gift exchanges took place with every marriage. Even when the boy's family do not "make demands," every girl's family nevertheless feels the obligation to give the traditional gifts, to the girl, to the boy, and to the boy's family. Particularly when the couple would be living in the joint family—that is, with the boy's parents and his married brothers and their families, as well as with unmarried siblings—which is still very common even among the urban, upper-middle class in India, the girl's parents are anxious to establish smooth relations between their family and that of the boy. Offering the proper gifts, even when not called "dowry," is often an important factor in influencing the relationship between the bride's and groom's families and perhaps, also, the treatment of the bride in her new home.

In a society where divorce is still a scandal and where, in fact, the divorce rate is exceedingly low, an arranged marriage is the beginning of a lifetime relationship not just between the bride and groom but between their families as well. Thus, while a girl's looks are important, her character is even more so, for she is being judged as a prospective daughter-in-law as much as a prospective bride. Where she would be living in a joint family, as was the case with my friend, the girl's ability to get along harmoniously in a family is perhaps the single most important quality in assessing her suitability.

My friend is a highly esteemed wife, mother, and daughter-in-law. She is religious, soft-spoken, modest, and deferential. She rarely gossips and never quarrels, two qualities highly desirable in a woman. A family that has the reputation for gossip and conflict among its womenfolk will not find it easy to get good wives for their sons. Parents will not want to send their daughter to a house in which there is conflict.

My friend's family were originally from North India. They had lived in Bombay, where her husband owned a business, for forty years. The family had delayed in seeking a match for their eldest son because he had been an Air Force pilot for several years, stationed in such remote places that it had seemed fruitless to try to find a girl who would be willing to accompany him. In their social class, a military career, despite its economic security, has little prestige and is considered a drawback in finding a suitable bride. Many families would not allow their daughters to marry a man in an occupation so potentially dangerous and which requires so much moving around.

The son had recently left the military and joined his father's business. Since he was a college graduate, modern, and well traveled, from such a good family, and, I thought, quite handsome, it seemed to me that he, or rather his family, was in a position to pick and choose. I said as much to my friend.

While she agreed that there were many advantages on their side, she also said, "We must keep in mind that my son is both short and dark; these are drawbacks in finding the right match." While the boy's height had not escaped my notice, "dark" seemed to me inaccurate; I would have called him "wheat" colored perhaps, and in any case, I did not realize that color would be a consideration. I discovered, however, that while a boy's skin color is a less important consideration than a girl's, it is still a factor.

An important source of contacts in trying to arrange her son's marriage was my friend's social club in Bombay. Many of the women had daughters of the right age, and some had already expressed an interest in my friend's son. I was most enthusiastic about the possibilities of one particular family who had five daughters, all of whom were pretty, demure, and well educated. Their mother had told my friend, "You can have your pick for your son, whichever one of my daughters appeals to you most."

I saw a match in sight. "Surely," I said to my friend, "we will find one there. Let's go visit and make our choice." But my friend held back; she did not seem to share my enthusiasm, for reasons I could not then fathom.

When I kept pressing for an explanation of her reluctance, she admitted, "See, Serena, here is the problem. The family has so many daughters, how will they be able to provide nicely for any of them? We are not making any demands, but still, with so many daughters to marry off, one wonders whether she will even be able to make a proper wedding. Since this is our eldest son, it's best if we marry him to a girl who is the only daughter, then the wedding will truly be a gala affair." I argued that surely the quality of the girls themselves made up for any deficiency in the elaborateness of the wedding. My friend admitted this point but still seemed reluctant to proceed.

"Is there something else," I asked her, "some factor I have missed?" "Well," she finally said, "there is one other thing. They have one daughter already married and living in Bombay. The mother is always complaining to me that the girl's in-laws don't let her visit her own family often enough. So it makes me wonder, will she be that kind of mother who always wants her daughter at her own home? This will prevent the girl from adjusting to our house. It is not a good thing." And so, this family of five daughters was dropped as a possibility.

Somewhat disappointed, I nevertheless respected my friend's reasoning and geared up for the next prospect. This was also the daughter of a woman in my friend's social club. There was clear interest in this family and I could see why. The family's reputation was excellent; in fact, they came from a subcaste slightly higher than my friend's own. The girl, who was an only daughter, was pretty and well educated and had a brother studying in the United States. Yet, after expressing an interest to me in this family, all talk of them suddenly died down and the search began elsewhere.

"What happened to that girl as a prospect?" I asked one day. "You never mention her any more. She is so pretty and so educated, what did you find wrong?"

"She is too educated. We've decided against it. My husband's father saw the girl on the bus the other day and thought her forward. A girl who 'roams about' the city by herself is not the girl for our family." My disappointment this time was even greater, as I thought the son would have liked the girl very much. But then I thought, my friend is right, a girl who is going to live in a joint family cannot be too independent or she will make life miserable for everyone. I also learned that if the family of the girl has even a slightly higher social status than the family of the boy, the bride may think herself too good for them, and this too will cause problems. Later my friend admitted to me that this had been an important factor in her decision not to pursue the match.

The next candidate was the daughter of a client of my friend's husband. When the client learned that the family was looking for a match for their son, he said, "Look no further, we have a daughter." This man then invited my friends to dinner to see the girl. He had already seen their son at the office and decided that "he liked the boy." We all went together for tea, rather than dinner—it was less of a commitment—and while we were there, the girl's mother showed us around the house. The girl was studying for her exams and was briefly introduced to us.

After we left, I was anxious to hear my friend's opinion. While her husband liked the family very much and was impressed with his client's business accomplishments and reputation, the wife didn't like the girl's looks. "She is short, no doubt, which is an important plus point, but she is also fat and wears glasses." My friend obviously thought she could do better for her son and asked her husband to make his excuses to his client by saying that they had decided to postpone the boy's marriage indefinitely.

By this time almost six months had passed and I was becoming impatient. What I had thought would be an easy matter to arrange was turning out to be quite complicated. I began to believe that between my friend's desire for a girl who was modest enough to fit into her joint family, yet attractive and educated enough to be an acceptable

partner for her son, she would not find anyone suitable. My friend laughed at my impatience: "Don't be so much in a hurry," she said. "You Americans want everything done so quickly. You get married quickly and then just as quickly get divorced. Here we take marriage more seriously. We must take all the factors into account. It is not enough for us to learn by our mistakes. This is too serious a business. If a mistake is made we have not only ruined the life of our son or daughter, but we have spoiled the reputation of our family as well. And that will make it much harder for their brothers and sisters to get married. So we must be very careful."

What she said was true and I promised myself to be more patient, though it was not easy. I had really hoped and expected that the match would be made before my year in India was up. But it was not to be. When I left India my friend seemed no further along in finding a suitable match for her son than when I had arrived.

Two years later, I returned to India and still my friend had not found a girl for her son. By this time, he was close to thirty, and I think she was a little worried. Since she knew I had friends all over India, and I was going to be there for a year, she asked me to "help her in this work" and keep an eye out for someone suitable. I was flattered that my judgment was respected, but knowing now how complicated the process was, I had lost my earlier confidence as a matchmaker. Nevertheless, I promised that I would try.

It was almost at the end of my year's stay in India that I met a family with a marriageable daughter whom I felt might be a good possibility for my friend's son. The girl's father was related to a good friend of mine and by coincidence came from the same village as my friend's husband. This new family had a successful business in a medium-sized city in central India and were from the same subcaste as my friend. The daughter was pretty and chic; in fact, she had studied fashion design in college. Her parents would not allow her to go off by herself to any of the major cities in India where she could make a career, but they had compromised with her wish to work by allowing her to run a small dressmaking boutique from their home. In spite of her desire to have a career, the daughter was both modest and home-loving and had had a traditional, sheltered upbringing. She had only one other sister, already married, and a brother who was in his father's business.

I mentioned the possibility of a match with my friend's son. The girl's parents were most interested. Although their daughter was not eager to marry just yet, the idea of living in Bombay—a sophisticated, extremely fashion-conscious city where she could continue her education in clothing design—was a great inducement. I gave the girl's father my friend's address and suggested that when they went to Bombay on some business or whatever, they look up the boy's family.

Returning to Bombay on my way to New York, I told my friend of this newly discovered possibility. She seemed to feel there was potential but, in spite of my urging, would not make any moves herself. She rather preferred to wait for the girl's family to call upon them. I hoped something would come of this introduction, though by now I had learned to rein in my optimism.

A year later I received a letter from my friend. The family had indeed come to visit Bombay, and their daughter and my friend's daughter, who were near in age, had become very good friends. During that year, the two girls had frequently visited each other. I thought things looked promising.

Last week I received an invitation to a wedding: My friend's son and the girl were getting married. Since I had found the match, my presence was particularly requested at the wedding. I was thrilled. Success at last! As I prepared to leave for India, I began thinking, "Now, my friend's younger son, who do I know who has a nice girl for him… ?"

This essay was written from the point of view of a family seeking a daughter-in-law. Arranged marriage looks somewhat different from the point of view of the bride and her family. Arranged marriage continues to be preferred, even among the more educated, Westernized sections of the Indian population. Many young women from these families still go along, more or less willingly, with the practice, and also with the specific choices of their families. Young women do get excited about the prospects of their marriage, but there is also ambivalence and increasing uncertainty, as the bride contemplates leaving the comfort and familiarity of her own home, where as a "temporary guest" she had often been indulged, to live among strangers. Even in the best situation she will now come under the close scrutiny of her husband's family. How she dresses, how she behaves, how she gets along with others, where she goes, how she spends her time, her domestic abilities—all of this and much more—will be observed and commented on by a whole new set of relations. Her interaction with her family of birth will be monitored and curtailed considerably. Not only will she leave their home, but with increasing geographic mobility, she may also live very far from them, perhaps even on another continent. Too much expression of her fondness for her own family, or her desire to visit them, may be interpreted as an inability to adjust to her new family and may become a source of conflict. In an arranged marriage the burden of adjustment is clearly heavier for a woman than for a man. And that is in the best of situations.

In less happy circumstances, the bride may be a target of resentment and hostility from her husband's family, particularly her mother-in-law or her husband's unmarried sisters, for whom she is now a source of competition for the affection, loyalty, and economic resources of their son or brother. If she is psychologically or even physically abused, her options are limited, as returning to her parent's home or divorce are still very stigmatized. For most Indians, marriage and motherhood are still considered the only suitable roles for a woman. Even for women who have careers, few women can comfortably contemplate remaining unmarried. Most families still consider "marrying off" their daughters as a compelling religious duty and social necessity. This increases a bride's sense of obligation to make the marriage a success, at whatever cost to her own personal happiness.

The vulnerability of a new bride may also be intensified by the issue of dowry, which, although illegal, has become a more pressing issue in the consumer conscious society of contemporary urban India. In many cases, where a groom's family is not satisfied with the amount of dowry a bride brings to her marriage, the young bride will be constantly harassed to get her parents to give more. In extreme cases, the bride may even be murdered and the murder disguised as an accident or suicide. This also offers the husband's family an opportunity to arrange another match for him, thus bringing in another dowry. This phenomenon, called dowry death, calls attention not just to the "evils of dowry" but also to larger issues of the powerlessness of women as well.

Afterword by Serena Nanda, 2007

DISCUSSION QUESTIONS

1. What are the advantages and disadvantages of arranged marriage? Do you feel that the disadvantages outweigh the advantages or vice versa?

2. What traits do parents in India look for when arranging a marriage for their sons and daughters?

3. When arranging a marriage for one's adult son, why would traditional Indian parents be reluctant to look for a bride from a family that has many daughters?

4. After reading this article, have you changed your mind about wanting an arranged marriage for yourself?

8

No More Angel Babies on the Alto do Cruzeiro

NANCY SCHEPER-HUGHES

Professor of Anthropology, University of California–Berkeley

Most social scientists acknowledge a special emotional mother–child bond that exists in all cultures, owing to the physical nature of pregnancy and birth. In a 1989 article in Natural History, titled "Death without Weeping," anthropologist Nancy Scheper-Hughes found that these strong emotional bonds between mother and child underwent significant changes in the face of severe socioeconomic conditions. Specifically, based on data collected in the 1960s and 1970s, Scheper-Hughes examines how extreme poverty, hunger, deprivation, and economic exploitation caused mothers in a shantytown in Northeast Brazil not to mourn the death of their infant children. She found that mothers living under these extreme conditions develop a strategy of delayed attachment to their children, withholding emotional involvement until they are reasonably certain that the child will survive. Such a strategy— while appearing cruel and unfeeling to those of us living in comfortable middle-class surroundings—is an emotional coping strategy for mothers living with extraordinarily high levels of infant and child mortality. Rather than seeing "mother love" as an absolute cultural universal, Scheper-Hughes suggested that, under these extreme conditions, it is a luxury reserved for only those children who survive. This article, which has appeared in the first three editions of Classic Readings in Cultural Anthropology, provided a thoughtful and wrenching analysis of how poverty, deprivations, and injustice can lead to the demise of a mother's basic human right of weeping for her dead child.

This selection, written nearly a quarter of a century after "Death without Weeping," is an update by Nancy Scheper-Hughes on the same theme of the mother–child bond in the same town of Timbauba where she first discovered this phenomenon in the mid-1960s. As her analysis progresses forward from 1964 through 2009, her central hypothesis of the relationship between mother love and extreme poverty is confirmed, and her story has a more uplifting ending. Using official data from the Brazilian Institute of Geography and Statistics, she was able to track the reduction of infant mortality in the town of Timbauba from 409 out of 1000 infants (41 percent of all newborns never made it to their first birthday) in 1977 to 357 out of 1000 in 1978, to 35 out of 1000 in 2001, and 25 out of 1000 in 2009. This dramatic reduction in the percentage of infants dying in the first year of life was largely the result of the Brazilian government's substantial success in creating a national

SOURCE: © 2013 by Nancy Scheper-Hughes. Reprinted with permission of the author.

health care system that, among other things, addressed issues of prenatal and post-natal care, and public nutrition programs as well as other initiatives to address the most debilitating consequences of extreme poverty. While conducting participant-observation research between 2001 and 2007, Scheper-Hughes interviewed expectant mothers who, unlike their own mothers' generation, "were confident in their ability to give birth to a healthy baby" and had "control over their reproductive lives in ways that (the author) could not have imagined (in 1964)."

It was almost fifty years ago that I first walked to the top of the Alto do Cruzeiro (the Hill of the Crucifix) in Timbaúba, a sugar-belt town in the state of Pernambuco, in Northeast Brazil. I was looking for the small mud hut, nestled in a cliff, where I was to live. It was December 1964, nine months after the coup that toppled the left-leaning president, João Goulart. Church bells were ringing, and I asked the woman who was to host me as a Peace Corps volunteer why they seemed to ring at all hours of the day. "Oh, it's nothing," she told me. "Just another little angel gone to heaven."

That day marked the beginning of my life's work. Since then, I've experienced something between an obsession, a trauma, and a romance with the shantytown. Residents of the newly occupied hillside were refugees from the military junta's violent attacks on the peasant league movement that had tried to enforce existing laws protecting the local sugarcane cutters. The settlers had thrown together huts made of straw, mud, and sticks, or, lacking that, lean-tos made of tin, cardboard, and scrap materials. They had thrown together families in the same makeshift fashion, taking whatever was at hand and making do. In the absence of husbands, weekend play fathers did nicely as long as they brought home the current baby's powdered milk, if not the bacon. Households were temporary; in such poverty women were the only stable force, and babies and fathers were circulated among them. A man who could not provide support would be banished to take up residence with another, even more desperate woman; excess infants and babies were often rescued by older women, who took them in as informal foster children.

Premature death was an everyday occurrence in a shantytown lacking water, electricity, and sanitation and beset with food scarcity, epidemics, and police violence. My assignment was to immunize children, educate midwives, attend births, treat infections, bind up festering wounds, and visit mothers and newborns at home to monitor their health and refer them as needed to the district health post or to the emergency room of the private hospital—owned by the mayor's brother—where charity cases were sometimes attended, depending on the state of local patron-client relations.

I spent several months making the rounds between the miserable huts on the Alto with a public-health medical kit strapped on my shoulder. Its contents were pathetic: a bar of soap, scissors, antiseptics, aspirin, bandages, a glass syringe, some ampules of vaccine, several needles, and a pumice stone to sharpen the needles, which were used over and over again for immunizations. Children ran away when they saw me coming, and well they might have.

But what haunted me then, in addition to my own incompetence, was something I did not have the skill or maturity to understand: Why didn't the women of the Alto grieve over the deaths of their babies? I tucked that question away. But as Winnicott, the British child psychoanalyst, liked to say, "Nothing is ever forgotten."

Sixteen years elapsed before I was able to return to the Alto do Cruzeiro, this time as a medical anthropologist. It was in 1982—during the period known as the abertura, or opening, the beginning of the end of the military dictatorship—that I made the first of the four trips that formed the basis for my 1992 book, *Death Without Weeping: The Violence of Everyday Life in Brazil*. My goal was to study women's lives, specifically mother love and child death under conditions so dire that the Uruguayan writer Eduardo Galeano once described the region as a concentration camp for 30 million people. It was not a gross exaggeration.

Decades of nutritional studies of sugarcane cutters and their families in Pernambuco showed hard evidence of slow starvation and stunting. These nutritional dwarfs were surviving on a daily caloric intake similar to that of the inmates of the Buchenwald concentration camp. Life on the Alto resembled prison-camp culture, with a moral ethic based on triage and survival.

If mother love is the cultural expression of what many attachment theorists believe to be a bioevolutionary script, what could this script mean to women living in these conditions? In my sample of three generations of mothers in the sugar plantation zone of Pernambuco, the average woman had 9.5 pregnancies, 8 live births, and 3.5 infant deaths. Such high rates of births and deaths are typical of societies that have not undergone what population experts call the demographic transition, associated with economic development, in which first death rates and, later, birth rates drop as parents begin to trust that more of their infants will survive. On the contrary, the high expectation of loss and the normalization of infant death was a powerful conditioner of the degree of maternal attachments. Mothers and infants could also be rivals for scarce resources. Alto mothers renounced breastfeeding as impossible, as sapping far too much strength from their own "wrecked" bodies.

Scarcity made mother love a fragile emotion, postponed until the newborn displayed a will to live—a taste (*gusto*) and a knack (*jeito*) for life. A high expectancy of death prepared mothers to "let go" of and to hasten the death of babies that were failing to thrive, by reducing the already insufficient food, water, and care. The "angel babies" of the Alto were neither of this Earth nor yet fully spirits. In appearance they were ghostlike: pale and wispy-haired; their arms and legs stripped of flesh; their bellies grossly distended; their eyes blank and staring; their faces wizened, a cross between startled primate and wise old sorcerer.

The experience of too much loss, too much death, led to a kind of patient resignation that some clinical psychologists might label "emotional numbing" or the symptoms of a "masked depression." But the mothers' resignation was neither pathological nor abnormal. Moreover, it was a moral code. Not only had a continual exposure to trauma obliterated rage and protest, it also minimized attachment so as to diminish sorrow.

Infant death was so commonplace that I recall a birthday party for a four-year-old in which the birthday cake, decorated with candles, was placed on the kitchen table next to the tiny blue cardboard coffin of the child's nine-month-old sibling, who had died during the night. Next to the coffin a single vigil candle was lit. Despite the tragedy, the child's mother wanted to go ahead with the party. "*Parabéns para você*," we sang, clapping our hands. "Congratulations to you!" the Brazilian birthday song goes. And on the Alto it had special resonance: "Congratulations, you survivor you—you lived to see another year!"

When Alto mothers cried, they cried for themselves, for those left behind to continue the struggle. But they cried the hardest for their children who had almost died, but who surprised everyone by surviving against the odds. Wiping a stray tear from her eye, an Alto mother would speak with deep emotion of the child who, given up for dead, suddenly beat death back, displaying a fierce desire for life. These tough and stubborn children were loved above all others.

Staying alive in the shantytown demanded a kind of egoism that often pits individuals against each other and rewards those who take advantage of those weaker than themselves. People admired toughness and strength; they took pride in babies or adults who were cunning and foxy. The toddler that was wild and fierce was preferred to the quiet and obedient child. Men and women with seductive charm, who could manipulate those around them, were better off than those who were kind. Poverty doesn't ennoble people, and I came to appreciate what it took to stay alive.

Theirs were moral choices that no person should be forced to make. But the result was that infants were viewed as limitless. There was a kind of magical replaceability about them, similar to what one might find on a battlefield. As one soldier falls, another takes his place. This kind of detached maternal thinking allowed the die-offs of shantytown babies—in some years, as many as 40 percent of all the infants born on the Alto died—to pass without shock or profound grief. A woman who had lost half her babies told me, "Who could bear it, Nancí, if we are mistaken in believing that God takes our infants to save us from pain? If that is not true, then God is a cannibal. And if our little angels are not in heaven flying around the throne of Our Lady, then where are they, and who is to blame for their deaths?"

If mothers allowed themselves to be attached to each newborn, how could they ever live through their babies' short lives and deaths and still have the stamina to get pregnant and give birth again and again? It wasn't that Alto mothers did not experience mother love at all. They did, and with great intensity. But mother love emerged as their children developed strength and vitality. The apex of mother love was not the image of Mary and her infant son, but a mature Mary, grieving the death of her young adult son. The Pietà, not the young mother at the crèche, was the symbol of motherhood and mother love on the Alto.

In *Death Without Weeping* I first told of a clandestine extermination group that had begun to operate in Timbaúba in the 1980s. The rise of these vigilantes seemed paradoxical, insofar as it coincided with the end of the twenty-year military dictatorship. What was the relationship between democracy and death squads? No one knew who was behind the extrajudicial *limpeza* ("street cleaning," as their supporters called it) that was targeting "dirty" street children and poor young black men from the shantytowns. But by 2000 the public was well aware of the group and the identity of its leader, Abdoral Gonçalves Queiroz. Known as the "Guardian Angels," they were responsible for killing more than 100 victims. In 2001 I was invited, along with my husband, to return to Timbaúba to help a newly appointed and tough minded judge and state prosecutor to identify those victims whose relatives had not come forward. In the interim, the death squad group had infiltrated the town council, the mayor's office, and the justice system. But eleven of them, including their semiliterate gangsterboss, Queiroz, had been arrested and were going on trial.

The death squad was a residue of the old military regime. For twenty years, the military police had kept the social classes segregated, with "dangerous" street youths and unemployed rural men confined to the hillside slums or in detention. When the old policing structures loosened following the democratic transition, the shantytowns ruptured and poor people, especially unemployed young men and street children, flooded downtown streets and public squares, once the preserve of *gente fina* (the cultivated people). Their new visibility betrayed the illusion of Brazilian modernity and evoked contradictory emotions of fear, aversion, pity, and anger.

Excluded and reviled, unemployed black youths and loose street kids of Timbaúba were prime targets of Queiroz and his gang. Depending on one's social class and politics, the band could be seen as hired serial killers or as *justiceiros* (outlaw heroes) who were protecting the community. Prominent figures—well-known businessmen and local politicians—applauded the work of the death squad, whom they also called "Police 2," and some of these leading citizens were active in the extrajudicial "courts" that were deciding who in Timbaúba should be the next to die.

During the 2001 death-squad field research expedition, I played cat-and-mouse with Dona Amantina, the dour manager of the *cartorio civil*, the official registry office. I was trying to assemble a body count of suspicious homicides that could possibly be linked to the death squad, focusing on the violent deaths of street kids and young black men. Since members of the death squad were still at large, I did not want to make public what I was doing. At first, I implied that I was back to count infant and child deaths, as I had so many years before. Finally, I admitted that I was looking into youth homicides. The manager nodded her head. "Yes, it's sad. But," she asked with a shy smile, "haven't you noticed the changes in infant and child deaths?" Once I began to scan the record books, I was wearing a smile, too.

Brazil's national central statistics bureau, the Instituto Brasileiro de Geografia e Estatística (IBGE), began reporting data for the municipality of Timbaúba in the late 1970s. In 1977, for example, IBGE reported 761 live births in the municipality and 311 deaths of infants (up to one year of age) for that same year, yielding an infant mortality rate of 409 per 1,000. A year later, the IBGE data recorded 896 live births and 320 infant deaths, an infant mortality rate of 357 per 1,000. If reliable, those official data indicated that between 36 and 41 percent of all infants in Timbaúba died in the first twelve months of life.

During the 1980s, when I was doing the research for *Death Without Weeping*, the then mayor of Timbaúba, the late Jacques Ferreira Lima, disputed those figures. "Impossible!" he fumed "This *município* is growing, not declining." He sent me to the local private hospital built by, and named for, his father, João Ferreira Lima, to compare the IBGE statistics with the hospital's records on births and deaths. There, the head nurse gave me access to her records, but the official death certificates only concerned stillbirths and perinatal deaths. In the end I found that the best source of data was the ledger books of the *cartorio civil*, where births and infant and child deaths were recorded by hand. Many births were not recorded until after a child had died, in order to register a death and receive a free coffin from the mayor's office. The statistics were as grim as those of the IBGE.

In 2001, a single afternoon going over infant and toddler death certificates in the same office was enough to document that something radical had since taken place—a revolution in child survival that had begun in the 1990s. The records now showed a completed birth rate of 3.2 children per woman, and a mortality rate of 35 per 1,000 births. Subsequent field trips in 2006 and 2007 showed even further reductions. The 2009 data from the IBGE recorded a rate of 25.2 child deaths per 1,000 births for Timbaúba.

Though working on other topics in my Brazilian field trips in 2001, 2006, and 2007, I took the time to interview several young women attending a pregnancy class at a newly constructed, government-run clinic. The women I spoke with—some first-time mothers, others expecting a second or third child—were confident in their ability to give birth to a healthy baby. No one I spoke to expected to have, except by accident, more than two children. A pair—that was the goal. Today, young women of the Alto can expect to give birth to three or fewer infants and to see all of them live at least into adolescence. The old stance of maternal watchful waiting accompanied by deselection of infants viewed as having no "talent" for life had been replaced by a maternal ethos of "holding on" to every infant, each seen as likely to survive. As I had noted in the past as well, there was a preference for girl babies. Boys, women feared, could disappoint their mothers—they could kill or be killed as adolescents and young men. The Alto was still a dangerous place, and gangs, drug dealers, and the death squads were still in operation. But women in the state-run clinic spoke of having control over their reproductive lives in ways that I could not have imagined.

By 2001 Timbaúba had experienced the demographic transition. Both infant deaths and births had declined so precipitously that it looked like a reproductive workers' strike. The numbers—though incomplete—were startling. Rather than the more than 200 annual infant and child mortalities of the early 1980s, by the late 1990s there were fewer than 50 childhood deaths recorded per year. And the causes of death were specific. In the past the causes had been stated in vague terms: "undetermined," "heart stopped, respiration stopped," "malnutrition," or the mythopoetic diagnosis of "acute infantile suffering."

On my latest return, just this June, the reproductive revolution was complete. The little two-room huts jumbled together on the back roads of the Alto were still poor, but as I visited the homes of dozens of Alto residents, sometimes accompanied by a local community health agent, sometimes dropping in for a chat unannounced, or summoned by the adult child of a former key informant of mine, I saw infants and toddlers who were plump and jolly, and mothers who were relaxed and breastfeeding toddlers as old as three years. Their babies assumed a high status in the family hierarchy, as precious little beings whose beauty and health brought honor and substance—as well as subsistence—to the household.

Manufactured cribs with pristine sheets and fluffy blankets, disposal diapers, and plastic rattles were much in evidence. Powdered milk, the number one baby killer in the past, was almost a banned substance. In contrast, no one, literally, breastfed during my early years of research on the Alto. It was breast milk that was banned, banned by the owners of the sugar plantations and by the bourgeois *patroas* (mistresses of the house) for whom the women of the Alto washed clothes and cleaned and cooked and served meals. Today, those jobs no longer exist. The sugar mills and sugar estates have closed down, and the landowning class has long since moved, leaving behind a population of working-class poor, a thin middle class (with washing machines rather than maids), and a displaced rural labor force that is largely sustained by the largesse of New Deal–style federal assistance.

Direct cash transfers are made to poor and unemployed families, and grants (*bolsas*, or "purses") are given to women, mothers, babies, schoolchildren, and youth. The grants come with conditions. The *bolsa familiar* (family grant), a small cash payment to each mother and up to five of her young children, requires the mother to immunize her babies, attend to their medical needs, follow medical directions, keep the children in school, monitor their homework, help them prepare for exams, and purchase school books, pens and pencils, and school clothes. Of the thirty Alto women between the ages of seventeen and forty my research associate, Jennifer S. Hughes, and I interviewed in June, the women averaged 3.3 pregnancies—higher than the national average, but the real comparison here is with their own mothers, who (based on the thirteen of the thirty who could describe their mothers' reproductive histories) averaged 13.6 pregnancies and among them counted sixty-one infant deaths. Jennifer is my daughter and a professor of colonial and postcolonial Latin American history at the University of California, Riverside. I like to think that her awesome archival skills were honed more than twenty years ago when I enlisted her, then a teenager, to help me count the deaths of Alto babies in the civil registry office. She agreed to help me on this most recent field trip, and it was our first professional collaboration.

Jennifer, for example, looked up Luciene, the firstborn daughter of Antonieta, one of my earliest key informants and my neighbor when I lived on the Alto do Cruzeiro. Now in her forties, Luciene had only one pregnancy and one living child. Her mother had given birth to fifteen babies, ten of whom survived. Daughter and mother now live next door to each other, and they spoke openly and emotionally about the "old days," "the hungry times," "the violent years," in comparison to the present. "Today we are rich," Antonieta declared, "*really* rich," by which she meant her modernized home on the Alto Terezinha, their new color television set, washing machine, and all the food and delicacies they could want.

Four of the thirty women we interviewed had lost an infant, and one had lost a two-year-old who drowned playing with a large basin of water. Those deaths were seen as tragic and painful memories. The mothers did not describe the deaths in a monotone or dismiss them as inevitable or an act of mercy that relieved their suffering. Rather, they recalled with deep sadness the date, the time, and the cause of their babies' deaths, and remembered them by name, saying that Gloria would be ten today or that Marcos would be eight years old today, had she or he lived.

What has happened in Timbaúba over the past decades is part of a national trend in Brazil. Over the past decade alone, Brazil's fertility rate has decreased from 2.36 to 1.9 children per family—a number that is below the replacement rate and lower than that of the United States. Unlike in China or India, this reproductive revolution occurred without state coercion. It was a voluntary transition, and a rapid one.

A footnote in *Death Without Weeping* records the most common requests that people made of me in the 1960s and again in the 1980s: Could I possibly help them obtain false teeth? a pair of eyeglasses? a better antibiotic for a sick older child? But most often I was asked—begged—by women to arrange a clandestine sterilization. In Northeast Brazil, sterilization was always preferable to oral contraceptives, IUDs, and condoms. Reproductive freedom meant having the children you wanted and then "closing down the factory." "*A fábrica é fechada!*" a woman would boastfully explain, patting her abdomen. Until recently, this was the privilege of the upper middle classes and the wealthy. Today, tubal ligations are openly discussed and arranged. One woman I interviewed, a devout Catholic, gushed that God was good, so good that he had given her a third son, her treasure trove, and at the same time had allowed her the liberty and freedom of a tubal ligation. "Praise to God!" she said. "Amen," I said.

In Brazil, the reproductive revolution is linked to democracy and the coming into political power of President Fernando Henrique Cardoso (1995–2002), aided by his formidable wife, the anthropologist and women's advocate Ruth Cardoso. It was continued by Luiz Inácio Lula da Silva, universally called "Lula," and, since 2011, by his successor, Dilma Rousseff. President Lula's Zero Hunger campaign, though much criticized in the popular media as a kind of political publicity stunt, in fact has supplied basic foodstuffs to the most vulnerable households.

Today food is abundant on the Alto. Schoolchildren are fed nutritious lunches, fortified with a protein mixture that is prepared as tasty milk shakes. There are food pantries and state and municipal milk distribution programs that are run by women with an extra room in their home. The monthly stipends to poor and single mothers to reward them for keeping their children in school has turned elementary school pupils into valuable household "workers," and literacy has increased for both the children and their mothers, who study at home alongside their children.

When I first went to the Alto in 1964 as a Peace Corps volunteer, it was in the role of a *visitadora*, a public-health community worker. The military dictatorship was suspicious of the program, which mixed health education and immunizations with advocating for water, street lights, and pit latrines as universal entitlements—owed even to those who had "occupied public land" (like the people of the Alto, who had been dispossessed by modernizing sugar plantations and mills). The *visitadora* program, Brazil's version of Chinese "barefoot doctors," was targeted by the military government as subversive, and the program ended by 1966 in Pernambuco. Many years later President Cardoso fortified the national health care system with a similar program of local "community health agents," who live and work in their micro-communities, visiting at-risk households, identifying crises, diagnosing common symptoms, and intervening to rescue vulnerable infants and toddlers from premature death. In Timbaúba, there are some 120 community health agents, male and female, working in poor micro-communities throughout the municipality, including dispersed rural communities. On the Alto do Cruzeiro twelve health agents each live and work in a defined area, each responsible for the health and well-being of some 150 families comprising 500 to 600 individuals. The basic requirement for a health worker is to have completed *ensino fundamental*, the equivalent of primary and middle school. Then, he or she must prepare for a public *concurso*, a competition based on a rigorous exam.

The community health agent's wage is small, a little more than the Brazilian minimum wage, but still less than US $700 a month for a forty-hour work week, most of it on foot up and down the hillside "slum" responding to a plethora of medical needs, from diaper rash to an emergency home birth. The agent records all births, deaths, illnesses, and other health problems in the micro- community; refers the sick to health posts, emergency rooms, and hospitals; monitors pregnancies and the health of newborns, the disabled, and the elderly. He or she identifies and reports communicable diseases and acts as a public-health and environmental educator. The agent participates in public meetings to shape health policies. Above all, the community health agent is the primary intermediary between poor people and the national health care system.

I am convinced that the incredible decline in premature deaths and useless suffering that I witnessed on the Alto is primarily the result of these largely unheralded medical heroes, who rescue mothers and their children in a large town with few doctors and no resident surgeons, pediatricians, and worst of all, obstetricians. A pregnant woman of the Alto suffers today from one of the worst dilemmas and anxieties a person in her condition can face: no certain location to give birth. The only solution at present is to refer women in labor to distant obstetric and maternity wards in public hospitals in Recife, the state capital, a sixty seven-mile drive away. The result can be fatal: at least one woman in the past year was prevented (by holding her legs together) from delivering her baby in an ambulance, and both mother and child died following their arrival at the designated hospital in Recife. For this reason Alto women and their health agents often choose prearranged cesarian sections well in advance of due dates, even though they know that C-sections are generally not in the best interest of mothers or infants.

Then, beyond the human factor, environmental factors figure in the decline in infant mortality in the shantytowns of Timbaúba and other municipalities in Northeast Brazil. The most significant of these is the result of a simple, basic municipal public-health program: the installation of water pipes that today reach nearly all homes with sufficient clean water. It is amazing to observe the transformative potential of material conditions: water = life!

Finally, what about the role of the Catholic Church? The anomaly is that, in a nation where the Catholic Church predominates in the public sphere and abortion is still illegal except in the case of rape or to save a mother's life, family size has dropped so sharply over the last two decades. What is going on? For one thing, Brazilian Catholics are independent, much like Catholics in the United States, going their own way when it comes to women's health and reproductive culture. Others have simply left Catholicism and joined evangelical churches, some of which proclaim their openness to the reproductive rights of women and men. Today only 60 percent of Brazilians identify as Roman Catholic. In our small sample of thirty women of the Alto, religion—whether Catholic, Protestant, Spiritist, or Afro-Brazilian—did not figure large in their reproductive lives.

The Brazilian Catholic Church is deeply divided. In 2009, the Archbishop of Recife announced the Vatican's excommunication of the doctors and family of a nine year-old girl who had had an abortion. She had been raped by her stepfather (thus the abortion was legal), and she was carrying twins—her tiny stature and narrow hips putting her life in jeopardy. After comparing abortion to the Holocaust, Archbishop José Cardoso Sobrinho told the media that the Vatican rejects believers who pick and choose their moral issues. The result was an immediate decline in church attendance throughout the diocese.

While the Brazilian Catholic hierarchy is decidedly conservative, the rural populace, their local clerics, and liberation theologians such as the activist ex-priest Leonardo Boff are open in their interpretations of Catholic spirituality and corporeality. The Jesus that my Catholic friends on the Alto embrace is a sensitive and sentient Son of God, a man of sorrows, to be sure, but also a man of compassion, keenly attuned to simple human needs. The teachings of liberation theology, while condemned by Pope John Paul II, helped to dislodge a baroque folk Catholicism in rural Northeast Brazil that envisioned God and the saints as authorizing and blessing the deaths of angel babies.

Padre Orlando, a young priest when I first met him in 1987, distanced himself from the quaint custom of blessing the bodies of dead infants as they were carried to the municipal graveyard in processions led by children. He also invited me and my Brazilian research assistant to give an orientation on family planning to poor Catholic women in the parish hall. When I asked what form of contraception I could teach, he replied, "I'm a celibate priest, how should I know? Teach it all, everything you know." When I reminded him that only the very unpredictable rhythm method was approved by the Vatican, he replied, "Just teach it all, everything you know, and then say, but the Pope only approves the not-so-safe rhythm method."

The people of the Alto do Cruzeiro still face many problems. Drugs, gangs, and death squads have left their ugly mark. Homicides have returned with a vengeance, but they are diffuse and chaotic, the impulsive murders one comes to expect among poor young men—the unemployed, petty thieves, and small-time drug dealers—and between rival gangs. One sees adolescents and young men of the shantytowns, who survived that dangerous first year of life, cut down by bullets and knives at the age of fifteen or seventeen by local gangs, strongmen, bandidos, and local police in almost equal measure. The old diseases also raise their heads from time to time: schistosomiasis, Chagas disease, tuberculosis, and even cholera.

But the bottom line is that women on the Alto today do not lose their infants. Children go to school rather than to the cane fields, and social cooperatives have taken the place of shadow economies. When mothers are sick or pregnant or a child is ill, they can go to the well-appointed health clinic supported by both state and national funds. There is a safety net, and it is wide, deep, and strong.

Just as we were leaving in mid-June, angry, insurgent crowds were forming in Recife, fed up with political corruption, cronyism, and the extravagant public expenditures in preparation for the 2014 World Cup in Brazil—when the need was for public housing and hospitals. Those taking to the streets were mostly young, urban, working-class and new middle-class Brazilians. The rural poor were generally not among them. The people of the Alto do Cruzeiro (and I imagine in many other communities like it) are strong supporters of the government led by the PT (*Partido dos Trabalhadores*, or Workers' Party). Under the PT the government has ended hunger in Pernambuco, and has opened family clinics and municipal schools that treat them and their children with respect for the first time in their lives.

The protesters in the streets are among the 40 million Brazilians who were added to the middle class between 2004 and 2010, under the government of President Lula, and whose rising expectations are combustible. When the healthy, literate children of the Alto do Cruzeiro grow up, they may yet join future protests demanding more accountability from their elected officials.

DISCUSSION QUESTIONS

1. Generally speaking, what is the relationship between *birth rates* and *high infant mortality*?

2. What were some of the socioeconomic changes occurring in Northeastern Brazil between 1964 and 2009 that radically altered how mothers related to their infant children?

3. How does Scheper-Hughes explain the radical reduction in birth rates over the past 45 years in Brazil, which has been, and still is, a predominantly Catholic country?

9

Society and Sex Roles

ERNESTINE FRIEDL

Professor Emerita of Anthropology, Duke University

Although it is possible to find societies in which gender inequalities are kept to a minimum, the overwhelming ethnographic and archaeological evidence suggests that females are subordinate to males in terms of exerting economic and political control. This gender asymmetry is so pervasive that some anthropologists have concluded that this gender inequality is the result of biological differences between men and women. That is, men are dominant because of their greater size, physical strength, and innate aggressiveness. In this selection, Ernestine Friedl argues that the answer to this near-universal male dominance lies more with economics than with biological predisposition.

Friedl, a former president of the American Anthropological Association, argues that men tend to be dominant because they control the distribution of scarce resources in the society, both within and outside of the family. Quite apart from who produces the goods, "the person controlling the distribution of the limited and valued resources possesses the currency needed to create the obligations and alliances that are at the center of all political relations." Using ethnographic examples from foraging societies, Friedl shows how women have relative equality in those societies where they exercise some control over resources. Conversely, men are nearly totally dominant in those societies in which women have no control over scarce resources.

"Women must respond quickly to the demands of their husbands," says anthropologist Napoleon Chagnon describing the horticultural Yanomamo Indians of Venezuela. When a man returns from a hunting trip, "the woman, no matter what she is doing, hurries home and quietly but rapidly prepares a meal for her husband. Should the wife be slow in doing this, the husband is within his rights to beat her. Most reprimands.... take the form of blows with the hand or with a piece of firewood.... Some of them chop their wives with the sharp edge of a machete or axe, or shoot them with a barbed arrow in some nonvital area, such as the buttocks or leg."

Among the Semai agriculturalists of central Malaya, when one person refuses the request of another, the offended party suffers *punan*, a mixture of emotional pain and frustration. "Enduring *punan* is commonest when a girl has refused the victim her sexual favors," reports Robert Dentan. "The jilted man's 'heart becomes sad.' He loses his energy and his appetite. Much of the time he sleeps, dreaming of his lost love. In this state he is in fact very likely to injure himself 'accidentally.'" The Semai are

SOURCE: From "Society and Sex Roles" by Ernestine Friedl in *Human Nature*, April 1978, 1(4), pp. 68–75. Reprinted with permission of the author.

afraid of violence; a man would never strike a woman.

The social relationship between men and women has emerged as one of the principal disputes occupying the attention of scholars and the public in recent years. Although the discord is sharpest in the United States, the controversy has spread throughout the world. Numerous national and international conferences, including one in Mexico sponsored by the United Nations, have drawn together delegates from all walks of life to discuss such questions as the social and political rights of each sex, and even the basic nature of males and females.

Whatever their position, partisans often invoke examples from other cultures to support their ideas about the proper role of each sex. Because women are clearly subservient to men in many societies, like the Yanomamo, some experts conclude that the natural pattern is for men to dominate. But among the Semai no one has the right to command others, and in West Africa women are often chiefs. The place of women in these societies supports the argument of those who believe that sex roles are not fixed, that if there is a natural order, it allows for many different arrangements.

The argument will never be settled as long as the opposing sides toss examples from the world's cultures at each other like intellectual stones. But the effect of biological differences on male and female behavior can be clarified by looking at known examples of the earliest forms of human society and examining the relationship between technology, social organization, environment, and sex roles. The problem is to determine the conditions in which different degrees of male dominance are found, to try to discover the social and cultural arrangements that give rise to equality or inequality between the sexes, and to attempt to apply this knowledge to our understanding of the changes taking place in modern industrial society.

As Western history and the anthropological record have told us, equality between the sexes is rare; in most known societies females are subordinate. Male dominance is so widespread that it is virtually a human universal; societies in which

women are consistently dominant do not exist and have never existed.

Evidence of a society in which women control all strategic resources like food and water, and in which women's activities are the most prestigious has never been found. The Iroquois of North America and the Lovedu of Africa came closest. Among the Iroquois, women raised food, controlled its distribution, and helped to choose male political leaders. Lovedu women ruled as queens, exchanged valuable cattle, led ceremonies, and controlled their own sex lives. But among both the Iroquois and the Lovedu, men owned the land and held other positions of power and prestige. Women were equal to men; they did not have ultimate authority over them. Neither culture was a true matriarchy.

Patriarchies are prevalent, and they appear to be strongest in societies in which men control significant goods that are exchanged with people outside the family. Regardless of who produces food, the person who gives it to others creates the obligations and alliances that are at the center of all political relations. The greater the male monopoly on the distribution of scarce items, the stronger their control of women seems to be. This is most obvious in relatively simple hunter-gatherer societies.

Hunter-gatherers, or foragers, subsist on wild plants, small land animals, and small river or sea creatures gathered by hand; large land animals and sea mammals hunted with spears, bows and arrows, and blow guns; and fish caught with hooks and nets. The 300,000 hunter-gatherers alive in the world today include the Eskimos, the Australian aborigines, and the Pygmies of Central Africa.

Foraging has endured for two million years and was replaced by farming and animal husbandry only 10,000 years ago; it covers more than 99 percent of human history. Our foraging ancestry is not far behind us and provides a clue to our understanding of the human condition.

Hunter-gatherers are people whose ways of life are technologically simple and socially and politically egalitarian. They live in small groups of 50 to 200 and have neither kings, nor priests, nor social classes. These conditions permit anthropologists to observe the essential bases for inequalities between the sexes without the distortions induced by the complexities of contemporary industrial society.

The source of male power among hunter-gatherers lies in their control of a scarce, hard to acquire, but necessary nutrient—animal protein. When men in a hunter-gatherer society return to camp with game, they divide the meat in some customary way. Among the !Kung San of Africa, certain parts of the animal are given to the owner of the arrow that killed the beast, to the first hunter to sight the game, to the one who threw the first spear, and to all men in the hunting party. After the meat has been divided, each hunter distributes his share to his blood relatives and his in-laws, who in turn share it with others. If an animal is large enough, every member of the band will receive some meat.

Vegetable foods, in contrast, are not distributed beyond the immediate household. Women give food to their children, to their husbands, to other members of the household, and rarely, to the occasional visitor. No one outside the family regularly eats any of the wild fruits and vegetables that are gathered by the women.

The meat distributed by the men is a public gift. Its source is widely known, and the donor expects a reciprocal gift when other men return from a successful hunt. He gains honor as a supplier of a scarce item and simultaneously obligates others to him.

These obligations constitute a form of power or control over others, both men and women. The opinions of hunters play an important part in decisions to move the village; good hunters attract the most desirable women; people in other groups join camps with good hunters; and hunters, because they already participate in an internal system of exchange, control exchange with other groups for flint, salt, and steel axes. The male monopoly on hunting unites men in a system of exchange and gives them power; gathering vegetable food does not give women equal power even among foragers who live in the tropics, where the food collected by women provides more than half the hunter-gatherer diet.

If dominance arises from a monopoly on big game hunting, why has the male monopoly remained unchallenged? Some women are strong enough to participate in the hunt and their endurance is certainly equal to that of men. Dobe San women of the Kalahari Desert in Africa walk an average of 10 miles a day carrying from 15 to 33 pounds of food plus a baby.

Women do not hunt, I believe, because of four interrelated factors: variability in the supply of game; the different skills required for hunting and gathering; the incompatibility between carrying burdens and hunting; and the small size of semi-nomadic foraging populations.

Because the meat supply is unstable, foragers must make frequent expeditions to provide the band with gathered food. Environmental factors such as seasonal and annual variation in rainfall often affect the size of the wildlife population. Hunters cannot always find game, and when they do encounter animals, they are not always successful in killing their prey. In northern latitudes, where meat is the primary food, periods of starvation are known in every generation. The irregularity of the game supply leads hunter-gatherers in areas where plant foods are available to depend on these predictable foods a good part of the time. Someone must gather the fruits, nuts, and roots and carry them back to camp to feed unsuccessful hunters, children, the elderly, and anyone who might not have gone foraging that day.

Foraging falls to the women because hunting and gathering cannot be combined on the same expedition. Although gatherers sometimes notice signs of game as they work, the skills required to track game are not the same as those required to find edible roots or plants. Hunters scan the horizon and the land for traces of large game; gatherers keep their eyes to the ground, studying the distribution of plants and the texture of the soil for hidden roots and animal holes. Even if a woman who was collecting plants came across the track of an antelope, she could not follow it; it is impossible to carry a load and hunt at the same time. Running with a heavy load is difficult, and should the animal be sighted, the hunter would be off balance and could neither shoot an arrow nor throw a spear accurately.

Pregnancy and child care would also present difficulties for a hunter. An unborn child affects a woman's body balance, as does a child in her arms, on her back, or slung at her side. Until they are two years old, many hunter-gatherer children are carried at all times, and until they are four, they are carried some of the time.

An observer might wonder why young women do not hunt until they become pregnant, or why mature women and men do not hunt and gather on alternate days, with some women staying in camp to act as wet nurses for the young. Apart from the effects hunting might have on a mother's milk production, there are two reasons. First, young girls begin to bear children as soon as they are physically mature and strong enough to hunt, and second, hunter-gatherer bands are so small that there are unlikely to be enough lactating women to serve as wet nurses. No hunter-gatherer group could afford to maintain a specialized female hunting force.

Because game is not always available, because hunting and gathering are specialized skills, because women carrying heavy loads cannot hunt, and because women in hunter-gatherer societies are usually either pregnant or caring for young children, for most of the last two million years of human history men have hunted and women have gathered.

If male dominance depends on controlling the supply of meat, then the degree of male dominance in a society should vary with the amount of meat available and the amount supplied by the men. Some regions, like the East African grasslands and the North American woodlands, abounded with species of large mammals; other zones, like tropical forests and semideserts, are thinly populated with prey. Many elements affect the supply of game, but theoretically, the less meat provided exclusively by the men, the more egalitarian the society.

All known hunter-gatherer societies fit into four basic types: those in which men and women work together in communal hunts and as teams gathering edible plants, as did the Washo Indians of North America; those in which men and

women each collect their own plant foods although the men supply some meat to the group, as do the Hadza of Tanzania; those in which male hunters and female gatherers work apart but return to camp each evening to share their acquisitions, as do the Tiwi of North Australia; and those in which the men provide all the food by hunting large game, as do the Eskimo. In each case the extent of male dominance increases directly with the proportion of meat supplied by individual men and small hunting parties.

Among the most egalitarian of hunter-gatherer societies are the Washo Indians, who inhabited the valleys of the Sierra Nevada in what is now southern California and Nevada. In the spring they moved north to Lake Tahoe for the large fish runs of sucker and native trout. Everyone—men, women, and children—participated in the fishing. Women spent the summer gathering edible berries and seeds while the men continued to fish. In the fall some men hunted deer but the most important source of animal protein was the jack rabbit, which was captured in communal hunts. Men and women together drove the rabbits into nets tied end to end. To provide food for the winter, husbands and wives worked as teams in the late fall to collect pine nuts.

Since everyone participated in most food gathering activities, there were no individual distributors of food and relatively little difference in male and female rights. Men and women were not segregated from each other in daily activities; both were free to take lovers after marriage; both had the right to separate whenever they chose; menstruating women were not isolated from the rest of the group; and one of the two major Washo rituals celebrated hunting while the other celebrated gathering. Men were accorded more prestige if they had killed a deer, and men directed decisions about the seasonal movement of the group. But if no male leader stepped forward, women were permitted to lead. The distinctive feature of groups such as the Washo is the relative equality of the sexes.

The sexes are also relatively equal among the Hadza of Tanzania but this near-equality arises because men and women tend to work alone to feed themselves. They exchange little food. The

Hadza lead a leisurely life in the seemingly barren environment of the East African Rift Gorge that is, in fact, rich in edible berries, roots, and small game. As a result of this abundance, from the time they are 10 years old, Hadza men and women gather much of their own food. Women take their young children with them into the bush, eating as they forage, and collect only enough food for a light family meal in the evening. The men eat berries and roots as they hunt for small game, and should they bring down a rabbit or a hyrax, they eat the meat on the spot. Meat is carried back to the camp and shared with the rest of the group only on those rare occasions when a poisoned arrow brings down a large animal—an impala, a zebra, an eland, or a giraffe.

Because Hadza men distribute little meat, their status is only slightly higher than that of the women. People flock to the camp of a good hunter and the camp might take on his name because of his popularity, but he is in no sense a leader of the group. A Hadza man and a woman have an equal right to divorce and each can repudiate a marriage simply by living apart for a few weeks. Couples tend to live in the same camp as the wife's mother but they sometimes make long visits to the camp of the husband's mother. Although a man may take more than one wife, most Hadza males cannot afford to indulge in this luxury. In order to maintain a marriage, a man must supply both his wife and his mother-in-law with some meat and trade goods, such as beads and cloth, and the Hadza economy gives few men the wealth to provide for more than one wife and mother-in-law. Washo equality is based on cooperation; Hadza equality is based on independence.

In contrast to both these groups, among the Tiwi of Melville and Bathurst Islands off the northern coast of Australia, male hunters dominate female gatherers. The Tiwi are representative of the most common form of foraging society, in which the men supply large quantities of meat, although less than half the food consumed by the group. Each morning Tiwi women, most with babies on their backs, scatter in different directions in search of vegetables, grubs, worms, and small game such as bandicoots, lizards, and opossums.

To track the game, they use hunting dogs. On most days women return to camp with some meat and with baskets full of *korka*, the nut of a native palm, which is soaked and mashed to make a porridge-like dish. The Tiwi men do not hunt small game and do not hunt every day, but when they do they often return with kangaroo, large lizards, fish, and game birds.

The porridge is cooked separately by each household and rarely shared outside the family, but the meat is prepared by a volunteer cook, who can be male or female. After the cook takes one of the parts of the animal traditionally reserved for him or her, the animal's "boss," the one who caught it, distributes the rest to all near kin and then to all others residing with the band. Although the small game supplied by the women is distributed in the same way as the big game supplied by the men, Tiwi men are dominant because the game they kill provides most of the meat.

The power of Tiwi men is clearest in their betrothal practices. Among the Tiwi, a woman must always be married. To ensure this, female infants are betrothed at birth and widows are remarried at the gravesides of their late husbands. Men form alliances by exchanging daughters, sisters, and mothers in marriage and some collect as many as 25 wives. Tiwi men value the quantity and quality of the food many wives can collect and the many children they can produce.

The dominance of the men is offset somewhat by the influence of adult women in selecting their next husbands. Many women are active strategists in the political careers of their male relatives, but to the exasperation of some sons attempting to promote their own futures, widowed mothers sometimes insist on selecting their own partners. Women also influence the marriages of their daughters and granddaughters, especially when the selected husband dies before the bestowed child moves to his camp.

Among the Eskimo, representative of the rarest type of forager society, inequality between the sexes is matched by inequality in supplying the group with food. Inland Eskimo men hunt caribou throughout the year to provision the entire society, and maritime

Eskimo men depend on whaling, fishing, and some hunting to feed their extended families. The women process the carcasses, cut and sew skins to make clothing, cook, and care for the young; but they collect no food of their own and depend on the men to supply all the raw materials for their work. Since men provide all the meat, they also control the trade in hides, whale oil, seal oil, and other items that move between the maritime and inland Eskimos.

Eskimo women are treated almost exclusively as objects to be used, abused, and traded by men. After puberty all Eskimo girls are fair game for any interested male. A man shows his intentions by grabbing the belt of a woman and if she protests, he cuts off her trousers and forces himself upon her. These encounters are considered unimportant by the rest of the group. Men offer their wives' sexual services to establish alliances with trading partners and members of hunting and whaling parties.

Despite the consistent pattern of some degree of male dominance among foragers, most of these societies are egalitarian compared with agricultural and industrial societies. No forager has any significant opportunity for political leadership. Foragers, as a rule, do not like to give or take orders, and assume leadership only with reluctance. Shamans (those who are thought to be possessed by spirits) may be either male or female. Public rituals conducted by women in order to celebrate the first menstruation of girls are common, and the symbolism in these rituals is similar to that in the ceremonies that follow a boy's first kill.

In any society, status goes to those who control the distribution of valued goods and services outside the family. Equality arises when both sexes work side by side in food production, as do the Washo, and the products are simply distributed among the workers. In such circumstances, no person or sex has greater access to valued items than do others. But when women make no contribution to the food supply, as in the case of the Eskimo, they are completely subordinate.

When we attempt to apply these generalizations to contemporary industrial society, we can predict that as long as women spend their discretionary income from jobs on domestic needs, they will gain little social recognition and power. To be an effective source of power, money must be exchanged in ways that require returns and create obligations. In other words, it must be invested.

Jobs that do not give women control over valued resources will do little to advance their general status. Only as managers, executives, and professionals are women in a position to trade goods and services, to do others favors, and therefore to obligate others to them. Only as controllers of valued resources can women achieve prestige, power, and equality.

Within the household, women who bring in income from jobs are able to function on a more nearly equal basis with their husbands. Women who contribute services to their husbands and children without pay, as do some middle-class Western housewives, are especially vulnerable to dominance. Like Eskimo women, as long as their services are limited to domestic distribution they have little power relative to their husbands and none with respect to the outside world.

As for the limits imposed on women by their procreative functions in hunter-gatherer societies, childbearing and child care are organized around work as much as work is organized around reproduction. Some foraging groups space their children three to four years apart and have an average of only four to six children, far fewer than many women in other cultures. Hunter-gatherers nurse their infants for extended periods, sometimes for as long as four years. This custom suppresses ovulation and limits the size of their families. Sometimes, although rarely, they practice infanticide. By limiting reproduction, a woman who is gathering food has only one child to carry.

Different societies can and do adjust the frequency of birth and the care of children to accommodate whatever productive activities women customarily engage in. In horticultural societies, where women work long hours in gardens that may be far from home, infants get food to supplement their mothers' milk, older children take care of younger children, and pregnancies are widely spaced. Throughout the world, if a society requires a woman's labor, it finds ways to care for her children.

In the United States, as in some other industrial societies, the accelerated entry of women with pre-school children into the labor force has resulted in the development of a variety of child-care arrangements. Individual women have called on friends, relatives, and neighbors. Public and private child-care centers are growing. We should realize that the declining birth rate, the increasing acceptance of childless or single-child families, and a de-emphasis on motherhood are adaptations to a sexual division of labor reminiscent of the system of production found in hunter-gatherer societies.

In many countries where women no longer devote most of their productive years to childbearing, they are beginning to demand a change in the social relationship of the sexes. As women gain access to positions that control the exchange of resources, male dominance may become archaic, and industrial societies may one day become as egalitarian as the Washo.

DISCUSSION QUESTIONS

1. How does Professor Friedl explain the pervasive inequality between men and women found in the world today?

2. Which societies does Friedl cite as having relative gender equality, and which societies does she cite as having high levels of inequality?

3. Based on her cross-cultural findings, what suggestions does Friedl make for Western women to acquire greater power and status?

What about placing a greater value on domestic work?

10

Do Muslim Women Really Need Saving?

LILA ABU-LUGHOD

Professor of Anthropology, Columbia University

This piece by anthropologist Lila Abu-Lughod, written shortly after 9/11, raises the question of whether it was legitimate, honest, or anthropologically informed for the US government (with First Lady Laura Bush as the principal spokesperson) to make the additional case for going to war with the Taliban-led government in Afghanistan, based on the desire to liberate or "save" the repressed Muslim women living under Taliban control.

Professor Abu-Lughod—who had conducted participant-observation research among Islamic women in Egypt for decades—discusses a number of issues suggesting that the First Lady's basic premise was ethnocentric, based on an oversimplification of the ethnographic realities, paternalistic, and self-servingly ideological. First, attempting to justify going to war with Afghanistan as a way of saving Muslim women from the "tyranny of the burqa" (1) fails to understand the sociocultural significance of the burqa or other forms of covering in traditional and contemporary Afghan society; (2) assumes that Afghan women would voluntarily choose to give up the burqa if given the choice; and (3) assumes that Muslim women, seeing themselves as "unfree" or repressed, believe that they need to be liberated in much the same way as women living in New York, Los Angeles, or London. And second, Mrs. Bush was relying on such misleading cultural dichotomies as (1) unliberated Muslim women versus women in the West living with a minimum of societal constraints and (2) the democratic United States versus the Taliban-terrorist axis in Afghanistan. By relying on these questionable (and certainly imperfect) cultural dichotomies, Mrs. Bush was diverting the public's attention away from examining the history of repressive regimes in Muslim countries (such as Afghanistan) and the role the United States played in this history.

What are the ethics of the current "War on Terrorism," a war that justifies itself by purporting to liberate, or save, Afghan women? Does anthropology have anything to offer in our search for a viable position to take regarding this rationale for war?

I was led to pose the question of my title in part because of the way I personally experienced the response to the U.S. war in Afghanistan. Like many colleagues whose work has focused on women and gender in the Middle East, I was deluged with invitations to speak—not just on news programs but also to various departments at colleges and universities, especially women's studies programs. Why did this not please me, a scholar who has devoted more than 20 years of her life to this

SOURCE: Abu-Lughod, Lila, "Do Muslim Women Really Need Saving? Anthropological Reflections on Cultural Relativism and its Others." AMERICAN ANTHROPOLOGIST, 104(3): 783–790, 2002.

subject and who has some complicated personal connection to this identity? Here was an opportunity to spread the word, disseminate my knowledge, and correct misunderstandings. The urgent search for knowledge about our sister "women of cover" (as President George Bush so marvelously called them) is laudable and when it comes from women's studies programs where "transnational feminism" is now being taken seriously, it has a certain integrity (see Safire 2001).

My discomfort led me to reflect on why, as feminists in or from the West, or simply as people who have concerns about women's lives, we need to be wary of this response to the events and aftermath of September 11, 2001. I want to point out the minefields—a metaphor that is sadly too apt for a country like Afghanistan, with the world's highest number of mines per capita—of this obsession with the plight of Muslim women. I hope to show some way through them using insights from anthropology, the discipline whose charge has been to understand and manage cultural difference, At the same time, I want to remain critical of anthropology's complicity in the reification of cultural difference.

CULTURAL EXPLANATIONS AND THE MOBILIZATION OF WOMEN

It is easier to see why one should be skeptical about the focus on the "Muslim woman" if one begins with the U.S. public response. I will analyze two manifestations of this response: some conversations I had with a reporter from the PBS *NewsHour with Jim Lehrer* and First Lady Laura Bush's radio address to the nation on November 17, 2001. The presenter from the *NewsHour* show first contacted me in October to see if I was willing to give some background for a segment on Women and Islam. I mischievously asked whether she had done segments on the women of Guatemala, Ireland, Palestine, or Bosnia when the show covered wars in those regions; but I finally agreed to look at the questions she was going to pose to panelists. The questions

were hopelessly general. Do Muslim women believe "x"? Are Muslim women "y"? Does Islam allow "z" for women? I asked her: If you were to substitute Christian or Jewish wherever you have Muslim, would these questions make sense? I did not imagine she would call me back. But she did, twice, once with an idea for a segment on the meaning of Ramadan and another time on Muslim women in politics. One was in response to the bombing and the other to the speeches by Laura Bush and Cherie Blair, wife of the British Prime Minister.

What is striking about these three ideas for news programs is that there was a consistent resort to the cultural, as if knowing something about women and Islam or the meaning of a religious ritual would help one understand the tragic attack on New York's World Trade Center and the U.S. Pentagon, or how Afghanistan had come to be ruled by the Taliban, or what interests might have fueled U.S. and other interventions in the region over the past 25 years, or what the history of American support for conservative groups funded to undermine the Soviets might have been, or why the caves and bunkers out of which Bin Laden was to be smoked "dead or alive, as President Bush announced on television, were paid for and built by the CIA.

In other words, the question is why knowing about the "culture" of the region, and particularly its religious beliefs and treatment of women, was more urgent than exploring the history of the development of repressive regimes in the region and the U.S. role in this history. Such cultural framing, it seemed to me, prevented the serious exploration of the roots and nature of human suffering in this part of the world. Instead of political and historical explanations, experts were being asked to give reliogiocultural ones. Instead of questions that might lead to the exploration of global interconnections, we were offered ones that worked to artificially divide the world into separate spheres—recreating an imaginative geography of West versus East, us versus Muslims, cultures in which First Ladies give speeches versus others where women shuffle around silently in burqas.

Most pressing for me was why the Muslim woman in general, and the Afghan woman in particular, were so crucial to this cultural mode of explanation, which ignored the complex entanglements in which we are all implicated, in sometimes surprising alignments. Why were these female symbols being mobilized in this "War against Terrorism" in a way they were not in other conflicts? Laura Bush's radio address on November 17 reveals the political work such mobilization accomplishes. On the one hand, her address collapsed important distinctions that should have been maintained. There was a constant slippage between the Taliban and the terrorists, so that they became almost one word—a kind of hyphenated monster identity: the Taliban-and-the-terrorists. Then there was the blurring of the very separate causes in Afghanistan of women's continuing malnutrition, poverty, and ill health, and their more recent exclusion under the Taliban from employment, schooling, and the joys of wearing nail polish. On the other hand, her speech reinforced chasmic divides, primarily between the "civilized people throughout the world" whose hearts break for the women and children of Afghanistan and the Taliban-and-the-terrorists, the cultural monsters who want to, as she put it, "impose their world on the rest of us."

Most revealingly, the speech enlisted women to justify American bombing and intervention in Afghanistan and to make a case for the "War on Terrorism" of which it was allegedly a part. As Laura Bush said, "Because of our recent military gains in much of Afghanistan, women are no longer imprisoned in their homes. They can listen to music and teach their daughters without fear of punishment. The fight against terrorism is also a fight for the rights and dignity of women" (U.S. Government 2002).

These words have haunting resonances for anyone who has studied colonial history. Many who have worked on British colonialism in South Asia have noted the use of the woman question in colonial policies where intervention into sati (the practice of widows immolating themselves on their husbands' funeral pyres), child marriage, and other practices was used to justify rule. As Gayatri Chakravorty Spivak (1988) has cynically put it: white men saving brown women from brown men. The historical record is full of similar cases,

including in the Middle East. In Turn of the Century Egypt, what Leila Ahmed (1992) has called "colonial feminism" was hard at work. This was a selective concern about the plight of Egyptian women that focused on the veil as a sign of oppression but gave no support to women's education and was professed loudly by the same Englishman, Lord Cromer, who opposed women's suffrage back home.

Sociologist Marnia Lazreg (1994) has offered some vivid examples of how French colonialism enlisted women to its cause in Algeria. She writes:

> Perhaps the most spectacular example of the colonial appropriation of women's voices, and the silencing of those among them who had begun to take women revolutionaries ... as role models by not donning the veil, was the event of May 16, 1958 [just four years before Algeria finally gained its independence from France after a long bloody struggle and 130 years of French control—L.A.]. On that day a demonstration was organized by rebellious French generals in Algiers to show their determination to keep Algeria French. To give the government of France evidence that Algerians were in agreement with them, the generals had a few thousand native men bused in from nearby villages, along with a few women who were solemnly unveiled by French women.... Rounding up Algerians and bringing them to demonstrations of loyalty to France was not in itself an unusual act during the colonial era. But to unveil women at a well-choreographed ceremony added to the event a symbolic dimension that dramatized the one constant feature of the Algerian occupation by France: its obsession with women. [Lazreg 1994:135]

Lazreg (1994) also gives memorable examples of the way in which the French had earlier sought to transform Arab women and girls. She describes skits at awards ceremonies at the Muslim Girls' School in Algiers in 1851 and 1852. In the first skit, written by "a French lady from Algiers," two

Algerian Arab girls reminisced about their trip to France with words including the following:

> Oh! Protective France: Oh! Hospitable France! …
> Noble land, where I felt free
> Under Christian skies to pray to our God: …
> God bless you for the happiness you bring us!
> And you, adoptive mother, who taught us
> That we have a share of this world,
> We will cherish you forever! [Lazreg 1994:68–69]

These girls are made to invoke the gift of a share of this world, a world where freedom reigns under Christian skies. This is not the world the Taliban-and-the-terrorists would "like to impose on the rest of us."

Just as I argued above that we need to be suspicious when neat cultural icons are plastered over messier historical and political narratives, so we need to be wary when Lord Cromer in British-ruled Egypt, French ladies in Algeria, and Laura Bush, all with military troops behind them, claim to be saving or liberating Muslim women.

POLITICS OF THE VEIL

I want now to look more closely at those Afghan women Laura Bush claimed were "rejoicing" at their liberation by the Americans. This necessitates a discussion of the veil, or the burqa, because it is so central to contemporary concerns about Muslim women. This will set the stage for a discussion of how anthropologists, feminist anthropologists in particular, contend with the problem of difference in a global world. In the conclusion, I will return to the rhetoric of saving Muslim women and offer an alternative.

It is common popular knowledge that the ultimate sign of the oppression of Afghan women under the Taliban- and-the-terrorists is that they were forced to wear the burqa. Liberals sometimes confess their surprise that even though Afghanistan has been liberated from the Taliban, women do not seem to be throwing off their burqas. Someone who has worked in Muslim regions must ask why this is so surprising. Did we expect that once "free" from the Taliban they would go "back" to belly shirts and blue jeans, or dust off their Chanel suits? We need to be more sensible about the clothing of "women of cover, and so there is perhaps a need to make some basic points about veiling.

First, it should be recalled that the Taliban did not invent the burqa. It was the local form of covering that Pashtun women in one region wore when they went out. The Pashtun are one of several ethnic groups in Afghanistan and the burqa was one of many forms of covering in the subcontinent and Southwest Asia that has developed as a convention for symbolizing women's modesty or respectability. The burqa, like some other forms of "cover" has, in many settings, marked the symbolic separation of men's and women's spheres, as part of the general association of women with family and home, not with public space where strangers mingled.

Twenty years ago the anthropologist Hanna Papanek (1982), who worked in Pakistan, described the burqa as "portable seclusion." She noted that many saw it as a liberating invention because it enabled women to move out of segregated living spaces while still observing the basic moral requirements of separating and protecting women from unrelated men. Ever since I came across her phrase "portable seclusion," I have thought of these enveloping robes as "mobile homes," Everywhere, such veiling signifies belonging to a particular community and participating in a moral way of life in which families are paramount in the organization of communities and the home is associated with the sanctity of women.

The obvious question that follows is this: If this were the case, why would women suddenly become immodest? Why would they suddenly throw off the markers of their respectability, markers, whether burqas or other forms of cover, which were supposed to assure their protection in the public sphere from the harassment of strange men by symbolically signaling to all that they were still in the inviolable space of their homes, even though moving in the public realm? Especially when these are forms of dress that had become so conventional that most women gave little thought to their meaning.

To draw some analogies, none of them perfect, why are we surprised that Afghan women do not throw off their burqas when we know perfectly well that it would not be appropriate to wear shorts to the opera? At the time these discussions of Afghan women's burqas were raging, a friend of mine was chided by her husband for suggesting she wanted to wear a pantsuit to a fancy wedding, "You know you don't wear pants to a WASP wedding," he reminded her. New Yorkers know that the beautifully coiffed Hasidic women, who look so fashionable next to their dour husbands in black coats and hats, are wearing wigs. This is because religious belief and community standards of propriety require the covering of the hair. They also alter boutique fashions to include high necks and long sleeves, As anthropologists know perfectly well, people wear the appropriate form of dress for their social communities and are guided by socially shared standards, religious beliefs, and moral ideals, unless they deliberately transgress to make a point or are unable to afford proper cover. If we think that U.S. women live in a world of choice regarding clothing, all we need to do is remind ourselves of the expression, "the tyranny of fashion."

What had happened in Afghanistan under the Taliban is that one regional style of covering or veiling, associated with a certain respectable but not elite class, was imposed on everyone as "religiously" appropriate, even though previously there had been many different styles, popular or traditional with different groups and classes—different ways to mark women's propriety, or, in more recent times, religious piety. Although I am not an expert on Afghanistan, I imagine that the majority of women left in Afghanistan by the time the Taliban took control were the rural or less educated, from nonelite families, since they were the only ones who could not emigrate to escape the hardship and violence that has marked Afghanistan's recent history. If liberated from the enforced wearing of

burqas, most of these women would choose some other form of modest headcovering, like all those living nearby who were not under the Taliban—their rural Hindu counterparts in the North of India (who cover their heads and veil their faces from affines) or their Muslim sisters in Pakistan.

Even *The New York Times* carried an article about Afghan women refugees in Pakistan that attempted to educate readers about this local variety (Fremson 2001). The article describes and pictures everything from the nowiconic burqa with the embroidered eyeholes, which a Pashtun woman explains is the proper dress for her community, to large scarves they call chadors, to the new Islamic modest dress that wearers refer to as *hijab*. Those in the new Islamic dress are characteristically students heading for professional careers, especially in medicine, just like their counterparts from Egypt to Malaysia. One wearing the large scarf was a school principal; the other was a poor street vendor. The telling quote from the young street vendor is, "If I did [wear the burqa] the refugees would tease me because the burqa is for 'good women' who stay inside the home" (Fremson 2001:14). Here you can see the local status associated with the burqa—it is for good respectable women from strong families who are not forced to make a living selling on the street.

The British newspaper *The Guardian* published an interview in January 2002 with Dr. Suheila Siddiqi, a respected surgeon in Afghanistan who holds the rank of lieutenant general in the Afghan medical corps (Goldenberg 2002). A woman in her sixties, she comes from an elite family and, like her sisters, was educated. Unlike most women of her class, she chose not to go into exile. She is presented in the article as "the woman who stood up to the Taliban" because she refused to wear the burqa. She had made it a condition of returning to her post as head of a major hospital when the Taliban came begging in 1996, just eight months after firing her along with other women. Siddiqi is described as thin, glamorous, and confident. But further into the article it is noted that her graying bouffant hair is covered in a gauzy veil. This is a reminder that though she refused the burqa, she had no question about wearing the chador or scarf.

Finally, I need to make a crucial point about veiling. Not only are there many forms of covering, which themselves have different meanings in the communities in which they are used, but also veiling itself must not be confused with, or made to stand for, lack of agency. As I have argued in my ethnography of a Bedouin community in Egypt in the late 1970s and 1980s (1986), pulling the black head cloth over the face in front of older respected men is considered a voluntary act by women who are deeply committed to being moral and have a sense of honor tied to family. One of the ways they show their standing is by covering their faces in certain contexts. They decide for whom they feel it is appropriate to veil.

To take a very different case, the modern Islamic modest dress that many educated women across the Muslim world have taken on since the mid-1970s now both publicly marks piety and can be read as a sign of educated urban sophistication, a sort of modernity (e.g., Abu-Lughod 1995, 1998; Brenner 1996; El Guindi 1999; MacLeod 1991; Ong 1990). As Saba Mahmood (2001) has so brilliantly shown in her ethnography of women in the mosque movement in Egypt, this new form of dress is also perceived by many of the women who adopt it as part of a bodily means to cultivate virtue, the outcome of their professed desire to be close to God.

Two points emerge from this fairly basic discussion of the meanings of veiling in the contemporary Muslim world. First, we need to work against the reductive interpretation of veiling as the quintessential sign of women's unfreedom, even if we object to state imposition of this form, as in Iran or with the Taliban. (It must be recalled that the modernizing states of Turkey and Iran had earlier in the century banned veiling and required men, except religious clerics, to adopt Western dress.) What does freedom mean if we accept the fundamental premise that humans are social beings, always raised in certain social and historical contexts and belonging to particular communities that shape their desires and understandings of the world? Is it not a gross violation of women's own understandings of what they are doing to simply denounce the

burqa as a medieval imposition? Second, we must take care not to reduce the diverse situations and attitudes of millions of Muslim women to a single item of clothing. Perhaps it is time to give up the Western obsession with the veil and focus on some serious issues with which feminists and others should indeed be concerned.

Ultimately, the significant political-ethical problem the burqa raises is how to deal with cultural "others." How are we to deal with difference without accepting the passivity implied by the cultural relativism for which anthropologists are justly famous—a relativism that says it's their culture and it's not my business to judge or interfere, only to try to understand. Cultural relativism is certainly an improvement on ethnocentrism and the racism, cultural imperialism, and imperiousness that underlie it; the problem is that it is too late not to interfere. The forms of lives we find around the world are already products of long histories of interactions.

I want to explore the issues of women, cultural relativism, and the problems of "difference" from three angles. First, I want to consider what feminist anthropologists (those stuck in that awkward relationship, as Strathern [1987] has claimed) are to do with strange political bedfellows. I used to feel torn when I received the e-mail petitions circulating for the last few years in defense of Afghan women under the Taliban. I was not sympathetic to the dogmatism of the Taliban; I do not support the oppression of women. But the provenance of the campaign worried me. I do not usually find myself in political company with the likes of Hollywood celebrities (see Hirschkind and Mahmood 2002). I had never received a petition from such women defending the right of Palestinian women to safety from Israeli bombing or daily harassment at checkpoints, asking the United States to reconsider its support for a government that had dispossessed them, closed them out from work and citizenship rights, refused them the most basic freedoms. Maybe some of these same people might be signing petitions to save African women from genital cutting, or Indian women from dowry deaths. However, I do not think that it would be as easy to mobilize so many of these American and European women if it were not a case of Muslim men oppressing Muslim women—women of cover for whom they can feel sorry and in relation to whom they can feel smugly superior. Would television diva Oprah Winfrey host the Women in Black, the women's peace group from Israel, as she did RAWA, the Revolutionary Association of Women of Afghanistan, who were also granted the *Glamour Magazine* Women of the Year Award? What are we to make of post-Taliban "Reality Tours" such as the one advertised on the internet by Global Exchange for March 2002 under the title "Courage and Tenacity: A Women's Delegation to Afghanistan"? The rationale for the $1,400 tour is that "with the removal of the Taliban government, Afghan women, for the first time in the past decade, have the opportunity to reclaim their basic human rights and establish their role as equal citizens by participating in the rebuilding of their nation," The tour's objective, to celebrate International Women's Week, is "to develop awareness of the concerns and issues the Afghan women are facing as well as to witness the changing political, economic, and social conditions which have created new opportunities for the women of Afghanistan" (Global Exchange 2002).

To be critical of this celebration of women's rights in Afghanistan is not to pass judgment on any local women's organizations, such as RAWA, whose members have courageously worked since 1977 for a democratic secular Afghanistan in which women's human rights are respected, against Soviet-backed regimes or U.S.-, Saudi-, and Pakistani- supported conservatives. Their documentation of abuse and their work through clinics and schools have been enormously important.

It is also not to fault the campaigns that exposed the dreadful conditions under which the Taliban placed women. The Feminist Majority campaign helped put a stop to a secret oil pipeline deal between the Taliban and the U.S. multinational Unocal that was going forward with U.S. administration support. Western feminist campaigns must not be confused with the hypocrisies of the new colonial feminism of a Republican president who was not elected for his progressive stance on feminist issues or of administrations that played

down the terrible record of violations of women by the United State's allies in the Northern Alliance, as documented by Human Rights Watch and Amnesty International, among others, Rapes and assaults were widespread in the period of infighting that devastated Afghanistan before the Taliban came in to restore order.

It is, however, to suggest that we need to look closely at what we are supporting (and what we are not) and to think carefully about why. How should we manage the complicated politics and ethics of finding ourselves in agreement with those with whom we normally disagree? I do not know how many feminists who felt good about saving Afghan women from the Taliban are also asking for a global redistribution of wealth or contemplating sacrificing their own consumption radically so that African or Afghan women could have some chance of having what I do believe should be a universal human right—the right to freedom from the structural violence of global inequality and from the ravages of war, the everyday rights of having enough to eat, having homes for their families in which to live and thrive, having ways to make decent livings so their children can grow, and having the strength and security to work out, within their communities and with whatever alliances they want, how to live a good life, which might very well include changing the ways those communities are organized.

Suspicion about bedfellows is only a first step; it will not give us a way to think more positively about what to do or where to stand. For that, we need to confront two more big issues. First is the acceptance of the possibility of difference. Can we only free Afghan women to be like us or might we have to recognize that even after "liberation" from the Taliban, they might want different things than we would want for them? What do we do about that? Second, we need to be vigilant about the rhetoric of saving people because of what it implies about our attitudes.

Again, when I talk about accepting difference, I am not implying that we should resign ourselves to being cultural relativists who respect whatever goes on elsewhere as "just their culture," I have already discussed the dangers of "cultural" explanations; "their" cultures are just as much part of history and an interconnected world as ours are. What I am advocating is the hard work involved in recognizing and respecting differences—precisely as products of different histories, as expressions of different circumstances, and as manifestations of differently structured desires. We may want justice for women, but can we accept that there might be different ideas about justice and that different women might want, or choose, different futures from what we envision as best (see Ong 1988)? We must consider that they might be called to personhood, so to speak, in a different language.

Reports from the Bonn peace conference held in late November to discuss the rebuilding of Afghanistan revealed significant differences among the few Afghan women feminists and activists present. RAWA's position was to reject any conciliatory approach to Islamic governance. According to one report I read, most women activists, especially those based in Afghanistan who are aware of the realities on the ground, agreed that Islam had to be the starting point for reform. Fatima Gailani, a U.S.-based advisor to one of the delegations, is quoted as saying, "If I go to Afghanistan today and ask women for votes on the promise to bring them secularism, they are going to tell me to go to hell." Instead, according to one report, most of these women looked for inspiration on how to fight for equality to a place that might seem surprising. They looked to Iran as a country in which they saw women making significant gains within an Islamic framework—in part through an Islamically oriented feminist movement that is challenging injustices and reinterpreting the religious tradition.

The situation in Iran is itself the subject of heated debate within feminist circles, especially among Iranian feminists in the West (e.g., Mir-Hosseini 1999; Moghissi 1999; Najmabadi 1998, 2000). It is not clear whether and in what ways women have made gains and whether the great increases in literacy, decreases in birthrates, presence of women in the professions and government, and a feminist flourishing in cultural fields like writing and filmmaking are because of or despite the establishment of a socalled Islamic Republic. The concept of an Islamic feminism itself is also controversial. Is it an oxymoron or does it refer to a viable movement forged by brave women who want a third way?

One of the things we have to be most careful about in thinking about Third World feminisms, and feminism in different parts of the Muslim world, is how not to fall into polarizations that place feminism on the side of the West. I have written about the dilemmas faced by Arab feminists when Western feminists initiate campaigns that make them vulnerable to local denunciations by conservatives of various sorts, whether Islamist or nationalist, of being traitors (Abu-Lughod 2001). As some like Afsaneh Najmabadi are now arguing, not only is it wrong to see history simplistically in terms of a putative opposition between Islam and the West (as is happening in the United States now and has happened in parallel in the Muslim world), but it is also strategically dangerous to accept this cultural opposition between Islam and the West, between fundamentalism and feminism, because those many people within Muslim countries who are trying to find alternatives to present injustices, those who might want to refuse the divide and take from different histories and cultures, who do not accept that being feminist means being Western, will be under pressure to choose, just as we are: Are you with us or against us?

My point is to remind us to be aware of differences, respectful of other paths toward social change that might give women better lives. Can there be a liberation that is Islamic? And, beyond this, is liberation even a goal for which all women or people strive? Are emancipation, equality, and rights part of a universal language we must use? To quote Saba Mahmood, writing about the women in Egypt who are seeking to become pious Muslims, "The desire for freedom and liberation is a historically situated desire whose motivational force cannot be assumed a priori, but needs to be reconsidered in light of other desires, aspirations, and capacities that inhere in a culturally and historically located subject" (2001:223). In other words, might other desires be more meaningful for different groups of people? Living in close families? Living in a godly way? Living without war? I have done fieldwork in Egypt over more than 20 years and I cannot think of a single woman I know, from the poorest rural to the most educated cosmopolitan, who has ever expressed envy of U.S. women, women they tend to perceive as bereft of community, vulnerable to sexual violence and social anomie, driven by individual success rather than morality, or strangely disrespectful of God.

Mahmood (2001) has pointed out a disturbing thing that happens when one argues for a respect for other traditions. She notes that there seems to be a difference in the political demands made on those who work on or are trying to understand Muslims and Islamists and those who work on secular-humanist projects. She, who studies the piety movement in Egypt, is consistently pressed to denounce all the harm done by Islamic movements around the world—otherwise she is accused of being an apologist. But there never seems to be a parallel demand for those who study secular humanism and its projects, despite the terrible violences that have been associated with it over the last couple of centuries, from world wars to colonialism, from genocides to slavery. We need to have as little dogmatic faith in secular humanism as in Islamism, and as open a mind to the complex possibilities of human projects undertaken in one tradition as the other.

BEYOND THE RHETORIC OF SALVATION

Let us return, finally, to my title, "Do Muslim Women Need Saving?" The discussion of culture, veiling, and how one can navigate the shoals of cultural difference should put Laura Bush's self-congratulation about the rejoicing of Afghan women liberated by American troops in a different light. It is deeply problematic to construct the Afghan woman as someone in need of saving. When you save someone, you imply that you are saving her from something. You are also saving her

to something. What violences are entailed in this transformation, and what presumptions are being made about the superiority of that to which you are saving her? Projects of saving other women depend on and reinforce a sense of superiority by Westerners, a form of arrogance that deserves to be challenged. All one needs to do to appreciate the patronizing quality of the rhetoric of saving women is to imagine using it today in the United States about disadvantaged groups such as African American women or working-class women. We now understand them as suffering from structural violence, We have become politicized about race and class, but not culture.

As anthropologists, feminists, or concerned citizens, we should be wary of taking on the mantles of those 19th-century Christian missionary women who devoted their lives to saving their Muslim sisters. One of my favorite documents fiom that period is a collection called *Our Moslem Sisters,* the proceedings of a conference of women missionaries held in Cairo in 1906 (Van Sommer and Zwemmer 1907). The subtitle of the book is *A Cry of Need from the Lands of Darkness Interpreted by Those Who Heard It.* Speaking of the ignorance, seclusion, polygamy, and veiling that blighted women's lives across the Muslim world, the missionary women spoke of their responsibility to make these women's voices heard. As the introduction states, "They will never cry for themselves, for they are down under the yoke of centuries of oppression" (Van Sommer and Zwemer 1907:15). "This book," it begins, "with its sad, reiterated story of wrong and oppression is an indictment and an appeal. It is an appeal to Christian womanhood to right these wrongs and enlighten this darkness by sacrifice and service" (Van Sommer and Zwemer 1907:5).

One can hear uncanny echoes of their virtuous goals today, even though the language is secular, the appeals not to Jesus but to human rights or the liberal West. The continuing currency of such imagery and sentiments can be seen in their deployment for perfectly good humanitarian causes. In February 2002, I received an invitation to a reception honoring an international medical humanitarian network called Médecins du Monde/ Doctors of the World (MdM). Under the sponsorship of the French Ambassador to the United States, the Head of the delegation of the European Commission to the United Nations, and a member of the European Parliament, the cocktail reception was to feature an exhibition of photographs under the cliched title "Afghan Women: Behind the Veil."

The invitation was remarkable not just for the colorful photograph of women in flowing burqas walking across the barren mountains of Afghanistan but also for the text, a portion of which I quote:

> For 20 years MdM has been ceaselessly struggling to help those who are most vulnerable. But increasingly, thick veils cover the victims of the war. When the Taliban came to power in 1996, Afghan Women became faceless. To unveil one's face while receiving medical care was to achieve a sort of intimacy, find a brief space for secret freedom and recover a little of one's dignity. In a country where women had no access to basic medical care because they did not have the right to appear in public, where women had no right to practice medicine, MdM's program stood as a stubborn reminder of human rights.... Please join us in helping to lift the veil.

Although I cannot take up here the fantasies of intimacy associated with unveiling, fantasies reminiscent of the French colonial obsessions so brilliantly unmasked by Alloula in *The Colonial Harem* (1986), I can ask why humanitarian projects and human rights discourse in the 21st century need rely on such constructions of Muslim women.

Could we not leave veils and vocations of saving others behind and instead train our sights on ways to make the world a more just place? The reason respect for difference should not be confused with cultural relativism is that it does not preclude asking how we, living in this privileged and powerful part of the world, might examine our own responsibilities for the situations in which others

in distant places have found themselves. We do not stand outside the world, looking out over this sea of poor benighted people, living under the shadow—or veil—of oppressive cultures; we are part of that world. Islamic movements themselves have arisen in a world shaped by the intense engagements of Western powers in Middle Eastern lives.

A more productive approach, it seems to me, is to ask how we might contribute to making the world a more just place. A world not organized around strategic military and economic demands; a place where certain kinds of forces and values that we may still consider important could have an appeal and where there is the peace necessary for discussions, debates, and transformations to occur within communities. We need to ask ourselves what kinds of world conditions we could contribute to making such that popular desires will not be over determined by an overwhelming sense of helplessness in the face of forms of global injustice. Where we seek to be active in the affairs of distant places, can we do so in the spirit of support for those within those communities whose goals are to make women's (and men's) lives better (as Walley has argued in relation to practices of genital cutting in Africa, [1997])? Can we use a more egalitarian language of alliances, coalitions, and solidarity, instead of salvation?

Even RAWA, the now celebrated Revolutionary Association of the Women of Afghanistan, which was so instrumental in bringing to U.S. women's attention the excesses of the Taliban, has opposed the U.S. bombing from the beginning. They do not see in it Afghan women's salvation but increased hardship and loss. They have long called for disarmament and for peacekeeping forces. Spokespersons point out the dangers of confusing governments with people, the Taliban with innocent Afghans who will be most harmed. They consistently remind audiences to take a close look at the ways policies are being organized around oil interests, the arms industry, and the international drug trade. They are not obsessed with the veil, even though they are the most radical feminists working for a secular democratic Afghanistan.

Unfortunately, only their messages about the excesses of the Taliban have been heard, even though their criticisms of those in power in Afghanistan have included previous regimes. A first step in hearing their wider message is to break with the language of alien cultures, whether to understand or eliminate them. Missionary work and colonial feminism belong in the past. Our task is to critically explore what we might do to help create a world in which those poor Afghan women, for whom "the hearts of those in the civilized world break, can have safety and decent lives.

NOTES

Acknowledgments. I want to thank Page Jackson, Fran Mascia-Lees, Tim Mitchell, Rosalind Morris, Anupama Rao, and members of the audience at the symposium "Responding to War," sponsored by Columbia University's Institute for Research on Women and Gender (where I presented an earlier version), for helpful comments, references, clippings, and encouragement.

REFERENCES

Abu-Lughod, Lila. 1986. *Veiled Sentiments: Honor and Poetry in a Bedouin Society.* Berkeley: University of California Press.

_____. 1995. Movie Stars and Islamic Moralism in Egypt. *Social Text* 42:53–67.

_____. 1998. *Remaking Women: Feminism and Modernity in the Middle East.* Princeton: Princeton University Press.

_____. 2001. Orientalism and Middle East Feminist Studies. *Feminist Studies* 27(1):101–113.

Ahmed, Leila. 1992. *Women and Gender in Islam.* New Haven, CT: Yale University Press.

Alloula, Malek. 1986. *The Colonial Harem.* Minneapolis: University of Minnesota Press.

Brenner, Suzanne. 1996. Reconstructing Self and Society: Javanese Muslim Women and "the Veil." *American Ethnologist* 23(4):673–697.

El Guindi, Fadwa. 1999. *Veil: Modesty, Privacy and Resistance.* Oxford: Berg.

Fremson, Ruth. 2001. Allure Must Be Covered. Individuality Peeks Through. *New York Times,* November 4:14.

Global Exchange. 2002. Courage and Tenacity: A Women's Delegation to Afghanistan. Electronic document, http://www.globalexchange.org/tours/auto/2002-03-05_CourageandTenacityAWomens-Dele. html. Accessed February 11.

Goldenberg, Suzanne. 2002. The Woman Who Stood Up to the Taliban. *The Guardian,* January 24. Electronic document, http://222guardian.co.uk/afghanistan/story/0,1284,63840.

Hirschkind, Charles, and Saba Mahmood. 2002. Feminism, the Taliban, and the Politics of Counter-Insurgency. *Anthropological Quarterly,* 75(2): 107–122.

Lazreg, Marnia. 1994. *The Eloquence of Silence: Algerian Women in Question.* New York: Routledge.

MacLeod, Arlene. 1991. *Accommodating Protest.* New York: Columbia University Press.

Mahmood, Saba. 2001. Feminist Theory, Embodiment, and the Docile Agent: Some Reflections on the Egyptian Islamic Revival. *Cultural Anthropology* 16(2):202–235.

Mir-Hosseini, Ziba. 1999. *Islam and Gender: The Religious Debate in Contemporary Iran.* Princeton: Princeton University Press.

Moghissi, Haideh. 1999. *Feminism and Islamic Fundamentalism,* London: Zed Books.

Najmabadi, Afsaneh. 1998. Feminism in an Islamic Republic. In *Islam, Gender and Social Change.* Yvonne Haddad and John Esposito, eds. pp. 59–84. New York: Oxford University Press.

_____. 2000. (Un)Veiling Feminism. *Social Text* 64:29–15.

Ong, Aihwa. 1988. Colonialism and Modernity: Feminist Re-Presentations of Women in Non-Western Societies. *Inscriptions* 3–4:79–93.

_____. 1990. State Versus Islam; Malay Families, Women's Bodies, and the Body Politic in Malaysia. *American Ethnologist* 17(2):258–276.

Papanek, Hanna. 1982. Purdah in Pakistan: Seclusion and Modern Occupations for Women. In *Separate Worlds*. Hanna Papanek and Gail Minault, eds. pp. 190–216. Columbus, MO: South Asia Books.

Safire, William. 2001. "On Language." *New York Times Magazine*, October 28: 22.

Spivak, Gayatri Chakravorty. 1988. Can the Subaltern Speak? In *Marxism and the Interpretation of Culture*, Cary Nelson and Lawrence

Grossberg, eds. pp. 271–313. Urbana: University of Illinois Press.

Strathern, Marilyn. 1987. An Awkward Relationship: The Case of Feminism and Anthropology. *Signs* 12:276–292.

U.S. Government. 1907. *Our Moslem Sisters: A Cry of Need from Lands of Darkness Interpreted by Those Who Heard It*. New York: Fleming H. Re veil Co.

_____. 2002. Electronic document, http://www.whitehouse.gov/news/releases/2001/11/20011117. Accessed January 10.

Walley, Christine. 1997. Searching for "Voices": Feminism, Anthropology, and the Global Debate over Female Genital Operations. *Cultural Anthropology* 12(3):405–438.

DISCUSSION QUESTIONS

1. Is there evidence from the Islamic world to suggest that there could be a form of Islamic feminism that could look appreciably different from feminism in the Western world?

2. Briefly describe how this same argument of "repressed Muslim women yearning to be free" was used by British colonialists in Southeast Asia and Egypt and French colonialists in Algeria to justify their colonial ambitions.

3. How can you explain the fact that most Afghan women—after the fall of the Taliban government—did not stop wearing their burqas?

11

Gypsy Identity, Names, and Social Security Numbers

ANNE SUTHERLAND

Professor Emerita, University of California–Riverside

Although the United States has frequently been referred to as a "melting pot," some would suggest that a more appropriate metaphor would be a "salad bowl," in which a number of ethnic groups retain a good deal of their cultural distinctiveness. Sometimes these distinct cultural practices come into conflict with the large body of civil and criminal statutes that make up our legal system. To illustrate, nineteenth-century Mormons, who valued the practice of having more than one wife at a time, came into conflict with the statutes of the state of Utah requiring monogamous marriage. More recently, we have seen that in the immediate aftermath of the 9/11 attacks in 2001, an Islamic woman in Florida was denied a driver's license because she refused to have her photo taken without a veil. Here was a situation where the state felt that it needed a full-face photo to verify her identity, whereas she claimed that it would violate her freedom of religion.

In this reading, applied anthropologist Anne Sutherland discusses a legal case of a Gypsy man in St. Paul, Minnesota, who was arrested for using someone else's Social Security number when purchasing an automobile. Sutherland, serving as an expert witness, testified that the defendant, as a member of the Gypsy culture, had no intention of defrauding anyone by using the Social Security number of a relative rather than his own. According to Sutherland's testimony, Gypsies in the United States routinely use false identification because, as members of a vitsa, or extended family group, a person's identity is, in actuality, corporate in nature, in much the same way that property is owned or controlled by the larger kinship and not the individual. As in many cases when laws of the state conflict with practices and beliefs of racial, ethnic, or religious minorities, it is the state laws that prevail.

It is often the case that a law made for one set of purposes has another, unintended impact on a particular group. A recent law making the use of a false social security number a federal felony is intended to help prosecution of major drug crime syndicates, but it has a special impact on Gypsies in the United States. Gypsies, traditionally a nomadic people, frequently borrow each others' "American" names and social security numbers, viewing them as a kind of corporate property of their kin group or *vitsa*. They also often lack birth certificates and must obtain midwife or baptismal certificates to use for

SOURCE: Reproduced by permission of the American Anthropological Association from POLAR: Political and Legal Anthropology Review, Volume 17, Issue 2, pages 75–84, November 1994. Not for sale or further reproduction.

identification purposes when they try to obtain credit, enter school, or apply for welfare.

In this article, I shall examine the case of a 19-year-old Gypsy man who was convicted under the new social security law and served 6 months in jail. Arguments for the defense in the case followed three lines of reasoning: 1) that this law unfairly singled out Gypsies for punishment; 2) that there was no intent to commit a crime; and 3) that in using the social security numbers of relatives, Gypsies were following a time-honored tradition to remain anonymous and separate from non-Gypsy society.

FACTS OF THE CASE

In the fall of 1991 in St. Paul, Minnesota, a 19-year-old Gypsy man was convicted of the crime of using his 5-year-old nephew's social security number to obtain credit to purchase a car. When the purchase was questioned by the car dealership, he returned the car and was arrested on a felony charge of using a false social security number. After he was arrested, police searched the apartment where he was staying. They found lists of names, addresses and social security numbers, leading them to suspect an organized crime ring.

In *The United States of America v. S. N,*[1] it was "alleged that the defendant, S.N., while in the process of obtaining a new Ford Mustang from a car dealership, used a social security number that was not his own with intent to deceive." Under the statute 42 U.S.C. 408 (g) (2), a person who, with intent to deceive, falsely represents his or her number to obtain something of value or for any other purpose, is a felon.

In Mr. S.N.'s case there is no specific allegation that he intended to deprive another person permanently of property because the focus of the charging statute is false representation of numbers. The underlying purpose which motivates a person to falsely represent his or her number may be an essentially innocent purpose, but the statute, at least as it has been interpreted, does not appear to impose a burden of proof as to wrongful purpose.

The statute punishes the means (false number) which a person may employ to achieve any number of ends and it punishes those means as a felony. The lawyer for the defense argued that the statute's failure to address the nature of the purpose to which false credentials are used is a serious flaw in the law and may punish those who would use the number for petty misconduct as felons. He also argued that there is a potential for discriminatory impact on Gypsies who use false credentials to conceal themselves from mainstream society. A Gypsy household may obtain a telephone by providing a false social security number and even if they pay the telephone bill without fail for years, they are felons under this law. S.N. not only made the payments for his car, but he returned it when the number was questioned. He is still a felon under this law.

The defense lawyer argued that the law is objectionable for two reasons. First, the law's disproportionate impact on the Gypsies is objectionable under the equal protection guarantees in the Fifth Amendment of the U.S. Constitution. He argued that the law denies Gypsies equal protection of the law by irrationally and disproportionately punishing at the felony level certain traditional Gypsy actions which cause no positive injury to anyone. As evidence he used material from my book, *Gypsies: The Hidden Americans,*[2] for testimony that Gypsies routinely use false social security numbers to acquire credit but do pay their bills and are available for repossession in case of default of payment. They get phone service, buy houses and cars and other household items on credit and have a record of payment that is probably better than the general population (*United States* v. *Sonny Nicholas,* 1991). They do this primarily to remain unknown by mainstream society rather than to cause loss or injury to any person.

1. *United States v. Sonny Nicholas,* U.S. District Court, State of Minnesota, CR 4-91-137 (1991). The following quotes are from a memorandum in support of a motion to declare 42 U.S.C. 408 (g) (2) unconstitutional, prepared by defense attorney Philip Leavenworth.

2. Sutherland, 1986.

Second, as the defense lawyer pointed out, there is a Supreme Court decision that requires the government to prove felonious intent when it seeks to punish a person for wrongful acquisition of another's property.[3] S.N. maintained that he used a false social security number because of a Gypsy tradition to remain anonymous and because his own number had been used by other Gypsies. The government argued that there was a "ring" of Gypsies in the area where S.N. was living. At S.N.'s residence a number of false credentials and social security numbers were found which had been used to obtain cars illegally. Some of these cars are still missing. In other words, there was evidence that false identity had been used recently in the area to steal. In this case, however, S.N. had not stolen anything and was not being accused of stealing, but only of using a false social security number.

Because of the evidence of a ring of car thieves in the area, the prosecution hoped to use the threat of prosecution against S.N., the only Gypsy they had been able to arrest, to plea bargain for information regarding the other people involved in the alleged ring. These other people had disappeared immediately as soon as S.N. was arrested.

One of the problems in the case was that both the prosecution and even the defense had difficulty obtaining complete and accurate information on S.N. For example, they had difficulty determining his "real" name, a moot point for the Gypsies since they have a practice of using many "American" names although they only have one "Gypsy" name (*nav romano*). The Gypsy name of *o Spiro le Stevanosko* (or Spiro the son of Stevan) uses the noun declension characteristic of the Sanskrit-rooted Rom language and is not immediately translatable into English since it does not employ a surname. Spiro's identity can be pinned down by finding out what *vitsa* (a cognatic descent group) he belongs to so that he will not be confused with any other Spiro le Stevanoskos. The Spiro of our example is a *Kashtare* which is part of a larger "nation" of Gypsies or *natsia* called *Kalderasha*

(coppersmith). For his "American" names he may take any of a number used by his relatives such as Spiro Costello, John Costello, John Marks, John Miller, Spiro John or Spiro Miller. His nickname is Rattlesnake Pete.

THE ANTHROPOLOGIST AS CULTURAL BROKER

S.N.'s defense attorney contacted me after finding that he was less confused about S.N. after reading my book about Gypsies. He sought my help in determining whether S.N. was a Gypsy, what his name was, and any other cultural information (such as the use of social security numbers by Gypsies) that would help him with his case.

Consequently, one cold autumn day I drove to the federal holding prison, one and a half hours from the city, and met S.N. He was a thin young man, perpetually fearful of pollution from contact with non-Gypsies and suffering from the effects of several months of what for him was solitary confinement since he had not seen any of his people since being incarcerated. The telephone was his only link with people to whom he could relate, people from his own culture who spoke his language. His main contact was with a non-Gypsy woman who lived with one of his relatives. She was his link with the world he had known and the only "American" household he had been in before prison. Since my primary task was to determine if he was a Gypsy, first 1 talked to him about his relatives in Los Angeles and his *vitsa* (Yowane) and tried to establish what section of the *vitsa* I personally knew. This exchange of information about *vitsa* and Gypsies of mutual acquaintance is a normal one between Gypsies. The purpose was to establish a link between us.

Then I asked him about why he was in Minnesota. He talked about a seasonal expedition he and his brothers and cousins make to Minnesota

3. See *Morrissette v. United States* 342 U.S. 246 (1952) in which the Supreme Court provided an examination of the issue of intent in criminal law. The court ruled that in the absence *of* an express element of felonious intent, intent will become an element to be proved (273). There must be some loss or injury to justify a felony conviction.

to buy and sell cars and fix fenders before winter sets in. He claimed not to know where his brothers and cousins had gone or how he got into his present predicament.

For S.N., the most immediately effective action I could take was to see that he got the food he needed to stay "clean" in jail. When I met him he had lost fifteen pounds and was suffering demonstrable distress and nervousness. He was upset at being cut off from his culture and people for the first time in his life. In addition, he was distressed at being incarcerated and fearful for his safety. More importantly, he was worried he would become defiled or *marime*. A major concern of his was that if he ate food prepared by non-Gypsies who did not follow rules of cleanliness considered essential in the Gypsy culture, he would become *marime*, a condition of ritual impurity that would result in his being shunned by his relatives and other Gypsies. To protect himself, he avoided eating prison food in the hopes that when he was released from prison he would be able to return to his family without a period of physical exile, also called *marime* (or "rejected" as the Gypsies translate it into English). I arranged for his lawyer to provide him with money to buy food from the concession because it is packaged and untouched by non-Gypsies and therefore considered clean by Gypsy standards. He bought milk in cartons, candy bars and soft drinks and other packaged foods that, though they may lack in nutrition, at least were not defiling and kept him from starvation.

A further complicating factor for S.N. was that he spoke English as a second language. He had only a rudimentary ability to read, thus straining his grasp of his defense. And his only contact with relatives was by telephone since neither he nor they could write with any ease. Even though his limited English made it difficult for him to follow his own trial, the court did not provide a translator.

THE TRIAL

The trial was held in Federal Court and centered around the constitutionality of a law that unfairly targets a particular ethnic group and the question of intent to commit a crime. My testimony was intended to establish that Gypsies may use false identification for a number of cultural reasons which may have no connection to any intent to commit a crime. For a traditionally nomadic group with pariah status in the wider society and a pattern of secretiveness and autonomy, concealing identity is a long-established pattern.

This pattern is widespread in all Gypsy groups in Eastern Europe, Western Europe, Russia, Latin America and the United States. It is a mechanism they have developed over centuries to protect themselves from a wider society that has persecuted them or driven them away. The recent case of the German government paying large sums to Romania to take back Gypsy refugees is only the latest in an historically established tradition of discrimination against Gypsies. The persecution of Gypsies in the Holocaust, in medieval Europe and in the early part of the 20th century in the United States has been well documented.[4] Current events in Eastern Europe have shown a resurgence of extreme prejudice against Gypsies. Interviews in recent New York Times articles have pointed to a hatred of Gypsies so deep that there is talk of extermination.[5] Because

4. See Donald Kenrick and Grattan Puxon, *The Destiny of Europe's Gypsies,* London: Heinemann Press, 1972; and Ian Hancock, *The Pariah Syndrome: An Account of Gypsy Slavery and Persecution,* Ann Arbor: Karoma Publishing, 1987. Because of the attempted extermination of Gypsies during the Holocaust, they are now represented at the United States Holocaust Memorial in Washington, D.C.

5. See *New York Times,* November 17, 1993 and November 28, 1993 for recent accounts of extreme prejudice against Gypsies. One Catholic parish priest in Slovakia is reported to have said, "I'm no racist, but some Gypsies you would have to shoot." (*New York Times,* November 28, 1993). For a recent book on the plight of Eastern European Gypsies who are returning to a nomadic life after decades of travel restrictions under Communist governments, see David Crowe and John Kolsti, *The Gypsies of Eastern Europe,* New York: M.E. Sharpe, Inc., 1991.

of the history of violence against them, Gypsies have developed elaborate mechanisms of secrecy and have hidden their identity in order to survive.[6]

The purpose of my testimony was to establish that S.N. *was* a Gypsy and that Gypsies often use false identification without intent to defraud. They do so because as members of a *vitsa,* or cognatic descent group, identification is corporate in nature. Members of the group have corporate access to property owned by other members of the group. That property includes forms of identification.

An additional problem in the S.N. case was the question of identification from photographs. Here we encountered the age-old problem that members of one culture and race have trouble identifying individuals from another culture and race. In simple terms, to many non-Gypsies, all Gypsies look alike. Part of the case involved clearing up erroneous identification of S.N. in photos provided by the prosecution.

I was also asked to testify on my own personal experience with discrimination against Gypsies by the Minneapolis Police Department. One instance of discrimination I related to the court occurred during a talk I gave to some twenty police officers to help them understand Gypsy culture. When I had spoken about the strong sense of family and community among the Gypsies and how much they value their children, a police officer suggested that since the main problem law enforcement officers have is how to detain the Gypsies long enough to prosecute them, removing Gypsy children from their homes on any pretext would be an effective way to keep the parents in town.

Prejudice against Gypsies often goes unrecognized even by culturally and racially sensitive people. The assistant district attorney prosecuting S.N. offered me an article that he used to understand the Gypsies, entitled "Gypsies, the People and their Criminal Propensity,"[7] which quotes extensively from my work, including the fact that Gypsies have several names and that the same or similar non-Gypsy names are used over and over. The article concentrates on "criminal" behavior and never mentions the possibility that there are Gypsies who may not engage in criminal activities. In one section, quotations from my book on the ways Gypsies deal with the welfare bureaucracy were placed under the title, "Welfare Fraud," although by far most of the practices I described were legal. These concluding words in Part II are representative of the tone of the article:

> Officers should not be misled into thinking these people are not organized. They are indeed organized and operate under established rules of behavior, including those that govern marriage, living quarters, child rearing, the division of money and participation in criminal acts.

The implication of such statements is inflammatory. Gypsies have a culture, history, language and social structure, but that fact is distorted to imply that their social organization is partly for the purpose of facilitating criminal behavior. Their culture is viewed as a criminal culture. Gypsies have been fighting this view for hundreds of years. It is the view that they still combat in their relations with law enforcement and the criminal justice system. It is the view that was promoted by the prosecution in this case.

In spite of the best efforts of S.N.'s attorney and my testimony that use of a false social security number did not necessarily indicate intent to commit a crime, he was convicted of illegally using a social security number and served about 6 months in jail.

CONCLUSIONS: ANTHROPOLOGY AND CULTURAL DIFFERENCES IN THE COURTROOM

Anthropologists are often called in as expert witnesses in cases involving cultural difference. Most

6. The literature on this phenomenon is huge. See Anne Sutherland, *Gypsies, the Hidden Americans,* Prospect Heights, IL: Waveland Press, 1986; Judith Okely, *The Traveller-Gypsies,* Cambridge: Cambridge University Press, 1983; George Gmelch, *The Irish Tinkers,* Prospect Heights, IL: Waveland Press, 1985.

7. See Terry Getsay, *Kansas State FOP Journal,* Parts I, II, and III 1982:18-30.

Native American legal cases, such as the *Mashpee* case reported by James Clifford,[8] center around Indian status, treaties and land rights. In St. Paul, a number of Hmong legal cases highlighted the conflict between traditional marriage (specifically, the age at which children may marry) and the legal status of minors in American law. With the Gypsies, there is yet another set of cultural issues in their contact with American law.

First is the question of the cultural conflict between a historically nomadic group and the state bureaucracy of settled people. Identification—a serious legal issue in a bureaucratic society composed of people with fixed abodes and a written language—has virtually no meaning for the nomadic Gypsies who consider descent and extended family ties the defining factor for identification.

Second is the conflict between Gypsy religious rules regarding ritual pollution and prison regulations. The Gypsies avoid situations, such as a job or jail, that require them to be in prolonged contact with non-Gypsies. Jail presents special problems for the Gypsies can become *marime*, that is, defiled by unclean food and living conditions. The psychological trauma that results from isolation from

their community is compounded if they then emerge from jail and have to undergo a further isolation from relatives because of becoming *marime* in jail.

Finally there is a cultural clash between the Gypsy value of corporate kinship and the American value of individual rights. The rights and status of an individual Gypsy are directly linked to his or her membership in a *vitsa* which is determined by birth. Furthermore, the status of the all members of the *vitsa* is effected by the behavior of each individual *vitsa* member. Since they are so intricately linked, reciprocity between *vitsa* members is expected. Members of a *vitsa* and family share economic resources, stay in each other's homes, help each other in work and preparation of rituals and loan each other cars, information, identification and money. They also share the shame of immoral or incorrect behavior by one member. For the Gypsies, the American idea that each individual has only one name, one social security number, or one medical identification number is contrary to their experience and culture. Unfortunately for the Gypsies in America, it is now a felony to think this way.

REFERENCES

Clifford, James. 1988. *The Predicament of Culture.* Cambridge: Harvard University Press.

Crowe, David and John Kolsti. 1991. *The Gypsies of Eastern Europe.* New York: M.E. Sharpe, Inc.

Getsay, Terry. 1982. Gypsies, the People and their Criminal Propensity. *Kansas State FOP Journal.*

Gmelch, George. 1985. *The Irish Tinkers.* Prospect Heights, IL: Waveland Press.

Hancock, Ian. 1987. *The Pariah Syndrome: An Account of Gypsy Slavery and Persecution.* Ann Arbor, MI: Karoma Publ.

Kenrick, Donald and Grattan Puxon. 1972. *The Destiny of Europe's Gypsies.* London: Heinemann Press.

Okely, Judith. 1983. *The Traveller-Gypsies.* Cambridge: Cambridge University Press.

Sutherland, Anne. 1986. *Gypsies: The Hidden American.* Prospect Heights, IL: Waveland Press.

United States v. Sonny Nicholas. 1991. U.S. District Court, State of Minnesota, CR 4-91-137. Affidavit of Janet Tompkins.

8. See "Identity in Mashpee", in *The Predicament of Culture,* Cambridge: Harvard University Press, 1988:277–346.

DISCUSSION QUESTIONS

1. In the case of *United States v. S.N.*, what three lines of reasoning were used by the defense?

2. Why have Gypsies traditionally wanted to remain anonymous and separate from the non-Gypsy society?

3. What was the defendant's main concern about being kept in jail away from people of his own culture?

12

Customary Law Development in Papua New Guinea

RICHARD SCAGLION

Professor of Anthropology, University of Pittsburgh

When European governments acquired colonies during the nineteenth century, they invariably superimposed upon the local populations their own Western legal systems, which often conflicted with local customary law. When these colonies became self-governing in the 1960s and 1970s, they were faced with the challenges of developing legal systems based on their own customs and traditions rather than those of their former colonial masters. One such former colony, Papua New Guinea, which won its independence from Australia in 1975, was faced with the daunting task of identifying the legal principles of over 750 local cultural-linguistic groups and reconciling them into a new national legal system.

This selection by Richard Scaglion serves as a classic example of how an applied (legal) anthropologist conducted research on local customary law to determine how, and to what extent, these many customary legal systems might serve as the basis for a new nationwide legal system. As head of the Customary Law Project (created and funded by the Papua New Guinea Parliament), Scaglion collected hundreds of detailed case studies of customary law. This data bank served two useful functions for the emerging national legal system. First, the case studies were immediately useful to lawyers in searching out legal precedents for their ongoing court cases. Second, the data bank helped to identify and subsequently alleviate certain problems arising from a conflict between customary law and the emerging national legal system.

PROBLEM AND CLIENT

After a long colonial history dating back to the nineteenth century, Papua New Guinea became an independent nation on September 16, 1975. For most of its history, the territories of Papua and New Guinea, which together constitute the eastern half of the island of New Guinea in the southwest Pacific, had been administered by Australia. Upon independence, national leaders adopted the Australian legal system then in force as an interim national legal system. This Western legal system often clashed with the customary law of tribal peoples within the new nation. National leaders,

SOURCE: *Anthropological praxis: translating knowledge into action* by Wulff, Robert M.; Fiske, Shirley J. Reproduced with permission of WESTVIEW PRESS in the format Republish in a book via Copyright Clearance Center.

therefore, wanted to develop a self-reliant national legal system based on their own customs and traditions rather than on those of their former colonial administrators. In 1979, I was hired by the government of the new nation to help bring about this development.

National leaders knew that this task would be prolonged and difficult. Papua New Guinea is well known for its cultural diversity. In a country of some three and one-half million people, there are at least 750 mutually unintelligible languages and probably about a thousand different customary legal systems. Amid such diversity, would it be possible to uncover basic legal principles common to all these Melanesian societies? If so, could the essence of Melanesian customary law, which functions smoothly in small-scale tribal societies, be reconciled with the requirements of a modern nation-state?

To investigate these issues on a long-term basis, the Papua New Guinea government established a Law Reform Commission as a constitutional body whose special responsibility was to "investigate and report to the Parliament and to the National Executive on the development, and on the adaptation to the circumstances of the country, of the underlying law, and on the appropriateness of the rules and principles of the underlying law to the circumstances of the country." Recognizing that customary law was essential in creating an underlying law appropriate for Papua New Guinea, the Law Reform Commission designed a basic framework for a Customary Law Project to conduct research on the nature of customary law and the extent to which it could form the basis for a unique national legal system. The commission hoped that some of the problems with the interim legal system could be resolved through this project.

In 1978 I was a relatively new assistant professor of anthropology at the University of Pittsburgh. My PhD research had been a study of customary law and legal change among the Abelam people of Papua New Guinea (Scaglion 1976). During that study, I became aware of many of the problems faced by the Abelam in reconciling their customs and traditions with imposed Australian law

(Scaglion 1985). Knowing of my interest in legal development in Papua New Guinea, officers of the Law Reform Commission asked me to direct their Customary Law Project for a few years. I was expected to design an ongoing research strategy to gather data on customary law patterns of different tribes, analyze the data, identify problem areas, and help create draft legislation designed to alleviate such problems. Officials also hoped that I could train other people to carry on the work after I left. In other words, I would help design and initiate a broad policy direction for legal development in Papua New Guinea. I found this prospect very exciting.

While I was gathering data for my PhD research on the early period of contact with the government, an Abelam man told me that he had been jailed for burying his deceased mother inside her house. Under Abelam custom, corpses were laid to rest in the houses in which the people had slept and worked. The corpses were covered with only a thin layer of soil, and the houses were allowed to fall into disrepair and eventually collapse. Australian patrol officers wanted this practice discontinued because of potential health problems. My informant was not really aware of the "new" rules or the reasons behind them. Furthermore, to bury his mother's body outside the house, somewhere in the jungle, would be disrespectful. By following customary law, he broke national law.

I also remembered a discussion with another informant, an elderly man who had two wives to whom he had been married for many years. Although many Abelam marriages are monogamous, polygyny is also customary. I explained that in my own country, the United States, men were permitted only one wife under the law of most areas, and he asked me if this were also true of the Australians. I explained that it was and that technically it was also true in Papua New Guinea. I felt bad when he became upset that he might be arrested, but he declared that he could never choose between his wives, both of whom he loved.

I was greatly interested in the prospect of working on problems like these. I had heard of Bernard Narakobi, the chairman of the Law Reform

Commission, when I was first contacted about this work. Although he was an indigenous lawyer, he had a social science background, and I expected him to be receptive to an anthropological approach. After working out the scheduling, I began a fifteen-month period of initial research in May 1979 under a leave of absence from the University of Pittsburgh.

PROCESS AND PLAYERS

The Customary Law Project staff consisted of myself as project director, supervising a full-time Papua New Guinea project officer (Bospidik Pilokos). Secretarial and support functions were performed by Law Reform Commission staff. The project was designed to be fairly autonomous but was under the supervision of the secretary of the Law Reform Commission (Samson Kaipu for most of the project) and ultimately under the chairman of the Law Reform Commission, the secretary for justice, and the minister for justice. A separate fund was available for the project director on behalf of the project, subject to normal financial approval.

I spent the first several months of the project organizing activities. Initially, I conducted extensive bibliographical research and identified hundreds of sources on customary law in Papua New Guinea. The project officer catalogued these references according to subject matter and geographical area. My examination of these bibliographic sources underlined the need for more detailed and more complete research on the subject of customary law in specific Papua New Guinea societies.

Many if not most of the materials on customary law unearthed in the bibliographic search had been gathered by anthropologists working in relatively unacculturated parts of the country. What was missing was a corpus of case studies from rural areas that had had a longer history of contact with the government and had begun the process of reconciling customary law with a national legal system. Several alternative strategies for gathering this primary data were investigated, including the use of

magistrates, foreign anthropologists, lawyers, and student researchers. To make the best use of available resources I hired students from the University of Papua New Guinea to work in their home areas during their long year-end break. These students already spoke the local language and were familiar with their own cultures. I also felt that their descriptions of their own customary legal systems would be more likely to reflect indigenous categories than if, say, Australian lawyers had done the research.

To develop a comparative methodology for the project, I tested several research strategies in the Maprik area of the East Sepik Province, where the Abelam live, and did preliminary analyses of the data collected. To make these results available to interested parties, and also to publicize the project, I published articles in both the *Melanesian Law Journal* (Scaglion 1979) for the legal community and *Oceania* (Scaglion 1981a) for applied anthropologists working in legal development in the Pacific. Based on this preliminary research, we decided that the overall data-gathering strategy should focus on the collection of original conflict case studies from which principles of customary law in particular societies could be extracted. These cases could then be analyzed as a homogeneous data base to investigate possibilities for cross-cultural national unification of customary law.

After selecting twenty university students to form the first research group, I designed a format and minicourse for training and conducted training sessions at the university. Bospidik Pilokos, the project officer, later used the minicourse training format to train the next group of ten student researchers. We tried to supervise researchers in the field as much as possible; however, many of the research locations were relatively remote and required considerable time and travel to visit. Transportation proved to be a problem for our researchers as well.

Despite these problems, our student researchers gathered a corpus of roughly 600 extended case studies from all parts of the country. We then coded these cases according to such variables as type of case, geographical area, remedy agents used, and decision reached. I wrote a computer retrieval system to allow legal researchers to scan various types of cases and to receive a printout of summary information about the cases, together with individual case numbers. These case identification numbers can now be used to retrieve the original cases from Law Reform Commission files for further study. In this way, a basic corpus of customary law cases has been created for use in developing the underlying law of Papua New Guinea.

We also initiated a Law Reform Commission monograph series to disseminate certain materials from our research. The first volume in this series (Scaglion 1981b), which contains anthropologists' reactions to certain provisions of a draft bill on customary compensation, is described in the next section. The second volume (Scaglion 1983) contains background materials related to the case materials. The student researchers have described their field-sites, including the conditions under which the cases were gathered and, where possible, have provided broad summaries of principles of customary law in their areas.

Toward the end of my active involvement in the project, I experienced scheduling problems. I had initially agreed to a two-year commitment for this research, consisting of a fifteen-month initial period of residence in Papua New Guinea to get the project under way, followed by a return to Pittsburgh to resume my teaching duties and to analyze preliminary data, and ending with another nine-month period of residence in Papua New Guinea. Although officials of the Law Reform Commission had agreed to this schedule, it subsequently turned out to violate certain Public Service Commission guidelines. Consequently, we could only negotiate a brief three-month return. As a result, much of the editing of monographs had to be done from abroad, and the writing of some of the results of the study has been delayed or abandoned.

RESULTS AND EVALUATION

Despite problems in completing the research, I feel that the original goals set for the early stages of the project were accomplished. These goals were (1) to create a database on Papua New Guinea case law and legal principles that would be useful to legal practitioners and (2) to begin to identify and investigate problem areas and facilitate the preparation of draft legislation to alleviate such problems.

The first goal was accomplished through the preparation of the computer retrieval system allowing legal researchers and practitioners to identify cases relevant to their problems. The actual extended cases can be researched at the Law Reform Commission. During my residence in Papua New Guinea, I helped a number of lawyers find customary precedent cases related to issues they were arguing in court. For example, one attorney asked me to help her find cases that might provide information about customary divorce practices in a particular region. Several such cases were in our files, and she referred to these in preparing her case. Thus our data have helped facilitate legal development through the use of customary law cases in court.

These data have also been useful in exploring a variety of problems in legal development. For example, the Institute for National Affairs and the Institute for Applied Social and Economic Research (INA 1984:209–226) used our case study data in examining law and order problems in the country. A colleague and I used these case studies to address problems of domestic violence and women's access to justice in rural Papua New Guinea (Scaglion and Wittingham 1985).

The second goal, the identification and alleviation of legislative problems, is an ongoing, long-range effort involving the Law Reform Commission, the Justice Department, and the National Parliament. A three-part structure consisting of research, preparation of sample legislation circulated for comments, and preparation of final draft legislation is being followed. During my involvement with the Customary Law Project, a number of problem areas were identified.

For example, my Abelam friend who was concerned about the possible legal consequences of his bigamy turned out to have a lot of company. The project identified family law as an area in which customary principles were often at variance with statute law. A wide range of customary arrangements were technically illegal. A draft family law bill has been prepared that would formally recognize customary marriages as legal marriages and would provide for polygamous customary marriages under certain conditions. I am happy to say these conditions would include my old informant and his wives.

Customary compensation, particularly homicide compensation, was identified as another specific problem area. Compensation is a form of conflict management, common in Melanesian societies, in which an aggrieved party demands payment of some sort from another party. The payment demanded is generally thought to be proportionate to the severity of the act that precipitated the dispute and is usually proportionate to the magnitude of the dispute as well. Payment of compensation generally implies acceptance of responsibility by the donors and willingness to terminate the dispute by the recipients. However, such arrangements are not generally recognized under the law.

Unfortunately, it was not a simple matter of just recognizing the legality of these arrangements. A series of cases, recently popularized by the local news media, showed the complexity of the problem. These cases involved huge groups of people and "excessive" compensation demands. In one case a man from one province had been driving a vehicle that struck and killed a man from another province. Representatives from the clan of the victim were demanding hundreds of thousands of kina (Papua New Guinea currency roughly equivalent to the Australian dollar) from the whole of the driver's province.

Thus, homicide compensation appeared to be an area in which social development had outstripped the ability of small-scale customary legal systems to adapt. Inflationary compensation demands had created law and order problems and diverted cash away from development in large sections of the country. Although the basic customary law patterns were worth preserving, how could they be adapted to modern conditions?

A draft bill (Law Reform Commission 1980) was prepared that provided for the formal recognition of customary compensation as an institution for dispute resolution. Exchanges of wealth and services as a means for settling compensation claims for deaths, injuries, and property damage were recognized, and appropriate tribunals modeled on customary conflict management were provided. The bill tried to control and regulate claims and payments by specifying circumstances and amounts for such payments. I solicited further anthropological input by asking anthropologists to prepare papers commenting on the draft bill from the viewpoint of their fieldsites. Papers were collected, edited, and published as a monograph (Scaglion 1981b). Anthropologists identified particular geographical areas where such legislation might cause problems, as well as possible unintended consequences of stipulating maximum payments. For example, anthropologist Andrew Strathern (1981) showed that in Hagen society compensation was part of a system of escalating competitive exchange called *moka* and cautioned against setting limits on *moka* or confusing it with the compensation payments related to it. As a result, a revised version recommending regional legislation and revised conflict management strategies is currently being prepared.

Domestic violence was another problem area in parts of the country that had experienced culture change. Traditional cultures often practice patrilocal residence, in which newly married couples live near the husband's family. However, in customary situations, the bride is rarely far from her own family and can usually return home easily if her husband becomes physically abusive. However, as couples take up residence in new locations to pursue opportunities in the cash labor sector, wives cannot easily return home to avoid beatings. The same situation can occur when a man and a woman from widely different locations meet in a town, marry, and go to live with the husband's family. Again, the woman is far from her supportive kinship group. This broad problem, which formed the basis for the third monograph in our series (Toft 1985), was researched by my successor at the Law Reform Commission.

THE ANTHROPOLOGICAL
DIFFERENCE

The Customary Law Project applied anthropological knowledge by making use of theory, concepts, and methods derived from anthropology. These are described in the following section.

Theory

Legal anthropologists often distinguish between substantive law (rules for normative behavior, infractions of which are negatively sanctioned) and procedural law (mechanisms through which legal issues are handled). Lawyers tend to stress the substantive aspects of the legal process. They often see "law" as the relatively rigid application of rules to a given fact situation. Individuals are considered equal before the law, and rules should be impartially applied. In Papua New Guinea, however, customary law is a system of ensuring a just solution through compromise. Customary law recognizes the social uniqueness of each individual, and each case is considered separately without regard to precedents. Thus Melanesian customary law lends itself to analysis as procedural law, and anthropological theory is particularly useful in this endeavor.

Legal anthropologists tend to study interpersonal conflict in a processual sense. They are less concerned with substantive rules of law than with strategies for conflict management. Anthropological theories of law suggest that we study techniques rather than rules and that customary law is flexible and responsive to changing social situations—an important factor in contemporary Papua New Guinea. Consequently the customary law project did not undertake to prepare formal and detailed restatements of customary law as was done in certain African nations. It was thought that in Papua New Guinea, where social change continues to be rapid, this approach would freeze customary law at a single and quickly outdated point in time. Thus the anthropological theory of law was used in broad project planning.

Concepts

Anthropological concepts consonant with the anthropological view of law were used throughout the project. The research focused on extended cases as a basis for extrapolating legal principles—an attempt to elicit real rather than ideal principles. Because Melanesians do not seem to think in terms of abstract rules for behavior in the legal sense, when pressed to describe rules they often give ideal moral precepts or religious obligations that Westerners do not consider strictly legal rules. This problem was noticed by Malinowski in his classic studies of the Trobriand Islands area of Papua New Guinea in 1914–1918.

Pospisil (1971:2) has frequently pointed out that the English term "law" really consists of two separate concepts that are distinguished in many other languages. One, which in Latin is called *ius*, means law in terms of the underlying principles implied in legal precedents, whereas *lex* means an abstract rule usually made explicit in a legal code. Lawyers often are preoccupied with *leges* (plural of *lex*: the statutory rules); anthropologists tend to uncover the *ius* or the underlying law. The Customary Law Project made use of such anthropological distinctions. Also, a wide variety of concepts from legal anthropology were used to provide direction for the project. Examples of such concepts are "moot courts" (informal meetings for conflict management; see Gibbs 1963) or "negotiation," "mediation," "arbitration," and "adjudication" (procedures for settling conflicts which involve varying involvements of a third party; see Koch 1974:29–30).

Methods

In addition to standard anthropological techniques such as participant-observation, the Customary Law Project used the case method of legal anthropology as a primary data-gathering technique. First popularized by Llewellyn and Hoebel (1941) in their classic work *The Cheyenne Way*, and refined by Laura Nader and her students (see Nader and Todd 1978:5–8), the methodology involves gathering detailed data on all aspects of conflict cases according to a carefully prepared schedule. The four basic types of cases collected are observed cases, cases taken from recorded materials, memory cases, and hypothetical cases. Elicitation of all types of cases provides a corpus of information from which "law" (*ius*) can be abstracted. The Customary Law Project employed this methodology throughout the research phase of the project.

The anthropological difference, or the effects of anthropological theory, concepts, and methods on the Customary Law Project was quite significant and derived mainly from taking an anthropological attitude toward law. Virtually all the senior legal officers and research officers in the Justice Department in Papua New Guinea are lawyers rather than social scientists. Most are from Commonwealth countries. By providing an anthropological view of law, and one flavored with American jurisprudence, the Customary Law Project succeeded in presenting an alternative point of view for consideration.

Initially many of the officers of the Justice Department assumed that the project could or would provide them with discrete compendiums of principles of customary law in various societies. However, the results of the Customary Law Project indicate that a Papua New Guinean common law

must be developed as the underlying law of the nation and that this objective would best be accomplished by reference to customary case law. Throughout the duration of the project, informal conflict management forums such as the village court system, designed to provide an interface between customary and introduced law, have been supported. Village courts give traditional leaders magisterial powers and permit them to arbitrate according to custom. Decisions or consensus solutions then have the weight of law. Research from the project indicated that such forums were much more successful than had been previously assumed. The village courts secretariat has received increased support, perhaps in part because of the Customary Law Project. It is felt that a legal approach stressing legal norms would have impeded the development of Papua New Guinea case law.

Research into customary law is ongoing. The anthropologist set up a basic structure for data collection and organization that could continue into the future. Thus, although the implementation phase has been completed, the anthropological input continues. In this way, anthropological concepts, theory, and methods have helped to develop a structure for ongoing legal change in Papua New Guinea.

REFERENCES

Gibbs, James L., Jr. 1963. The Kpelle Moot: A Therapeutic Model for the Informal Settlement of Disputes. *Africa* 33: 1–11.

INA. 1984. *Law and Order in Papua New Guinea*, vol. 2 Port Moresby: Institute for National Affairs.

Koch, K. F. 1974. *War and Peace in Jalemo: The Management of Conflict in Highland New Guinea*. Cambridge: Harvard University Press.

Law Reform Commission of Papua New Guinea.1980. Customary Compensation. Report no. 11. Port Moresby: PNG Government Printers.

Llewellyn, K., and E. A. Hoebel. 1941. *The Cheyenne Way: Conflict and Case Law in Primitive Jurisprudence*. Norman, OK: University of Oklahoma Press.

Nader, L., and H. F. Todd, Jr. 1978. *The Disputing Process: Law in Ten Societies*. New York: Columbia University Press.

Pospisil, L. 1971. *Anthropology of Law: A Comparative Theory*. New York: Harper and Row.

Scaglion, R. 1976. Seasonal Patterns in Western Abelam Conflict Management Practices. Ph.D. thesis, University of Pittsburgh.

_____. 1979. Formal and Informal Operations of a Village Court in Maprik. *Melanesian Law Journal* 7: 116–1291.

_____. 1981a. Samukundi Abelam Conflict Management: Implications for Legal Planning in Papua New Guinea. *Oceania* 52: 28–38.

_____. 1985. Kiaps as Kings: Abelani Legal Change in Historical Perspective. In D. Gewertz and E. Schieffelin, eds., *History and Ethnohistory in Papua New Guinea*, Oceania Monograph no. 28, Sydney, pp. 77–99.

_____, and R.Whittingham. 1985. Female Plaintiffs and Sex-Related Disputes in Rural Papua New Guinea. In S. Toft, ed., *Domestic Violence in Papua New Guinea*. Law Reform Commission of Papua New Guinea, Monograph no. 3, Port Moresby, pp. 120–133.

Scaglion, R., ed. 1981b. Homicide Compensation in Papua New Guinea: Problem and Prospects. Law Reform Commission of Papua New Guinea, Monograph no. 1, Port Moresby.

_____, ed. 1983. Customary Law in Papua New Guinea: A Melanesian View. Law Reform Commission of Papua New Guinea, Monograph no. 1, Port Moresby.

Strathern, A. 1981. Compensation: Should There be a New Law? In R. Scaglion, ed., *Homicide Compensation in Papua New Guinea: Problems and Prospects*. Law Reform Commission of Papua New Guinea, Monograph no. 3, Port Moresby, pp. 5–24.

Toft, S., ed. 1985. Domestic Violence in Papua New Guinea. Law Reform Commission of Papua New Guinea, Monograph no. 3, Port Moresby.

DISCUSSION QUESTIONS

1. Why was the government of Papua New Guinea faced with the particularly difficult challenge of developing a national legal system?

2. What was the purpose of the Customary Law Project?

3. How would you describe the anthropological contribution that Scaglion made to the Customary Law Project?

13

The Adaptive Value of Religious Ritual

RICHARD SOSIS

Professor of Anthropology, University of Connecticut

Although most cultural anthropologists can agree that every known society has some form of religion or supernatural belief system, there is less consensus on why this cultural universal exists. It is impossible to prove beyond a reasonable doubt that any supernatural powers (such as deities, witches, angels, or devils) actually exist or don't exist. Moreover, supernatural powers don't always operate as effectively as the faithful think they should. Nevertheless, the very existence of strong beliefs in supernatural beings and forces performs quite subtle or latent (not always understood) functions for both the individual and the society as a whole. For the individual, religion and systems of supernatural belief play a cognitive function (enabling humans to explain the unexplainable phenomena in their lives) and an emotional function (helping individuals to cope with the anxieties that often accompany illness, accidents, death, and other misfortunes).

The social functions of religion include (1) social control (religions tend to maintain social order by encouraging socially acceptable behavior, with the threat of supernatural sanctions); (2) conflict resolution (disenfranchised and powerless people in stratified societies oftentimes use religion as a means of diffusing their hostility toward the society as a whole); and (3) building group solidarity (powerful social bonds and allegiances are often created by people who share the experiences of supernatural beliefs, practices, and rituals).

Approaching religious/supernatural practices from the perspective of behavioral ecology, Richard Sosis goes beyond merely recognizing that religion contributes to group solidarity, to suggest that the primary adaptive benefit of religion is its capacity to reinforce group solidarity and cooperation. Even though much religious ritual and behavior appears to be maladaptive, Sosis, by studying ecology and animal communication, presents an interesting counter thesis—that is, that religious behavior tends to be highly adaptive.

I was 15 years old the first time I went to Jerusalem's Old City and visited the 2,000-year-old remains of the Second Temple, known as the Western Wall. It may have foreshadowed my future life as an anthropologist, but on my first glimpse of the ancient stones I was more taken by the people standing at the foot of the structure than by the wall itself. Women stood in the open sun, facing the Wall in solemn worship, wearing long-sleeved shirts, head coverings and heavy skirts that scraped the ground. Men in their thick beards, long black coats and fur hats also seemed oblivious to the

SOURCE: Richard Sosis, The Adaptive Value of Religious Ritual. AMERICAN SCIENTIST, Vol. 92, March/April 2004, pp. 166–172. Reprinted with permission of the publisher.

summer heat as they swayed fervently and sang praises to God. I turned to a friend, "Why would anyone in their right mind dress for a New England winter only to spend the afternoon praying in the desert heat?" At the time I thought there was no rational explanation and decided that my fellow religious brethren might well be mad.

Of course, "strange" behavior is not unique to ultraorthodox Jews. Many religious acts appear peculiar to the outsider. Pious adherents the world over physically differentiate themselves from others: Moonies shave their heads, Jain monks of India wear contraptions on their heads and feet to avoid killing insects, and clergy almost everywhere dress in outfits that distinguish them from the rest of society. Many peoples also engage in some form of surgical alteration. Australian aborigines perform a ritual operation on adolescent boys in which a bone or a stone is inserted into the penis through an incision in the urethra. Jews and Muslims submit their sons to circumcision, and in some Muslim societies daughters are also subject to circumcision or other forms of genital mutilation. Groups as diverse as the Nuer of Sudan and the Iatmul of New Guinea force their adolescents to undergo ritual scarification. Initiation ceremonies, otherwise known as rites of passage, are often brutal. Among Native Americans, Apache boys were forced to bathe in icy water, Luiseño initiates were required to lie motionless while being bitten by hordes of ants, and Tukuna girls had their hair plucked out.

How can we begin to understand such behavior? If human beings are rational creatures, then why do we spend so much time, energy and resources on acts that can be so painful or, at the very least, uncomfortable? Archaeologists tell us that our species has engaged in ritual behavior for at least 100,000 years, and every known culture practices some form of religion. It even survives covertly in those cultures where governments have attempted to eliminate spiritual practices. And, despite the unparalleled triumph of scientific rationalism in the 20th century, religion continued to flourish. In the United States a steady 40 percent of the population attended church regularly throughout the century. A belief in God (about

96 percent), the afterlife (about 72 percent), heaven (about 72 percent) and hell (about 58 percent) remained substantial and remarkably constant. Why do religious beliefs, practices and institutions continue to be an essential component of human social life?

Such questions have intrigued me for years. Initially my training in anthropology did not provide an answer. Indeed, my studies only increased my bewilderment. I received my training in a subfield known as human behavioral ecology, which studies the adaptive design of behavior with attention to its ecological setting. Behavioral ecologists assume that natural selection has shaped the human nervous system to respond successfully to varying ecological circumstances. All organisms must balance trade-offs: Time spent doing one thing prevents them from pursuing other activities that can enhance their survival or reproductive success. Animals that maximize the rate at which they acquire resources, such as food and mates, can maximize the number of descendants, which is exactly what the game of natural selection is all about.

Behavioral ecologists assume that natural selection has designed our decision-making mechanisms to optimize the rate at which human beings accrue resources under diverse ecological conditions—a basic prediction of *optimal foraging theory*. Optimality models offer predictions of the "perfectly adapted" behavioral response, given a set of environmental constraints. Of course, a perfect fit with the environment is almost never achieved because organisms rarely have perfect information and because environments are always changing. Nevertheless, this assumption has provided a powerful framework to analyze a variety of decisions, and most research (largely conducted among foraging populations) has shown that our species broadly conforms to these expectations.

If our species is designed to optimize the rate at which we extract energy from the environment, why would we engage in religious behavior that seems so counterproductive? Indeed, some religious practices, such as ritual sacrifices, are a conspicuous display of wasted resources. Anthropologists can explain why foragers regularly share their food with others in the group, but why would anyone share their food with a dead ancestor by burning it to ashes on an altar? A common response to this question is that people believe in the efficacy of the rituals and the tenets of the faith that give meaning to the ceremonies. But this response merely begs the question. We must really ask why natural selection has favored a psychology that believes in the supernatural and engages in the costly manifestations of those beliefs.

RITUAL SACRIFICE

Behavioral ecologists have only recently begun to consider the curiosities of religious activities, so at first I had to search other disciplines to understand these practices. The scholarly literature suggested that I wasn't the only one who believed that intense religious behavior was a sign of madness. Some of the greatest minds of the past two centuries, such as Marx and Freud, supported my thesis. And the early anthropological theorists also held that spiritual beliefs were indicative of a primitive and simple mind. In the 19th century, Edward B. Tylor, often noted as one of the founding fathers of anthropology, maintained that religion arose out of a misunderstanding among "primitives" that dreams are real. He argued that dreams of deceased ancestors might have led the primitives to believe that spirits can survive death.

Eventually the discipline of anthropology matured and its practitioners moved beyond the equation that "primitive equals irrational." Instead, they began to seek functional explanations of religion. Most prominent among these early 20th-century theorists was the Polish-born anthropologist Bronislaw Malinowski. He argued that religion arose out of "the real tragedies of human life, out of the conflict between human plans and realities." Although religion may serve to allay our fears of death, and provide comfort from our incessant search for answers, Malinowski's thesis did not seem to explain the origin of rituals. Standing in the midday desert sun in several layers of black

clothing seems more like a recipe for increasing anxiety than treating it. The classical anthropologists didn't have the right answers to my questions. I needed to look elsewhere.

Fortunately, a new generation of anthropologists has begun to provide some explanations. It turns out that the strangeness of religious practices and their inherent costs are actually the critical features that contribute to the success of religion as a universal cultural strategy and why natural selection has favored such behavior in the human lineage. To understand this unexpected benefit we need to recognize the adaptive problem that ritual behavior solves. William Irons, a behavioral ecologist at Northwestern University, has suggested that the universal dilemma is the promotion of cooperation within a community. Irons argues that the primary adaptive benefit of religion is its ability to facilitate cooperation within a group—while hunting, sharing food, defending against attacks and waging war—all critical activities in our evolutionary history. But, as Irons points out, although everyone is better off if everybody cooperates, this ideal is often very difficult to coordinate and achieve. The problem is that an individual is even better off if everyone else does the cooperating, while he or she sits at home enjoying an afternoon siesta. Cooperation requires social mechanisms that prevent individuals from free riding on the efforts of others. Irons argues that religion is such a mechanism.

The key is that religious rituals are a form of communication, which anthropologists have long maintained. They borrowed this insight from ethologists who observed that many species engage in patterned behavior, which they referred to as "ritual." Ethologists recognized that ritualistic behaviors served as a form of communication between members of the same species, and often between members of different species. For example, the males of many avian species engage in courtship rituals— such as bowing, head wagging, wing waving and hopping (among many other gestures)— to signal their amorous intents before a prospective mate. And, of course, the vibration of a rattlesnake's tail is a powerful threat display to other species that enter its personal space.

Irons's insight is that religious activities signal commitment to other members of the group. By engaging in the ritual, the member effectively says, "I identify with the group and I believe in what the group stands for." Through its ability to signal commitment, religious behavior can overcome the problem of free riders and promote cooperation within the group. It does so because trust lies at the heart of the problem: A member must assure everyone that he or she will participate in acquiring food or in defending the group. Of course, hunters and warriors may make promises— "you have my word, I'll show up tomorrow"— but unless the trust is already established such statements are not believable.

It turns out that there is a robust way to secure trust. Israeli biologist Amotz Zahavi observes that it is often in the best interest of an animal to send a dishonest signal—perhaps to fake its size, speed, strength, health or beauty. The only signal that can be believed is one that is too costly to fake, which he referred to as a "handicap." Zahavi argues that natural selection has favored the evolution of handicaps. For example, when a springbok antelope spots a predator it often *stots*—it jumps up and down. This extraordinary behavior puzzled biologists for years: Why would an antelope waste precious energy that could be used to escape the predator? And why would the animal make itself more visible to something that wants to eat it? The reason is that the springbok is displaying its quality to the predator— its ability to escape, effectively saying, "Don't bother chasing me. Look how strong my legs are, you won't be able to catch me." The only reason a predator believes the springbok is because the signal is too costly to fake. An antelope that is not quick enough to escape cannot imitate the signal because it is not strong enough to repeatedly jump to a certain height. Thus, a display can provide honest information if the signals are so costly to perform that lower quality organisms cannot benefit by imitating the signal.

In much the same way, religious behavior is also a costly signal. By donning several layers of clothing and standing out in the midday sun, ultra-orthodox Jewish men are signaling to others: "Hey!

Look, I'm a *haredi* Jew. If you are also a member of this group you can trust me because why else would I be dressed like this? No one would do this *unless* they believed in the teachings of ultraorthodox Judaism and were fully committed to its ideals and goals." The quality that these men are signaling is their level of commitment to a specific religious group.

Adherence to a set of religious beliefs entails a host of ritual obligations and expected behaviors. Although there may be physical or psychological benefits associated with some ritual practices, the significant time, energy and financial costs involved serve as effective deterrents for anyone who does not believe in the teachings of a particular religion. There is no incentive for nonbelievers to join or remain in a religious group, because the costs of maintaining membership—such as praying three times a day, eating only kosher food, donating a certain part of your income to charity and so on— are simply too high.

Those who engage in the suite of ritual requirements imposed by a religious group can be trusted to believe sincerely in the doctrines of their respective religious communities. As a result of increased levels of trust and commitment among group members, religious groups minimize costly monitoring mechanisms that are otherwise necessary to overcome free-rider problems that typically plague communal pursuits. Hence, the adaptive benefit of ritual behavior is its ability to promote and maintain cooperation, a challenge that our ancestors presumably faced throughout our evolutionary history.

BENEFITS OF MEMBERSHIP

One prediction of the "costly signaling theory of ritual" is that groups that impose the greatest demands on their members will elicit the highest levels of devotion and commitment. Only committed members will be willing to dress and behave in ways that differ from the rest of society. Groups that maintain more-committed members can also offer more because it's easier for them to attain their collective goals than groups whose members are less committed. This may explain a paradox in the religious marketplace: Churches that require the most of their adherents are experiencing rapid rates of growth. For example, the Church of Jesus Christ of Latter-day Saints (Mormons), Seventh-day Adventists and Jehovah's Witnesses, who respectively abstain from caffeine, meat and blood transfusions (among other things), have been growing at exceptional rates. In contrast, liberal Protestant denominations such as the Episcopalians, Methodists and Presbyterians have been steadily losing members.

Economist Lawrence Iannaccone, of George Mason University, has also noted that the most demanding groups also have the greatest number of committed members. He found that the more distinct a religious group was—how much the group's lifestyle differed from mainstream America—the higher its attendance rates at services. Sociologists Roger Finke and Rodney Stark, of Penn State and the University of Washington, respectively, have argued that when the Second Vatican Council in 1962 repealed many of the Catholic Church's prohibitions and reduced the level of strictness in the church, it initiated a decline in church attendance among American Catholics and reduced the enrollments in seminaries. Indeed, in the late 1950s almost 75 percent of American Catholics were attending Mass weekly, but since the Vatican's actions there has been a steady decline to the current rate of about 45 percent.

The costly signaling theory of ritual also predicts that greater commitment will translate into greater cooperation within groups. My colleague Eric Bressler, a graduate student at McMaster University, and I addressed this question by looking at data from the records of 19th-century communes. All communes face an inherent problem of promoting and sustaining cooperation because individuals can free-ride on the efforts of others. Because cooperation is key to a commune's survival, we employed commune longevity as a measure of cooperation. Compared to their secular counterparts, the religious communes did indeed demand more of their members, including such behavior as celibacy, the surrender of all material

possessions and vegetarianism. Communes that demanded more of their members survived longer, overcoming the fundamental challenges of cooperation. By placing greater demands on their members, they were presumably able to elicit greater belief in and commitment toward the community's common ideology and goals.

I also wanted to evaluate the costly signaling theory of ritual within modern communal societies. The kibbutzim I had visited in Israel as a teenager provided an ideal opportunity to examine these hypotheses. For most of their 100-year history, these communal societies have lived by the dictum, "From each according to his abilities, to each according to his needs." The majority of the more than 270 kibbutzim are secular (and often ideologically antireligious); fewer than 20 are religiously oriented. Because of a massive economic failure— a collective debt of more than $4 billion—the kibbutzim are now moving in the direction of increased privatization and reduced communality. When news of the extraordinary debt surfaced in the late 1980s, it went largely unnoticed that the religious kibbutzim were financially stable. In the words of the Religious Kibbutz Movement Federation, "the economic position of the religious kibbutzim is sound, and they remain uninvolved in the economic crisis."

The success of the religious kibbutzim is especially remarkable given that many of their rituals inhibit economic productivity. For example, Jewish law does not permit Jews to milk cows on the Sabbath. Although rabbinic rulings now permit milking by kibbutz members to prevent the cows from suffering, in the early years none of this milk was used commercially. There are also significant constraints imposed by Jewish law on agricultural productivity. Fruits are not allowed to be eaten for the first few years of the tree's life, agricultural fields must lie fallow every seven years, and the corners of fields can never be harvested—they must be left for society's poor. Although these constraints appear detrimental to productivity, the costly signaling theory of ritual suggests that they may actually be the key to the economic success of the religious kibbutzim.

I decided to study this issue with economist Bradley Ruffle of Israel's Ben Gurion University. We developed a game to determine whether there were differences in how the members of secular and religious kibbutzim cooperated with each other. The game involves two members from the same kibbutz who remain anonymous to each other. Each member is told there are 100 shekels in an envelope to which both members have access. Each participant decides how many shekels to withdraw and keep. If the sum of both requests exceeds 100 shekels, both members receive no money and the game is over. However, if the requests are less than or equal to 100 shekels, the money remaining in the envelope is increased by 50 percent and divided evenly among the participants. Each member also keeps the original amount he or she requested. The game is an example of a common-pool resource dilemma in which publicly accessible goods are no longer available once they are consumed. Since the goods are available to more than one person, the maintenance of the resources requires individual self-restraint; in other words, cooperation.

After we controlled for a number of variables, including the age and size of the kibbutz and the amount of privatization, we found not only that religious kibbutzniks were more cooperative with each other than secular kibbutzniks, but that male religious kibbutz members were significantly more cooperative than female members. Among secular kibbutzniks we found no sex differences at all. This result is understandable if we appreciate the types of rituals and demands imposed on religious Jews. Although there are a variety of requirements that are imposed equally on males and females, such as keeping kosher and refraining from work on the Sabbath, male rituals are largely performed in public, whereas female rituals are generally pursued privately. Indeed, none of the three major requirements imposed exclusively on women—attending a ritual bath, separating a portion of dough when baking bread and lighting Shabbat and holiday candles—are publicly performed. They are not rituals that signal commitment to a wider group; instead they appear to signal commitment to the family.

Men, however, engage in highly visible rituals, most notably public prayer, which they are expected to perform three times a day. Among male religious kibbutz members, synagogue attendance is positively correlated with cooperative behavior. There is no similar correlation among females. This is not surprising given that women are not required to attend services, and so their presence does not signal commitment to the group. Here the costly signaling theory of ritual provides a unique explanation of these findings. We expect that further work will provide even more insight into the ability of ritual to promote trust, commitment and cooperation.

We know that many other species engage in ritual behaviors that appear to enhance trust and cooperation. For example, anthropologists John Watanabe of Dartmouth University and Barbara Smuts at the University of Michigan have shown that greetings between male olive baboons serve to signal trust and commitment between former rivals. So why are human rituals often cloaked in mystery and the supernatural? Cognitive anthropologists Scott Atran of the University of Michigan and Pascal Boyer at Washington University in St. Louis have pointed out that the counterintuitive nature of supernatural concepts are more easily remembered than mundane ideas, which facilitates their cultural transmission. Belief in supernatural agents such as gods, spirits and ghosts also appears to be critical to religion's ability to promote long-term cooperation. In our study of 19th-century communes, Eric Bressler and I found that the strong positive relationship between the number of costly requirements imposed on members and commune longevity only held for religious communes, not secular ones. We were surprised by this result because secular groups such as militaries and fraternities appear to successfully employ costly rituals to maintain cooperation. Cultural ecologist Roy Rappaport explained, however, that although religious and secular rituals can both promote cooperation, religious rituals ironically generate greater belief and commitment because they sanctify unfalsifiable statements that are beyond the possibility of examination. Since statements containing supernatural elements, such as "Jesus is the son of God," cannot be proved or disproved, believers verify them "emotionally." In contrast to religious propositions, the kibbutz's guiding dictum, taken from Karl Marx, is not beyond question; it can be evaluated by living according to its directives by distributing labor and resources appropriately. Indeed, as the economic situation on the kibbutzim has worsened, this fundamental proposition of kibbutz life has been challenged and is now disregarded by many who are pushing their communities to accept differential pay scales. The ability of religious rituals to evoke emotional experiences that can be associated with enduring supernatural concepts and symbols differentiates them from both animal and secular rituals and lies at the heart of their efficiency in promoting and maintaining long-term group cooperation and commitment.

Evolutionary research on religious behavior is in its infancy, and many questions remain to be addressed. The costly signaling theory of ritual appears to provide some answers, and, of course, it has given me a better understanding of the questions I asked as a teenager. The real value of the costly signaling theory of ritual will be determined by its ability to explain religious phenomena across societies. Most of us, including ultraorthodox Jews, are not living in communes. Nevertheless, contemporary religious congregations that demand more of their members are able to achieve a close-knit social community—an impressive accomplishment in today's individualistic world.

Religion has probably always served to enhance the union of its practitioners; unfortunately, there is also a dark side to this unity. If the intragroup solidarity that religion promotes is one of its significant adaptive benefits, then from its beginning religion has probably always played a role in intergroup conflicts. In other words, one of the benefits for individuals of intragroup solidarity is the ability of unified groups to defend and compete against other groups. This seems to be as true today as it ever was, and is nowhere more apparent than the region I visited as a 15-year-old boy—which is where I am as I write these words. As I conduct my fieldwork in the center of this war zone, I hope that by appreciating the depth of the religious need in the human psyche, and by understanding this powerful adaptation, we can learn how to promote cooperation rather than conflict.

REFERENCES

Atran, S. 2002. *In Gods We Trust*. New York: Oxford University Press.

Iannaccone, L. 1992. Sacrifice and stigma: Reducing free-riding in cults, communes, and other collectives. *Journal of Political Economy* 100:271–291.

Iannaccone, L. 1994. Why strict churches are strong. *American Journal of Sociology* 99:1180–1211.

Irons, W. 2001. Religion as a hard-to-fake sign of commitment. In "Evolution and the Capacity for Commitment," ed. R. Nesse, pp. 292–309. New York: Russell Sage Foundation.

Rappaport, R. 1999. *Ritual and Religion in the Making of Humanity*. Cambridge: Cambridge University Press.

Sosis, R. 2003. Why aren't we all Hutterites? Costly signaling theory and religious behavior. *Human Nature* 14:91–127.

Sosis, R., and C. Alcorta. 2003. Signaling, solidarity, and the sacred: The evolution of religious behavior. *Evolutionary Anthropology* 12:264–274.

Sosis, R., and E. Bressler. 2003. Cooperation and commune longevity: A test of the costly signaling theory of religion. *Cross-Cultural Research* 37:211–239.

Sosis, R., and B. Ruffle. 2003. Religious ritual and cooperation: Testing for a relationship on Israeli religious and secular kibbutzim. *Current Anthropology* 44:713–722.

Zahavi, A., and A. Zahavi. 1997. *The Handicap Principle*. New York: Oxford University Press.

DISCUSSION QUESTIONS

1. What does Sosis mean by his claim that some religious behavior is "too costly to fake?"

2. What does the "stotting behavior" of springboks have in common with bearded Jews in Jerusalem wearing heavy black coats and fur hats in the desert?

3. What does Sosis mean by the "dark side of religion?"

14

Baseball Magic

GEORGE GMELCH

Professor of Anthropology, University of San Francisco

Americans like to think of themselves as being grounded in scientific rationality rather than in superstition, magic, and ritual. Yet, when we turn the anthropological lens upon our own culture, we can see that magic and appeals to supernatural forces are employed in the United States for the same reasons they are in the Trobriand Islands or among the Azande in the Southern Sudan—that is, to ensure success in human activities. Middle-class North Americans—and others—are likely to call on supernatural forces in those situations that are unpredictable and over which they have relatively little control.

In this article, George Gmelch, an anthropologist and former professional baseball player, reminds us that US baseball players are more likely to use magic (ritual, taboos, and fetishes) on those aspects of the game that are unpredictable (hitting and pitching) than on fielding, over which players have greater control. Even if this baseball magic doesn't always produce the desired outcome, it continues to be used because it functions to reduce anxiety and provide players with at least the illusion of control.

> *We find magic wherever the elements of chance and accident, and the emotional play between hope and fear[,] have a wide and extensive range. We do not find magic wherever the pursuit is certain, reliable, and well under the control of rational methods.*
>
> —*Bronislaw Malinowski*

Professional baseball is a nearly perfect arena in which to test Malinowski's hypothesis about magic. The great anthropologist was not, of course, talking about sleight of hand but of rituals, taboos and fetishes that men resort to when they want to ensure that things go their own way. Baseball is rife with this sort of magic, but, as we shall see, the players use it in some aspects of the game far more than in others.

Everyone knows that there are three essentials of baseball—hitting, pitching and fielding. The point is, however, that the first two, hitting and pitching, involve a high degree of chance. The pitcher is the player least able to control the outcome of his own efforts. His best pitch may be hit for a bloop single while his worst pitch may be hit directly to one of his fielders for an out. He may limit the opposition to a single hit and lose, or he

SOURCE: Reprinted by permission of Springer-SBM, B.V. "Superstition and Ritual in American Baseball" by George Gmelch in *Society*, 8(8): 39–41. Reprinted with permission of the author.

may give up a dozen hits and win. It is not uncommon for pitchers to perform well and lose, and vice versa; one has only to look at the frequency with which pitchers end a season with poor won-lost percentages but low earned run averages (number of runs given up per game). The opposite is equally true: some pitchers play poorly, giving up many runs, yet win many games. In brief, the pitcher, regardless of how well he performs, is dependent upon the proficiency of his teammates, the inefficiency of the opposition and the supernatural (luck).

But luck, as we all know, comes in two forms, and many fans assume that the pitcher's tough losses (close games in which he gave up very few runs) are eventually balanced out by his "lucky" wins. This is untrue, as a comparison of pitchers' lifetime earned run averages to their overall won-lost records shows. If the player could apply a law of averages to individual performance, there would be much less concern about chance and uncertainty in baseball. Unfortunately, he cannot and does not.

Hitting, too, is a chancy affair. Obviously, skill is required in hitting the ball hard and on a line. Once the ball is hit, however, chance plays a large role in determining where it will go, into a waiting glove or whistling past a falling stab.

With respect to fielding, the player has almost complete control over the outcome. The average fielding percentage or success rate of .975 compared to a .245 success rate for hitters (the average batting average), reflects the degree of certainty in fielding. Next to the pitcher or hitter, the fielder has little to worry about when he knows that better than 9.7 times in ten he will execute his task flawlessly. If Malinowski's hypothesis is correct, we should find magic associated with hitting and pitching, but none with fielding. Let us take the evidence by category—ritual, taboo and fetish.

RITUAL

After each pitch, ex-major leaguer Lou Skeins used to reach into his back pocket to touch a crucifix, straighten his cap and clutch his genitals. Detroit

Tiger infielder Tim Maring wore the same clothes and put them on exactly in the same order each day during a batting streak. Baseball rituals are almost infinitely various. After all, the ballplayer can ritualize any activity he considers necessary for a successful performance, from the type of cereal he eats in the morning to the streets he drives home on.

Usually, rituals grow out of exceptionally good performances. When the player does well he cannot really attribute his success to skill alone. He plays with the same amount of skill one night when he gets four hits as the next night when he goes hitless. Through magic, such as ritual, the player seeks greater control over his performance, actually control over the elements of chance. The player, knowing that his ability is fairly constant, attributes the inconsistencies in his performance to some form of behavior or a particular food that he ate. When a player gets four hits in a game, especially "cheap" hits, he often believes that there must have been something he did, in addition to his ability, that shifted luck to his side. If he can attribute his good fortune to the glass of iced tea he drank before the game or the new shirt he wore to the ballpark, then by repeating the same behavior the following day he can hope to achieve similar results. (One expression of this belief is the myth that eating certain foods will give the ball "eyes," that is, a ball that seeks the gaps between fielders.) In hopes of maintaining a batting streak, I once ate fried chicken every day at 4:00 P.M., kept my eyes closed during the national anthem and changed sweat shirts at the end of the fourth inning each night for seven consecutive nights until the streak ended.

Fred Caviglia, Kansas City minor league pitcher, explained why he eats certain foods before each game: "Everything you do is important to winning. I never forget what I eat the day of a game or what I wear. If I pitch well and win I'll do it all exactly the same the next day I pitch. You'd be crazy not to. You just can't ever tell what's going to make the difference between winning and losing."

Rituals associated with hitting vary considerably in complexity from one player to the next, but they have several components in common. One of the most popular is tagging a particular base when leaving and returning to the dugout each inning. Tagging second base on the way to the outfield is habitual with some players. One informant reported that during a successful month of the season he stepped on third base on his way to the dugout after the third, sixth and ninth innings of each game. Asked if he ever purposely failed to step on the bag he replied, "Never! I wouldn't dare, it would destroy my confidence to hit." It is not uncommon for a hitter who is playing poorly to try different combinations of tagging and not tagging particular bases in an attempt to find a successful combination. Other components of a hitter's ritual may include tapping the plate with his bat a precise number of times or taking a precise number of warm-up swings with the leaded bat.

One informant described a variation of this in which he gambled for a certain hit by tapping the plate a fixed number of times. He touched the plate once with his bat for each base desired: one tap for a single, two for a double and so on. He even built in odds that prevented him from asking for a home run each time. The odds of hitting a single with one tap were one in three, while the chances of hitting a home run with four taps were one in 12.

Clothing is often considered crucial to both hitters and pitchers. They may have several athletic supporters and a number of sweat shirts with ritual significance. Nearly all players wear the same uniform and undergarments each day when playing well, and some even wear the same street clothes. In 1954, the New York Giants, during a 16-game winning streak, wore the same clothes in each game and refused to let them be cleaned for fear that their good fortune might be washed away with the dirt. The route taken to and from the stadium can also have significance; some players drive the same streets to the ballpark during a hitting streak and try different routes during slumps.

Because pitchers only play once every four days, the rituals they practice are often more complex than the hitters', and most of it, such as tugging the cap between pitches, touching the rosin bag after each bad pitch or smoothing the dirt on the mound before each new batter, takes place on the field. Many baseball fans have observed this behavior never realizing that it may be as important to the pitcher as throwing the ball.

Dennis Grossini, former Detroit farmhand, practiced the following ritual on each pitching day for the first three months of a winning season. First, he arose from bed at exactly 10:00 A.M. and not a minute earlier or later. At 1:00 P.M. he went to the nearest restaurant for two glasses of iced tea and a tuna fish sandwich. Although the afternoon was free, he observed a number of taboos such as no movies, no reading and no candy. In the clubhouse he changed into the sweat shirt and jock he wore during his last winning game, and one hour before the game he chewed a wad of Beechnut chewing tobacco. During the game he touched his letters (the team name on his uniform) after each pitch and straightened his cap after each ball. Before the start of each inning he replaced the pitcher's rosin bag next to the spot where it was the inning before. And after every inning in which he gave up a run he went to the clubhouse to wash his hands. I asked him which part of the ritual was most important. He responded: "You can't really tell what's most important so it all becomes important. I'd be afraid to change anything. As long as I'm winning I do everything the same. Even when I can't wash my hands [this would occur when he must bat] it scares me going back to the mound.... I don't feel quite right."

One ritual, unlike those already mentioned, is practiced to improve the power of the baseball bat. It involves sanding the bat until all the varnish is removed, a process requiring several hours of labor, then rubbing rosin into the grain of the bat before finally heating it over a flame. This ritual treatment supposedly increases the distance the ball travels after being struck. Although some North Americans prepare their bats in this fashion it is more popular among Latin Americans. One informant admitted that he was not certain of the effectiveness of the treatment. But, he added, "There may not be a God, but I go to church just the same."

Despite the wide assortment of rituals associated with pitching and hitting, I never observed any ritual related to fielding. In all my 20 interviews only one player, a shortstop with acute fielding problems, reported any ritual even remotely connected to fielding.

TABOO

Mentioning that a no-hitter is in progress and crossing baseball bats are the two most widely observed taboos. It is believed that if the pitcher hears the words "no-hitter" his spell will be broken and the no-hitter lost. As for the crossing of bats, that is sure to bring bad luck; batters are therefore extremely careful not to drop their bats on top of another. Some players elaborate this taboo even further. On one occasion a teammate became quite upset when another player tossed a bat from the batting cage and it came to rest on top of his. Later he explained that the top bat would steal hits from the lower one. For him, then, bats contain a finite number of hits, a kind of baseball "image of limited good." Honus Wagner, a member of baseball's Hall of Fame, believed that each bat was good for only 100 hits and no more. Regardless of the quality of the bat he would discard it after its 100th hit.

Besides observing the traditional taboos just mentioned, players also observe certain personal prohibitions. Personal taboos grow out of exceptionally poor performances, which a player often attributes to some particular behavior or food. During my first season of professional baseball I once ate pancakes before a game in which I struck out four times. Several weeks later I had a repeat performance, again after eating pancakes. The result was a pancake taboo in which from that day on I never ate pancakes during the season. Another personal taboo, born out of similar circumstances, was against holding a baseball during the national anthem.

Taboos are also of many kinds. One athlete was careful never to step on the chalk foul lines or the chalk lines of the batter's box. Another would never put on his cap until the game started and would not wear it at all on the days he did not pitch. Another had a movie taboo in which he refused to watch a movie the day of a game.

Often certain uniform numbers become taboo. If a player has a poor spring training or a bad year, he may refuse to wear the same uniform number again. I would not wear double numbers, especially 44 and 22. On several occasions, teammates who were playing poorly requested a change of uniform during the middle of the season. Some players consider it so important that they will wear the wrong size uniform just to avoid a certain number or to obtain a good number.

Again, with respect to fielding, I never saw or heard of any taboos being observed, though of course there were some taboos, like the uniform numbers, that were concerned with overall performance and so included fielding.

FETISHES

These are standard equipment for many baseball players. They include a wide assortment of objects: horsehide covers of old baseballs, coins, bobby pins, protective cups, crucifixes and old bats. Ordinary objects are given this power in a fashion similar to the formation of taboos and rituals. The player during an exceptionally hot batting or pitching streak, especially one in which he has "gotten all the breaks," credits some unusual object, often a new possession, for his good fortune. For example, a player in a slump might find a coin or an odd stone just before he begins a hitting streak. Attributing the improvement in his performance to the new object, it becomes a fetish, embodied with supernatural power. While playing for Spokane, Dodger pitcher Alan Foster forgot his baseball shoes on a road trip and borrowed a pair from a teammate to pitch. That night he pitched a no-hitter and later, needless to say, bought the shoes from his teammate. They became his most prized possession.

Fetishes are taken so seriously by some players that their teammates will not touch them out of fear of offending the owner. I once saw a fight caused by the desecration of a fetish. Before the game, one player stole the fetish, a horsehide baseball cover, out of a teammate's back pocket. The prankster did not return the fetish until after the game, in which the owner of the fetish went hitless, breaking a batting streak. The owner, blaming his inability to hit on the loss of the fetish, lashed out at the thief when the latter tried to return it.

Rube Waddel, an old-time Philadelphia Athletic pitching great, had a hairpin fetish. However, the hairpin he possessed was only powerful as long as he won. Once he lost a game he would look for another hairpin, which had to be found on the street, and he would not pitch until he found another.

The use of fetishes follows the same pattern as ritual and taboo in that they are connected only with hitting or pitching. In nearly all cases the player expressed a specific purpose for carrying a fetish, but never did a player perceive his fetish as having any effect on his fielding.

I have said enough, I think, to show that many of the beliefs and practices of professional baseball players are magical. Any empirical connection between the ritual, taboo and fetishes and the desired event is quite absent. Indeed, in several instances the relationship between the cause and effect, such as eating tuna fish sandwiches to win a ball game, is even more remote than is characteristic of primitive magic. Note, however, that unlike many forms of primitive magic, baseball magic is usually performed to achieve one's own end and not to block someone else's. Hitters do not tap their bats on the plate to hex the pitcher but to improve their own performance.

Finally, it should be plain that nearly all the magical practices that I participated in, observed or elicited, support Malinowski's hypothesis that magic appears in situations of chance and uncertainty. The large amount of uncertainty in pitching and hitting best explains the elaborate magical practices used for these activities. Conversely, the high success rate in fielding, .975, involving much less uncertainty offers the best explanation for the absence of magic in this realm.

DISCUSSION QUESTIONS

1. How would you distinguish among a ritual, a taboo, and a fetish?

2. Of the three aspects of the game of baseball (fielding, hitting, and pitching), which are the most susceptible to baseball magic?

3. Can you think of how magic is used in other US sports?

15

Dharavi: Mumbai's Shadow City

MARK JACOBSON
National Geographic Society

Traditional anthologies in cultural anthropology, like this one, have been composed of selected readings written by anthropologists that have remained relevant over the years. With the increased interest of applied anthropology in recent decades, some anthropologists have made their findings available to policy makers seeking to address a wide variety of societal problems, including public health, education, adaptation to climate change, and economic development, among others. Yet many anthropologists have remained content to report their research findings in scholarly journals, emphasize the theoretical and methodological signif-icance of their work, and leave to others the translation of the practical implications for programs of social change.

Fortunately, anthropologists are not the only people able to understand the practical ramifications of their ethnographic findings. Often, novelists, philosophers, and journalists are keen observers of cultural realities and, as such, can show policy makers and agents of sociocultural change how to both avoid cultural gaffes as well as plan programs that would maximize the benefits for all stakeholders.

In this selection, journalist Mark Jacobson, who has spent considerable time conducting his own ethnographic study of the largest "slum" in Mumbai, India, tells a compelling story through the eyes of a well-meaning urban land developer and the local residents of the "slum" he would like to gentrify. Jacobson digs deeply into the different (and often com-peting) values and perspectives of the residents of impoverished urban neighborhoods and those who would want to reshape these urban spaces for the better. Surely, this piece of writing, which appeared in the National Geographic Magazine in May 2007, should be required reading for everyone involved in the politics of urban economic development.

All cities in India are loud, but nothing matches the 24/7 decibel level of Mumbai, the former Bombay, where the traffic never stops and the horns always honk. Noise, however, is not a prob-lem in Dharavi, the teeming slum of one million souls, where as many as 18,000 people crowd into a single acre (0.4 hectares). By nightfall, deep inside the maze of lanes too narrow even for the putt-putt of auto rickshaws, the slum is as still as a verdant glade. Once you get accustomed to sharing 300 square feet (28 square meters) of floor with 15 humans and an uncounted number of mice, a strange sense of relaxation sets in–ah, at last a moment to think straight.

SOURCE: From National Geographic Learning. National Geographic Learning Reader: Cultural Anthropology (with Bind-In eBook Printed Access Card), 1E. © 2013 South-Western, a part of Cengage Learning, Inc. Reproduced by permission. www.cengage.com/permissions.

Dharavi is routinely called "the largest slum in Asia," a dubious attribution sometimes conflated into "the largest slum in the world." This is not true. Mexico City's Neza-Chalco-Itza barrio has four times as many people. In Asia, Karachi's Orangi Township has surpassed Dharavi. Even in Mumbai, where about half of the city's swelling 12 million population lives in what is euphemistically referred to as "informal" housing, other slum pockets rival Dharavi in size and squalor.

Yet Dharavi remains unique among slums. A neighborhood smack in the heart of Mumbai, it retains the emotional and historical pull of a subcontinental Harlem—a square-mile (three square kilometers) center of all things, geographically, psychologically, spiritually. Its location has also made it hot real estate in Mumbai, a city that epitomizes India's hopes of becoming an economic rival to China. Indeed, on a planet where half of humanity will soon live in cities, the forces at work in Dharavi serve as a window not only on the future of India's burgeoning cities, but on urban space everywhere.

Ask any longtime resident-some families have been here for three or more generations–how Dharavi came to be, and they'll say, "We built it." This is not far off. Until the late 19th century, this area of Mumbai was mangrove swamp inhabited by Koli fishermen. When the swamp filled in (with coconut leaves, rotten fish, and human waste), the Kolis were deprived of their fishing grounds–they would soon shift to bootlegging liquor–but room became available for others. The Kumbhars came from Gujarat to establish a potters' colony. Tamils arrived from the south and opened tanneries. Thousands traveled from Uttar Pradesh to work in the booming textile industry. The result is the most diverse of slums, arguably the most diverse neighborhood in Mumbai, India's most diverse city.

Stay for a while on the three-foot-wide (one meter) lane of Rajendra Prasad Chawl, and you become acquainted with the rhythms of the place. The morning sound of devotional singing is followed by the rush of water. Until recently few people in Dharavi had water hookups. Residents such as Meera Singh, a wry woman who has lived on the lane for 35 years, used to walk a mile (two

kilometers) to get water for the day's cleaning and cooking. At the distant spigot she would have to pay the local "goons" to fill her buckets. This is how it works in the bureaucratic twilight zone of informal housing. Deprived of public services because of their illegal status, slum dwellers often find themselves at the mercy of the "land mafia." There are water goons, electricity goons. In this regard, the residents of Rajendra Prasad Chawl are fortunate. These days, by DIY hook or crook, nearly every household on the street has its own water tap. And today, like every day, residents open their hoses to wash down the lane as they stand in the doorways of their homes to brush their teeth.

This is how Dharavi wakes up. On 90 Feet Road, named for its alleged width (even if 60 Feet Road, the slum's other main drag, is considerably wider), the cab drivers coax their battered Fiats to life. In the potters' neighborhood, black smoke is already pouring from six-foot-square (one square meter) kilns. By the mucky industrial canal, the recyclers are in full swing. In Dharavi nothing is considered garbage. Ruined plastic toys are tossed into massive grinders, chopped into tiny pieces, melted down into multicolored pellets, ready to be refashioned into knockoff Barbie dolls. Here every cardboard box or 55-gallon (208 liters) oil drum has another life, and another one after that.

Mornings at Rajendra Prasad Chawl are equally hectic. With the eight furniture makers to whom she rents part of her apartment gone for the day, Meera Singh combs the hair of her grandchildren: Atul, 7, Kanchan, 10, and Jyoti, 12. Soon the apartment, home to 15, is empty, save for Meera and her twentysomething son, Amit, he of the dashing mustache and semi-hipster haircut. A couple of years ago, the Singh family, like everyone else in Dharavi, sat in front of the television to see local singer Abhijit Sawant win the first Indian Idol contest. But now Meera is watching her favorite TV personality, the orange-robed yoga master, Baba Ramdev, who demonstrates an antiaging technique: rubbing your fingernails against each other at a rapid pace.

"Why listen to this fool?" dismisses Amit.

"You know nothing," Meera shoots back. "His hair is black, and he is more than 80 years old."

"Eighty? He's no more than 40. Don't fall for these cheating tricks."

Meera shakes her head. She gave up trying to talk sense to Amit long ago. "His head is in the clouds," she says. She wishes he'd get a job as did his brother Manoj, who sews jeans in one of Dharavi's kaarkhanas, or sweatshops. But this is not for him, Amit says. A thinker, he sees his life in terms of "a big picture." Central to this conceit is the saga of how the Singhs came to Dharavi in the first place. Members of the Kshatriyas, regarded as second only to Brahmans in the caste system, Amit's great uncles were zamindars, or landlords, in the service of the British. Stripped of privilege after independence, the family moved from Uttar Pradesh to Mumbai, where Amit's father worked in the textile mills. The collapse of the mills in the 1970s landed the family in Dharavi.

It is this story of chance and fate ("A hundred years ago we would have been bosses," he says) that spurs Amit's outsize sense of self. He's always got a dozen things going. There's his soap powder pyramid scheme, his real estate and employment agency gambits. New is his exterminator firm, for which he has distributed hundreds of handbills ("No bedbug! No rat!"), claiming to be Dharavi's "most trusted" vermin remover, despite having yet to exterminate one cockroach.

Also on Amit's agenda is the Janhit Times, a tabloid he envisions as a hard-hitting advocate of grassroots democracy. The first edition featured a story about an allegedly corrupt Dharavi policeman. Amit's headline: "A Giant Bastard, a Dirty Corrupted Devil, and Uniformed Goon." Cooler heads, pointing out the policeman wielded a lethal lathi (bamboo nightstick), suggested a milder approach. Reluctantly Amit went with "A Fight for Justice."

Even though the paper has yet to print its first edition, Amit carries a handsome press pass, which he keeps with his stack of business cards. This leads his mother to remark, "That's you, many cards, but no businesses." Looking at her son, she says, "You are such a dreamer."

It is an assessment that Amit, who just decided to open a rental car agency in hopes of diversifying his portfolio in the mode of "a Richard Branson of Dharavi," does not dispute.

"Talk about doing something about Mumbai slums, and no one pays attention. Talk about Dharavi, and it is Mission Impossible, an international incident," says Mukesh Mehta as he enters the blond-paneled conference room of the Maharashtra State Administration Budding. For nine years, Mehta, a 56-year-old architect and urban designer, has honed his plan for "a sustainable, mainstreamed, slum-free Dharavi." At today's meeting, after many PowerPoint presentations, the plan is slated for approval by the state chief minister, Vilasrao Deshmukh.

Dharavi is to be divided into five sectors, each developed with the involvement of investors, mostly nonresident Indians. Initially, 57,000 Dharavi families will be resettled into high-rise housing close to their current residences. Each family is entitled to 225 square feet (21 square meters) of housing, with its own indoor plumbing. In return for erecting the "free" buildings, private firms will be given handsome incentives to build for-profit housing to be sold at (high) market rates.

"All that remains is the consent," Mehta tells Deshmukh, a sour-looking gentleman in a snow-white suit sitting with his advisers at the 40-foot (12 meters) conference table. Normally, it is required that 60 percent of Dharavi residents approve of the plan.

But Deshmukh announces that formal consent is not needed because Mehta's plan is a government-sponsored project. All he must do is give the residents a month to register complaints. "A 30-day window, not a day more," Deshmukh says with impatient finality.

Later, as his driver pilots his Honda Accord through traffic, Mehta is smiling. "This is a good day," he says. "A dream come true."

At first glance, Mehta, resident of an elegant apartment building on swank Napean Sea Road, a longtime member of the British Raj–era Bombay Gymkhana and Royal Bombay Yacht Club, does not appear to be a Dharavi dreamer.

"You could say I was born with a golden spoon in my mouth," he remarks at his West Bandra office overlooking the Arabian Sea. "My father came to Bombay from Gujarat without a penny and built a tremendous steel business. An astrologer told him his youngest son—me—would be the most successful one, so I was afforded everything." These perks included a top education, plus a sojourn in the U.S., where Mehta studied architecture at Pratt Institute in Brooklyn.

"For me, America has always been the inspiration," says Mehta, who made a fortune managing his father's steel business before deciding to develop real estate on Long Island's exclusive North Shore. "Great Gatsby country," he says, detailing how he built high-end houses and lived in Centre Island, a white community with "the richest of the rich"—such as Billy Joel, who recently listed his mansion for 37.5 million dollars.

"The slums were the furthest thing from my mind," Mehta says. This changed when he returned to Mumbai. He saw what everyone else did—that the city was filled with a few rich people, a vast number of poor people, and hardly anyone in the middle. This was most evident in the appalling housing situation. The city was split between the Manhattan-priced high-rises that dotted the south Mumbai skyline and those brownish areas on the map marked with the letters ZP for zopadpatti, aka slums.

Downtown business people railed that the slums were choking the life out of the city, robbing it of its rightful place in the 21st century. After all, India was no longer a post-colonial backwater famous only for the most wretched people of the Earth and the gurus who appealed to gullible Beatles. Now, when a computer broke in Des Moines, the help desk was in Bangalore. Economists were predicting exactly when the Indian GNP was likely to surpass that of the United States. If Mumbai was going to achieve its stated destiny of becoming a world-class metropolis, a rival to China's soaring Shanghai, how could that happen when every bit of open space was covered with these eyesores, these human dumps where no one paid taxes? For Mukesh Mehta, if India were to become the ideal

consumer society, it would have to develop a true middle class—and housing would be the engine. The slums would have to be reclaimed.

But which slums? There were so many of them. Then it jumped out, as clear as real estate's incontrovertible first axiom, location, location, location: Dharavi, right in the middle of the map. It was a quirk of geography and history, as any urban planner will tell you (the American inner city aside): Large masses of poor people are not supposed to be in the center of the city. They are supposed to be on the periphery, stacked up on the outskirts. Dharavi had once been on the northern fringe, but ever growing Mumbai had sprawled toward the famous slum, eventually surrounding it.

It didn't take a wizard to see the advantages of Dharavi's position. Served by two railway lines, it was ideally situated for middle-class commuters. Added to this was the advent of the Bandra-Kurla Complex, a global corporate enclave located directly across the remaining mangrove swamps, as dose to Dharavi as Wall Street is to Brooklyn Heights. Sterile and kempt, the BKC was the future, right on the doorstep of the zopadpatti.

"I approached it as a developer. In other words, as a mercenary," says Mehta, satellite images of Dharavi spread across his desk. "But something happened. I opened an office in Dharavi, started talking to people, seeing who they were, how hard they worked, and how you could be there for months and never once be asked for a handout."

It was then, Mehta says, "I had an epiphany. I asked myself if these people were any different from my father when he first came from Gujarat. They have the same dreams. That was when I decided to dedicate the rest of my life to fixing the slums. Because I realized: The people of Dharavi—they are my genuine heroes."

Back on Rajendra Prasad Chawl, news of the plan's approval was met with a decidedly mixed response. Meera Singh barely looked up from Baba Ramdev's lecture. She had heard often the stories about Dharavi's supposed transformation. Nothing much ever happened. Why should Mukesh Mehta's scheme be any different? Moreover, what reason would possess her to move into a 225-square-foot (21 square meters) apartment, even if it were free? She has nearly 400 square feet (40 square meters). "Informal housing" has been good to her. She receives 1,100 rupees a month from the furniture workers and another thousand from renting her basement. Why should she give this up for a seven-story apartment building where she'll be saddled with fees, including "lift" charges? She doesn't like to ride in elevators. They give her the creeps.

Amit Singh was more outspoken. Mehta's plan was nothing more than "a scam, a chunk of fool's gold." Amit was already drafting an editorial in the Janhit Times demanding a citizen's arrest of "the gangster Mehta."

In a place with one toilet for every few hundred people (the so-called politics of defecation is a perennial hot button in India), the prospect of having one's own bathroom would seem to be a powerful selling point for the plan. But even if a stir broke out last summer when gurus declared that the waters of Mahim Creek, the slum's reeking unofficial public toilet, had miraculously turned "sweet" (leading to much gastrointestinal trauma), many Dharavi locals were unmoved by the idea of a personal loo.

"What need do I have of my own toilet?" asks Nagamma Shilpiri, who came to Dharavi from Andhra Pradesh 20 years ago and now lives with her crippled father and 13 other relatives in two 150-square-foot (14 square meters) rooms. Certainly, Shilpiri is embarrassed by the lack of privacy when she squats in the early morning haze beside Mahim Creek. But the idea of a personal flush toilet offends her. To use all that water for so few people seems a stupid, even sinful, waste.

Everyone in Dharavi had their own opinion about how and why the plan was concocted to hurt them in particular. The most nuanced assessment came from Shaikh Mobin, a plastics recycler in his mid-30s. Mobin has lived his whole life in Dharavi, but he'd never call himself a slum dweller. His recycling business, started by his grandfather, passed to his father, and now to him ("the post-consumer economy, turning waste into wealth," he says), had made Mobin a relatively rich man.

He and his family live in a marble-floored flat at the 13-floor Diamond Apartments, "Dharavi's number one prestige address."

Mobin is a supporter of development in Dharavi. Change is necessary. Polluting industries like recycling have no business being in the center of a modern metropolis. Mobin was already making plans to move his factory several miles to the north. But this didn't mean he is happy with what is happening in the place of his birth.

Much of his critique is familiar. The government's failure to create housing for middle-income people was responsible for the existence of the slums, Mobin contends. Many people in Dharavi make enough money to live elsewhere, "a house like you see on TV." But since no such housing exists, they are doomed to the slum. Mobin doubts Mukesh Mehta's private developers will help. All over Dharavi are reminders of developmental disasters. Near Dharavi Cross Road, members of the L.P.T. Housing Society, their houses torn down in preparation for their promised apartments, have spent the past eight years living in a half-finished building without steady electricity or water, at the mercy of the goons and the malarial Mumbai heat.

But when it comes down to it, Mobin says, Dharavi's dilemma is at once much simpler and infinitely more complex: "This is our home." This is what people such as Chief Minister Deshmukh and Mukesh Mehta will never understand, Mobin says. "Mukesh Mehta says I am his hero, but what does he know of my life? He is engaged in shaikhchilli, which is dreaming, dreaming in the day. Does it occur to him that we do not wish to be part of his dream?"

Such sentiments cause Mukesh Mehta distress. "If someone calls me a dreamer, I plead guilty," he says, finishing his crème caramel at the Bombay Yacht Club. To be sure, Mehta has made some fanciful statements regarding Dharavi's future. His idea to install a golf driving range has met with widespread guffaws. "Golf? What is this golf?" asked Shilpiri's crippled father. The other day Mehta was fantasizing about constructing a 120,000-seat cricket stadium in the slum. Asked where fans would park, Mehta looked stricken.

"Parking! Oh, my God," he exclaimed. "I'm going to be up all night trying to figure that out."

But being a dreamer doesn't mean he is "unrealistic," Mehta says. He has been around the block of India's bruising bureaucracy. He has learned hard lessons along the way. One is that "sometimes the last thing people in power want is to get rid of slums." Much of what Mehta calls "slum perpetuation" has to do with the infamous "vote bank"—a political party, through a deep-rooted system of graft, lays claim to the vote of a particular neighborhood. As long as the slum keeps voting the right way, it's to the party's advantage to keep the community intact. A settlement can remain in the same place for years, shelters passing from makeshift plastic tarps to corrugated metal to concrete. But one day, as in the case of Dharavi, the slum might find itself suddenly in the "wrong" place. Once that happens, the bulldozer is always a potential final solution. A few years ago, the Maharashtra government, under the direction of Chief Minister Deshmukh, in a spasm of upgrading supposedly aimed at closing the "world-class" gap, demolished 60,000 hutments, some in place for decades. As many as 300,000 people were displaced.

This, Mehta says, is what his plan is devised to avoid. "No one wants to be that unhappy guy driving the bulldozer." Preferring "the talking cure," Mehta says if anyone, anywhere, doesn't think his plan is the best possible outcome for Dharavi, he will sit with them for as long as it takes, to convince them. A few days later, at Kumbharwada, he got his chance.

To many, the Kumbhar potters are the heart and soul of Dharavi. Their special status derives not only from their decades-long residence but also from the integrity of their work. While Dharavi is famous for making use of things everyone throws away, the Kumbhars create the new.

Savdas family members have been Dharavi potters for generations, but Tank Ranchhod Savdas once imagined another kind of life. "I had big dreams," he says. "I thought I would be a lawyer." But Tank's father died in 1986, and "as the oldest son I took up this business." Not that he has any regrets. "During busy times, I make hundreds of

pots a day, and I get pleasure from each one," he says.

Recently, however, the fortyish "Mr. Tank" has begun to fear for the future of Kumbhars in Dharavi. Increasing numbers of the community's young men have become merchant seamen, or computer specialists at the Bandra-Kurla Complex. Kumbharwada is full of teenage boys who have never used a potter's wheel, unthinkable only a few years ago.

And now there is this plan. Just talking about "a slum-free Dharavi" is enough to make Tank shake with anger. How dare anyone claim that Kumbharwada is "a slum" in need of rehabilitation! Kumbharwada is home to working people, men and women who have always made their own way. If Mukesh Mehta was so enamored of the U.S., couldn't he see Kumbharwada was a sterling example of the supposed American dream?

"Look at my house," Tank demands, showing off the 3,000-square-foot (280 square meters) home and workshop he built and now shares with his two brothers and their families. "Why should we move from here, to there?"

By "there," Tank means the Slum Rehabilitation Authority high-rise under construction behind Kumbharwada. Freshly painted, the building has a sprightly look, but soon lack of maintenance will turn it into a replica of every other SRA building: a decaying Stalinist-styled pile, covered with Rorschach-like mildew stains. Inside is a long, dank hallway with 18 apartments on either side, which Amit Singh calls "36 rooms of gloom."

"That is a slum," says Tank, "a vertical slum." Told that Mehta says he's willing to talk with anyone unhappy with the plan, Tank says, "Then bring him here. Tomorrow."

On his cell phone from Hyderabad, Mehta, "not risk averse," says "ten o'clock." But he is skeptical the meeting will accomplish much. He's spoken with the potters many times. Proposals allowing them to keep the majority of their space have been rejected, as was his idea to maximize the potters' profits by adding ornamental ceramics to their traditional vessels and religious objects. "I've offered them the moon and been repaid with crushing indifference," Mehta bemoans. Plus, he never knows which alleged leadership group represents whom. It's a frustrating situation that one afternoon causes the Americanized Mehta to shout, "Your trouble is you have too many chiefs and not enough Indians!"

Yet when ten o'clock rolls around, there he is, impeccably attired in a tan suit, cuff links gleaming in the sunlight, in the courtyard in front of Tank's house. Perhaps a hundred people have assembled, sitting on plastic chairs. Most are potters, but there are others, too, such as Amit Singh and several colleagues from the Janhit Times. After politely listening to Mehta's short form of the plan (he has brought his PowerPoint presentation, but sunlight prevents its deployment), the objections begin. It is outrageous that this was even being discussed, people say. "We have been making pots for 130 years," one man shouts. "This land is ours."

Mehta is sympathetic to the Kumbhar position. But there are a few "realities" they must understand. First, the assumption that the community owns the Kumbharwada grounds by virtue of the British Raj–era Vacant Land Tenancy act is incorrect. Mehta says the Kumbhars' long-term lease ran out when the act was repealed in 1974. Also, there is the pollution issue. Every day the potters' brick kilns send huge black clouds into the air. It's gotten so bad that nearby Sion Hospital is complaining that the smoke is aggravating patients' pulmonary ailments.

The Kumbhars are vulnerable on these issues, Mehta says. Chief Minister Deshmukh would be within his rights to send the dreaded bulldozers rolling down 90 Feet Road. The Kumbhars should trust him, Mehta says. His very presence proves his sincerity. "People said if I came here, I should wear a hard hat. But you see me, bareheaded." At the very least, the Kumbhars should allow him to conduct a census of the area. This information would help him fight for them, get them the best deal.

With the return of the late monsoon rains, the session breaks up. Mehta gets back into his chauffeured car feeling upbeat. "A good meeting," he says. The fact that the Kumbhars seemed to agree to the census was a good sign, Mehta says, driving off through puddles.

Back at Kumbharwada, Tank is asked what he has learned from the meeting. Surrounded by perhaps 20 potters, Tank says, "We have learned that Mukesh Mehta's plan is of no use to us." Would they participate in the census? "Well think about it," says Tank.

In any event, there is no time to talk about it now. The meeting has taken almost two hours. With orders piling up, there is work to be done.

Mukesh Mehta's plan is scheduled to be implemented sometime this year, not that Dharavi is excessively fixated on it during holiday season, a time to, as a sign in the window of Jayanthian fireworks store on 90 Feet Road says, "enjoy the festivals with an atom bomb." Today is Ganesh Chaturthi, and much of Dharavi (the Hindus, anyway) are in the streets beating giant drums and blaring Bollywood-inflected songs on car-battery-powered speakers in celebration of Lord Ganesh. Ganesh, the roly-poly elephant god, has special significance in Dharavi, being considered the deity of "removing obstacles."

One such obstacle is in evidence at the outset of the parade marking the end of the ten-day festival for which people make giant murtis, or likenesses, of the god. These effigies are borne through the streets to Mahim Beach and then tossed into the water. One group has constructed a ten-foot-high (three meters) Ganesh from silvery papier-mâché. They have not, however, bothered to measure the narrow lane through which the Ganesh will need to pass to reach Dharavi Main Road. After much discussion and a tortuous 50-foot (15 meters) journey during which many Dharavian "obstacles," including a ganglia of illegally connected electric wires, needed to be removed, the murti makes it through with a quarter inch to spare. Not a bit of the god's silvery skin is nicked.

As the Ganesh is lifted onto a flatbed truck for its journey to Mahim Beach, one resident turns and says, "You see. The Ganesh is undamaged. This is our talent. We deal with what is."

DISCUSSION QUESTIONS

1. How would you describe the contrasting views of "slums" like Dharavi held by (a) government officials and urban developers on the one hand and (b) residents of these low-income urban enclaves on the other?

2. Why were most local Dharavi residents opposed to the "renewal" of their community?

3. Why is it critical for urban planners and real estate developers to understand the culture(s) of the urban areas they are trying to gentrify?

16

The Glaciers of the Andes Are Melting: Indigenous and Anthropological Knowledge Merge in Restoring Water Resources

INGE BOLIN
Vancouver Island University, Canada

Cultural anthropologists have known for years that climate change is a reality and not merely the opinion of paranoid physical scientists. Unlike other social scientists, cultural anthropologists study and live with those populations that are the first to experience the negative consequences of climate change. Because these small-scale societies (such as pastoralists, hunters, fishers, and subsistence farmers) live close to the earth, they are sensitive to minute changes in animal behavior, water temperatures, amounts of rainfall, planting cycles, climate changes, and soil conditions. In fact, this accumulated knowledge about their ecology has enabled them to make the appropriate cultural changes needed to successfully adapt to their changing environments over the past millennia. Owing to their close relationship with their natural environment, these small-scale societies are the first to pick up the early warning signs of climate change and, unfortunately, are the first to experience the negative consequences.

In this selection, Inge Bolin introduces us to the Quechua people of the high Peruvian Andes, who are facing severe water shortages brought about by the rapidly retreating glaciers. Bolin discusses how the Quechua are reinstating, in the twenty-first century, certain ancient Incan practices of water conservation, such as garden terracing and the revitalization of ancient irrigation canals and reservoirs used in earlier times. Although anthropologists such as Bolin have served as liaisons between the Quechua people and local and regional officials, much more needs to be done by global organizations to prevent these rapidly occurring water shortages from becoming catastrophic. And as Bolin reminds us, this is not a problem facing just the Quechua people of Peru. Rather, more than one-sixth of the world's population depends on glaciers and seasonal snow packs for its basic water supply.

The indigenous Quechua people of the high Peruvian Andes are worried as they look at their mountain peaks. Never in their lifetimes have they witnessed environmental changes of such drastic dimensions. One village elder expressed his concern by telling me: "Our *Apus* (sacred mountain deities)

SOURCE: From "The Glaciers of the Andes Are Melting: Indigenous and Anthropological Knowledge Merge in Restoring Water Resources" by Inge Bolin. In Susan A. Crate and Mark Nuttall (eds.), *Anthropology and Climate Change: From Encounters to Actions*. Walnut Creek, CA: Left Coast Press, 2009, pp. 228–239. Reprinted by permission of Left Coast Press and the author.

have always had sparkling white ponchos. Now some of their ponchos have brown stripes. Other peaks have shed their ponchos altogether" (Bolin 2001, 25). His feelings resonate throughout the hills and valleys where one often hears people say, "When all the snow is gone from the mountain tops the end of the world as we know it is near, because there is no life without water" (Bolin 2003).

I first encountered the problem of melting glaciers in 1984–85 when I researched the organization of irrigation along the Vilcanota/Urubamba Valleys (Bolin 1987, 1990, 1992, 1994). At that time Peruvian geologist Dr. Carlos Kalofatovich told me that the Chicon glacier above the Urubamba Valley had receded sixty meters in fifty years (personal communication). During the next two decades I continued to observe how glaciers melted in this and other adjacent regions. This process became much more visible starting in the

mid-1990s, at which time my research and applied work among high-altitude pastoralists was focused on ritual activities (Bolin 1998), environmental issues (Bolin 1999, 2002; Bolin and Bolin 2006) and child rearing (Bolin 2006). Starting in 2004 when glacial retreat and water shortages had reached serious proportions, I shifted my research focus more directly to the problems of climate change, concentrating on melting glaciers, water shortages, and solutions that could improve the chances for the survival of the indigenous peoples and their cultures.

In this chapter I discuss glacial retreat in the high Andes with focus on the provinces of Quispicanchis and Uruhamba in the Cusco region of southeast Peru (Figure 16.1). The people living in these areas deal with a rainy season that lasts from roughly October to the end of March, and a dry season from April to the end of September. During the dry season almost all the water that people and

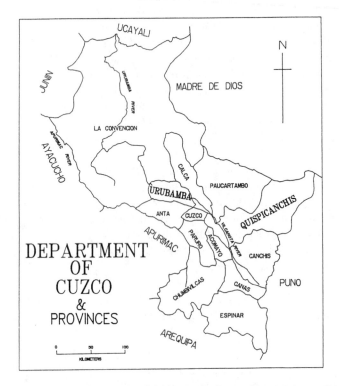

F I G U R E 16.1 Map of the Cuzco region and its provinces. © Inge Bolin.

animals use throughout the Andes is derived from the glaciers in the mountains' high peaks. The indigenous people who reside along the hillsides of these provinces, between 3,000 and 5,000 meters above sea level, live primarily from working the land and pasturing their animals. I will describe how the melting process affects the natural environment, the livelihood of agriculturists and high-altitude pastoralists, and the impact it has on their culture and religious beliefs. The discussion will center on my role as a collaborative researcher and mediator between the local and the global by describing my interactions with the indigenous people as climate change intensified and we were forced to seek ways to mitigate the impending crisis caused by glacial retreat and water shortage. Together we started to consider local adaptive strategies and globally devised methods to preserve, capture, recycle, purify, and distribute water, and adjust irrigation and agricultural practices in ways that may allow the Andean people to remain in their homeland instead of migrating to overcrowded cities. As a collaborative researcher I have helped with such projects in the past; some are being implemented at the present time as discussed below; others will follow.

CHANGES IN ANDEAN GLACIAL TOPOGRAPHY AND ITS REPERCUSSIONS

What can science tell us about the changes that have occurred within the Andean glacial topography? At 7,250 kilometers in length, the Andean Cordillera is the longest mountain chain in the world. Within it, Peru's glaciers alone account for 70 percent of the tropical mountain glaciers of the planet (González 2003). Given their tropical latitudes, these glaciers are very close to the melting point and are therefore extremely sensitive to changes in the earth's temperature. Since climate change is greatest at high altitudes, it makes them prime indicators of global warming (Vásquez

Ruesta et al. 2002). In the last twenty years the ice of the Peruvian Andes has been reduced by 20 percent, and this process is accelerating (González 2003). Renowned glaciologist Lonnie Thompson found that the Qori Kalis glacier, the largest glacier of the Quelccaya ice cap in the southern Andes mountains, which had been retreating an average of six meters per year between 1963 and 1978, has since retreated on average sixty meters a year (personal communication, 2007; see also Thompson et al. 2006). In a 2007 CBC News report, he and a team of scientists relayed evidence that Qori Kalis could be gone in five years (CBC News, February 16, 2007).

The Quelccaya ice cap, the world's largest tropical ice mass, covers 44 square kilometers and is located about 125 miles north-northeast of Lake Titicaca (Bowen 2005, 166). Thompson warns that it is the unprecedented rate of ice loss that concerns him most in the Andes and in other parts of the world where he and his crew have been working. Other leading scientists of the Intergovernmental Panel on Climate Change (IPCC) reported in 2007 that "warming of the climate system is unequivocal given increases in average air and ocean temperatures, widespread melting of snow and ice and rising sea levels" (CTV News, March 26, 2007).

The smaller glaciers that make up 80 percent of the glaciers within the Andean Cordillera may vanish in ten to fifteen years as predicted by Francou (2001) and Francou et al. (2003). But many of these small glaciers have already melted or are melting at a much faster rate than ever predicted. The forecast for rainfall, which is hoped to makeup for at least part of the water loss from glaciers, is equally alarming. According to the fourth assessment report of the IPCC, the annual precipitation is likely to decrease in the southern Andes (Matthews 2007). More scientists now join indigenous peoples in their concern about glacial retreat and its consequences. During November and December of 2007 I discussed the issue of melting glaciers and water scarcity in the Andes with directors and scientists of environmental agencies in Cuzco, Peru, among them IMA (Instituto del Manejo de Agua), CONAM (Consejo Nacional del Ambiente),

ANDES (Asociación para la Naturaleza y el Desarrollo Sostenible), Plan MERISS (International Irrigation), and Ayllus Ecológicos del Cusco. They unanimously agree that the situation is very serious and that steps must be taken at once to slow down the disastrous consequences of global warming.

IMPACT OF GLACIAL RETREAT ON THE LOCAL POPULATIONS

Since virtually all the water available to Andean peasant farmers and pastoralists in the dry season comes from the snow and ice fields of their high mountains, the repercussions of melting glaciers are immense for local communities. Melting glaciers may provide added water in the short run, but they also cause rock falls, landslides, and floods. As snow masses diminish, however, mountain lakes and creeks shrink or disappear, and rivers no longer receive enough water from the glaciers to irrigate fields and meadows, which require 70 percent of the water supply, or to generate hydroelectric power. Water scarcity, combined with extreme weather conditions, result in bad or lost harvests. In addition, increasingly higher temperatures require that tender new plants be irrigated more frequently, though not enough irrigation water is available. To make matters worse, multinationals are building luxury hotels that use much of the precious water in the province of Urubamba, while international mining companies destroy the glaciers of many sacred mountains in the Andes and elsewhere to extract minerals, thereby poisoning water and land. The smaller mountain glaciers above the Urubamba Valley, which had receded slightly more than one meter in 1985, are now receding twelve meters each year (Tupayachi Herrera, personal communication, 2007); the last ones will soon be gone.

The unprecedented melting of the Andean glaciers is also posing serious drinking water problems

for local inhabitants. Drinking water becomes scarce where springs dry up, and lower water levels in lakes and rivers are causing disease vectors from animal feces to increase. This requires that water be thoroughly boiled, but firewood is scarce. As a result, many people drink raw water, putting themselves at risk of contracting gastrointestinal ailments. These, in turn, require natural medicines that must be derived from plants that are increasingly scarce due to the uncertain water regime.

Furthermore, weather patterns in the Andes now tend to reverse, a trend also found in other climate-sensitive areas of the world. The absence of rain during part of the rainy season has interfered with the growing of food plants, while rains during the dry season have barely allowed for the freeze-drying of potatoes, the staple of the herders' diet. Hunger, combined with extreme temperatures, has caused much sickness, and led to new diseases (e.g., *Verruga peruana*) and new pests. Until a few years ago potatoes and other high-altitude tuber crops (*oqa, ulluku,* and *maswa*) were free from pests. Recently, however, some high-altitude communities have been forced to spray their potato crop, which has caused financial hardships for most families.

VIEWS EXPRESSED BY INDIGENOUS ANDEAN PEOPLE

Inhabitants of the Andean Cordilleras have been concerned about water scarcity for a long time. Myths and legends tell about courageous young people who dared to face severe obstacles to bring much-needed water from snowfields and high mountain lakes to villages in the valley. Water was sacred to pre-Columbian civilizations as it is to many indigenous people today. Pre-Columbian religions and the beliefs of today's indigenous societies have been based on the benevolence of Mother Earth, and the sacred Apus, those mountains whose snow and ice fields provide the life-giving waters, and on the mountain lakes that retain it. As the snowfields melt due to global climate change, these deities lose their powers. Eventually Andean religion may erode and these legends will become meaningless. Some indigenous people have wondered what they have done wrong to deserve the wrath of the gods who began to restrict the water that flows from their mountainsides. Although elders are often aware of the effects of El Niño that can cause havoc in the weather patterns, few know of the problems underlying global climate change and of those responsible for causing such a devastating process. Yet, the local knowledge of the Quechua people of the high Andes is invaluable to their survival. The slightest changes in the environment tell them when something goes wrong. Thus, for example, the people living along the hillsides above the Vilcanota and Urubamba valleys observed already in the mid-1980s (and perhaps earlier) that important medicinal plants became increasingly hard to find, and even where they persisted, their growth was stunted, usually because of water scarcity during at least part of the year. The Andean mountains that contain the most extreme range of landscape types, climates, and vegetation communities in the world are rapidly losing their biodiversity (Brack, Egg, and Noriega 2000). Since biodiversity is highest at high altitudes, indigenous knowledge in this area is paramount in our struggle to help preserve these plants (Gade 1975; Tupayachi Herrera 1997, 2005).

With the same degree of precision as with medicinal plants, the Quechua people's local knowledge tells about past weather patterns, either seen in their own lifetimes or learned through oral history. They know whether a change that is happening now has occurred before or in such an extreme form within living memory. When it comes to rainfall, for example, the Andean people refer to *veranillos,* which are dry periods that can last for three weeks and have occurred mainly during the height of the rainy season in January and February. Within recent years, however, *veranillos* have also appeared earlier. I experienced two *vera-nillos* within six weeks in November and December 2007. Abnormalities such as torrential rains, snow, and hail falling during the dry season

have occurred increasingly within the last decade or two. These weather anomalies seriously affect the herds and crops, mainly the preservation of potatoes, the staple of high Andeans' diet. The freeze-drying process of potatoes can only take place between May and July when the days are sunny and the nights are frosty. Now this weather pattern can no longer be relied on. The rains that fall in the rainy season also tend to be stronger now, washing the potatoes out of their steep beds into the rivers. These situations have caused several years of hunger in high-altitude regions (Bolin 1999; see also Winterhalder 1994 on rainfall patterns). Also, during drought conditions high-altitude pastoralists often point to grasses that are of such weak texture that they break apart and even pulverize when grazed by llamas and alpacas. Melting glaciers and drying creeks and mountain lakes all add to the problems caused by drought.

Peruvian environmental organizations and village leaders are becoming increasingly concerned about the local and regional impacts of global climate change and in some cases have taken action. Attempts to slow down glacial retreat started several years ago along Peru's Sinakara mountain range. Here tens of thousands of pilgrims flock from high-altitude regions of Peru and Bolivia to celebrate at the sanctuary of Qoyllur Rit'i with ancient Andean and Christian rituals. Hundreds of *ukukus* who represent spiritual figures dressed in shaggy alpaca robes with masks of alpaca wool ascend to the glaciers under the full moon for initiation and other ceremonies. They leave a few drops of blood in the snow as a sacrifice to the mountain. In return, they used to chop off large chunks of ice and bring this potent medicine to the people in their villages (see Figure 16.2). Beginning in the year 2000, as the melting of glaciers became a frightening reality for many, the indigenous leaders who organized this great pilgrimage announced that the ancient custom of collecting ice from the glaciers must be abandoned. Since 2003 this law has been strictly enforced. Now each *ukuku* is allowed to fill only a tiny bottle with snow or water to bring to the valley.

FIGURE 16.2 Ukukus (bear men) bring ice, believed to be medicine, from the glacier to their villages in 1991. This age-old custom was abandoned in 2000 because of alarming glacial retreat. © Inge Bolin.

LOCAL RESPONSES

Indigenous peoples live in close association with their land. In the high Andes the Quechua revere Pachamama or Mother Earth, the sacred mountains they call Apus, and lakes and meadows. These are omnipresent deities. Yet, in places where water became too scarce to make a living, families were forced to move to find a better environment in which to plant their crops or herd their animals. But few have been successful, relocating only to find similar issues with water or lack of land. Those who sold or abandoned their land and moved to the overcrowded cities were for the most part equally disappointed. Without extended families and *compadrazgo*, networks of fictive kinship ties, they found no support when they most needed it in an unknown environment.

Yet, Andean peasants and herders have been very resourceful throughout history in adapting to environmental changes. In order to defend themselves against the vagaries of the weather, for example, they have always used small parcels of land at different altitudes and within different microenvironments to ensure that at least part of a year's potato harvest can be saved. Now, with much greater changes in the weather pattern, with hotter summers and colder winters, with more variable precipitation, and with less or no water flowing from their mountain peaks, they contemplate growing drought-resistant species of food plants and think about methods of storing water. But the manifold effects of climate change, the activities that contribute to it, and governments that are not responding to the policy challenges are all too distant for most local people to comprehend. It is here that the role of an anthropologist or other professional as mediator between the local, national, and global levels becomes important.

COLLABORATION BETWEEN INDIGENOUS PEOPLES AND ANTHROPOLOGISTS

Just as many anthropologists have learned the strategies of survival in marginal environments from indigenous and other local peoples, indigenous peoples now need information from anthropologists about global climate change, the way it affects humanity, how future trends are detected and forecast, and new coping strategies. We all must understand, for example, that the disappearance of glaciers is not only felt locally, but also at the national and worldwide levels. Glacial retreat in the Andes causes mountain lakes and creeks to dry up, becoming unable to provide water to fill the rivers that make their way throughout the country to the dry, rainless coast or to the jungle regions. As aquifers also drop, even drinking water can become scarce during the dry season or whenever the rains do not arrive on time.

During more than two decades of research and applied work in the Andes, it became clear to me that migration to the cities or other parts of Peru is not the answer for people who want to get a better chance at survival. Andean people are attached to their land, lifeways, and religious beliefs, and it is here where efforts must begin. Since most of the world's leaders are doing little to curb climate change through implementing policies that restrict emissions from vehicles, factories, and billions of animals kept under atrocious conditions,[1] local people must become innovative and self-empowered to implement both short-term emergency projects

to survive and projects that are sustainable in the long term. In most cases, indigenous inhabitants have a wealth of knowledge already available to them based on how their ancestors dealt with and adapted to weather extremes, like the scarcity of water.

In 1984–85, the villages along the hillsides above the Sacred Valley of the Incas in the province of Urubamba suffered from a serious water shortage that resulted in conflicts over the last few drops of water during the dry season. Given this emergency, the indigenous population asked for international cooperation to improve irrigation canals and reconstruct small Inca reservoirs. At various occasions the local people told me that their Inca ancestors knew the most stable regions along the mountainsides, where remnants of ancient canals and reservoirs could still be seen. Since many of these structures had for centuries been trampled on by animals, they were no longer functional.

The elders of the village of Yanahuara along the hillsides of the Sacred Valley of the Incas, where I studied the ways by which they organized their irrigation activities, approached me to assist them in writing a proposal to the international developers who were working in the Vilcanota Valley, 400 kilometers away. The elders requested that their broken ancient canals and reservoirs be repaired. Together with the local population, I wrote a proposal to get the necessary funding, which I took to the GTZ (Gesellschaft für Technische Zusammenarheit, German International Development Corporation) in Germany who discussed the issues with their Peruvian counterparts.

The people of Yanahoara and adjacent regions rejoiced when in 1986 the international development agency Plan MERIS II (now Plan MERISS) in Cuzco, through which Peru and Germany cooperate, accepted our proposal to improve canals and reservoirs to provide enough water year round, and

---

1. The suffering of billions of animals in animal factories is a disgrace to humanity and also a major contributor to our environmental dilemma. In a groundbreaking 2006 report, the UN declared that raising animals for food generates more greenhouse gases than all the cars and trucks in the world combined. Senior UN Food and Agriculture Organization official Henning Steinfeld reported that the meat industry is "one of the most significant contributors to today's most serious environment problems." Yet, this most significant issue is seldom, if ever, discussed at environmental conferences or elsewhere. Should we close our eyes to an issue that is at the very heart of global warming? Should we continue to waste 2,500 gallons of water required to produce one pound of beef?

to also add complementary projects (e.g., a school building). Yet, within the last five years, with the glaciers along the Cordillera de Uruhamba melting much faster and retreating at an average of twelve meters a year (Tupayachi Herrera, personal communication), water scarcity has again been sorely felt by the local people, especially during planting time. Within the last decade, climatic extremes here and elsewhere in the Andes have contributed to floods, catastrophic droughts, heat waves, and cold spells as never seen before. Among other drastic events, in 1998 and 1999 harvests were destroyed by extreme weather conditions throughout large parts of the Andes (Bolin 1999). In 2005 an immense avalanche of snow and ice, estimated at about two hundred tons, tumbled from Mount Veronica, destroying everything in its path and finally obstructing the train tracks in the valley leading to Machu Picchu (Tupayachi Herrera, personal communication). The recent cold spell in May 2007 was more extreme than any previous one experienced by the Quechua people, killing some of the very old and very young. (See also Suarez 2008.) Yet, as soon as this natural catastrophe was over, glacial melting continued as before.

With some peaks now free of ice and snow and others losing their glaciers at a rapid rate, major efforts are necessary to curb further destruction. Together with the volunteer organization Yachaq Runa, which I founded in 1992 in Cuzco, we have embarked on a program to help stop local environmental degradation and, hopefully, reverse it. The indigenous Quechua people along the hillsides of the Vilcanota and Urubamba Valleys have been eager to revert to Inca ways of managing the environment by planting native trees, recreating small forests on the hillsides and around their homesteads, and by planting bushes alongside irrigation canals to keep water evaporation low (see also Bolin 1987). Although Australian eucalyptus trees grow fastest and continue growing after being cut, they need much water, and their enormous roots destroy plants and buildings in their close proximity. Therefore reforestation with indigenous trees,

such as Q'euña (*Polylepis incana*) and Quiswar *(Buddleja incana)*, and indigenous shrubs, such as Tayanka (*Baccharis odorata*) and Chilika (*Baccharis latifolia*), is environmentally much more beneficial. These reforestation projects were started by the villagers of Chillihuani, in the province of Quispicanchis, in cooperation with the Yachaq Runa volunteer group and with international funding.[2] Reforestation in Challwaqocha and five other villages in the province of Urubamba is now underway. As soil and waterways are stabilized through reforestation, the simultaneous planting of the highly nutritious Maca tuber and other food plants is becoming more successful.

Since increasing water scarcity is already starting to affect the potential of hydroelectric plants, indigenous people in several of my study communities are happy as we cooperate to provide solar cookers, photovoltaic lights, and solar hot water to the health stations, schools, shower houses, and other facilities we help to build and equip. Yet, many more efforts are necessary to assure the survival of the Andean people should global climate change continue at the present rate. Unless precipitation patterns change to become more beneficial to agriculture and pastoralism, much more must be done to provide the amount and quality of water necessary for survival. We must consider primarily indigenous Andean knowledge—known in some areas, but forgotten in others—as waterways are restored, agricultural practices are adapted to prevailing climatic conditions, and new methods are devised to collect water and use it sparingly throughout the dry season. In cooperation with the indigenous population, and based largely on their ancestral knowledge system, we arrived at the following priorities: a) the reconstruction of ancient and building of new terraces, b) the use of conservation tillage, and, c) the rejuvenation of ancient irrigation systems.

Irrigation uses around 70 percent of the available water. Water is saved and erosion largely prevented when peasant farmers use terraces built by their forefathers and/or construct new ones. Where

2. Funding for this and other projects was provided by the Red Cross and Landkreis Böblingen, both of Germany, and by private donors; formerly also by Change for Children in Canada.

slopes are not terraced, fields must be leveled in such a way that water seeps to the root system without eroding the soil. The Incas did this masterfully, as seen on ancient fields. Secondly, to prevent runoff and erosion and keep soil and plants from drying out, contour drenches must be dug. Conservation till age, used in pre-Columbian times and sometimes today, leaves the soil undisturbed and moist, as seeds are placed into narrow slits.

Above all, changes must be made in the way water is transported. The ancient Andeans used a variety of methods, including subterranean water channels, to bring water from the mountains to the dry, rainless coast. The ancient and venerated site of Tipon, 20 kilometers south of Cuzco, consists of a network of narrow irrigation canals that crisscross the region, providing the fields with small amounts of water throughout extended periods of time, causing no erosion and little evaporation. Modern drip irrigation systems are ideal, but still too expensive for most peasant communities (see also Schreier, Brown, and MacDonald 2006).

CONCLUSION

Anthropologists working with indigenous and other place-based peoples have a critical role in the issue of climate change, working as research collaborators and mediators between the local and the global. In this chapter I have shown how, in collaboration with the Andean people and in the context of Yachaq Runa, we continue to look into both old and new ways of collecting, using, and transporting as well as recycling and purifying water. Increasingly more reservoirs will have to be built to store water collected in the rainy season. Individuals and national and international nongovernmental organizations, those mentioned above and others, have been cooperating successfully with indigenous and other local people. Yet, much more help is required in the Andes and worldwide to guarantee survival. The situation is extremely serious (see also Hansen 2007) and it is unimaginable what will happen in the Andes and other parts of this planet if governments do not begin to act quickly: "With more than one-sixth of the Earth's population relying on glaciers and seasonal snow packs for their water supply, the consequences of these hydrological changes for future water availability are likely to be severe" (Barnett, Adam, and Lettenmaier 2005). For example, "Up to three billion people live from the food and energy produced by the Himalayan rivers" (Schild 2007). In the Andes, "glaciers feed the rivers that feed the sprawling cities and shantytowns on Peru's bone-dry Pacific coast. Two-thirds of Peru's 27 million people live on the coast where just 1.8 percent of the nation's water supply is found" (CBS News 2007/02/11). The people of the high Andes have no choice but to remain in their mountains, keeping them moist, planting trees, digging trenches, collecting rain water, and hoping that the world's leaders will finally wake up and give all they have to help avert the worst disaster humankind ever had to face.

REFERENCES

Barnett, T. P., J. C. Adam, and D. P. Lettenmaier. 2005. Potential impacts of a warming climate on water availability in snow-dominated regions. *Nature* 438: 303–309.

Bolin, I. 1987. The organization of irrigation in the Vilcanota Valley of Peru: Local autonomy, development and corporate group dynamics. PhD diss., University of Alberta.

_____. 1990. Upsetting the power balance: Cooperation, competition and conflict along an Andean irrigation system. *Human Organization* 49(2): 140–148.

_____. 1992. Achieving reciprocity: Anthropological research and development assistance. *Practicing Anthropology*. 14(4): 12–15.

_____. 1994. Levels of autonomy in the organization of irrigation in Peru. In: *Irrigation at high altitudes: The* social organization of water control systems in the Andes, eds. W. P. Mitchell, and D. Guillet, 14 1–66, vol. 12, Society for Latin American Anthropology Publication Series.

_____. 1998. *Rituals of respect: The secret of survival in the high Peruvian Andes.* Austin: University of Texas Press.

_____. 1999. Survival in marginal lands: Climate change in the high Peruvian Andes. *Development and Cooperation.* 5: 25–26.

_____. 2001. When Apus are losing their white ponchos: Environmental dilemmas and restoration efforts in Peru. *Development and Cooperation.* 6: 25–26.

_____. 2002. Melting glaciers in the Andes and the future of the water supply. Paper presented at the meetings of IMA (Instituto de Manejo de Agua), October 31, Cusco, Peru.

_____. 2003. Our Apus are dying: Glacial retreat and its consequences for life in the Andes. Paper presented at the annual meeting of the American Anthropological Association, Nov. 19–23, Chicago, Illinois.

Bolin, I. 2006. *Growing up in a culture of respect: Child rearing in Highland Peru.* Austin: The University of Texas Press.

Bolin, I., and G. Bolin. 2006. Solar solution for Andean people. *Development and Cooperation* 2: 74–75.

Bowen, M. 2005. Thin ice: Unlocking the secrets of climate in the world's highest mountains. New York: Henry Holt and Company.

Brack, E., A. Bravo, and A. Belen Noriega Bravo, 2000. Gestión Sostenible de los Ecosistemas de Montaña. *In Memoria del Taller Internacional de Ecosistemas de Montaña. Cuseo, Peru.*

CBC News. 2007. Peru's glacier vanishing scientists warn. www.cbc.ca/technology/story/2007/02/16.

CBS News. 2007. Warming threatens double-trouble in Peru: Shrinking glaciers and a water shortage, by Leslie Josephs.

CTV News. 2007. Regional Climates may change radically. http://www.ctv.ca/servlet/ArticleNews/story/CTVNews/2007/03/26.

Francou, B. 2001. Small glaciers of the Andes may vanish in 10–15 years. http://unisci.com.stories/20011/0117013.htm.

Francou, B., M. Vuille, P. Wagnon, J. Mendoza, and J.-E. Sicart, 2003. Tropical climate change recorded

by a glacier in the central Andes during the last decades of the twentieth century. Chacaltaya, Bolivia, l6oS. *Journal of Geophysical Research* 108(5): 4154.

Gade, D. 1975. *Plants, man and the land in the Vilcanota Valley of Peru.* The Hague: W. Junk.

González, G. 2003. Desaparecen Glaciares de Montaña Tierramérica—Medio Ambiente y Desarrollo, August 21, 2003.

Hansen, J. 2007. Scientific reticence and sea level rise. *Environ. Res. Lett,* 2(2007).

Matthews, J. H. 2007. What you should know. *WWF* Summary for Policymakers. IPCC Fourth Assessment Report—Climate Change, 2007.

Schild, A. 2007. Climate change, glaciers, and water resources in the Himalayan region. Speech given at the First Asia-Pacific Water Summit, December 3–4, Japan.

Schreier, H., S. Brown, and J. R. MacDonald, 2006. *Too little and too much: Water and development in a Himalayan watershed.* Vancouver: University of British Columbia.

Suarez, L. 2008. Climate change: Opportunity or threat in the central Andean region of Peru. *Mountain Forum Bulletin* (Jan.): 18–19.

Thompson, L. G., E. Mosley-Thompson, H. Brecher, M. Davis, B. León, D. Les, P. NanLin, T. Mashiotta, and K. Mountain. 2006. Abrupt tropical climate change: Past and present. http://www.pnas.org/cgi/doi/1o.1073.

Tupayachi Herrera, A. 1997. Diversidad arbórea en las microcuencas transversales al rio Urubamba en el valle sagrado de los Incas. *Opciones* 7: 41–46. Inandes UNSAAC, Cusco

_____. 2005. Flora de Ia Cordillera de Vilcanota. ARNALDOA 12 (1–2): 126–144.

Vásquez Ruesta, P., with S. Isola Elias, J. Chang Olivas, and A. Tovar Narváez. 2002. *Cambio climático y sus efectos en las montañas sudamericanas.* Lima: Universidad Agraria La Molina.

Winterhalder, B. 1994. The ecological basis of water management in the central Andes: Rainfall and temperature in southern Peru. In *Irrigation at high altitudes: The social organization of water control systems in the Andes,* eds. W. P. Mitchell and D. Guillet, 21–67, vol. 12, Society for Latin American Anthropology Publication Series.

DISCUSSION QUESTIONS

1. What role should cultural anthropologists play helping to solve problems stemming from global warming and climate change?

2. In addition to retreating glaciers, what other water-related problems stemming from global warming are negatively affecting small-scale societies throughout the world?

3. Many anthropologists would argue that local populations such as the Quechua are in the best position to know what needs to be done to ameliorate the negative effects of climate change. How would you explain this position?